A Tolkienian Mathomium

ᚨ:ᛏᛟᛚᚲᛁᛖᚾᛁᚨᚾ:ᛗᚨᛏᚺᛟᛗᛁᚢᛗ:

A Collection of Articles on J.R.R. Tolkien
and His Legendarium

Mark T. Hooker

[signature]

Llyfrawr 2006

Library of Congress Cataloging-in-Publication Data

Hooker, Mark T.

    A Tolkienian Mathomium : A Collection of Articles on J.R.R. Tolkien and His Legendarium / Mark T. Hooker

    Includes bibliographic references and index

Subject headings:

Tolkien, J.R.R. (John Ronald Reuel), 1892-1973—Criticism and interpretation

Tolkien, J.R.R. (John Ronald Reuel), 1892-1973—Translations of

Fantasy fiction, English—History and criticism

Middle Earth (Imaginary place)

All rights reserved. No portion of this book may be reproduced, by any process or technique, without the express written consent of the author.

First published in 2006 by Llyfrawr, the academic imprint of CV&M.

Printed by www.lulu.com in the United States.

10—9—8—7—6—5—4—3—2—1

Preface

In a *Letter to the Editor* published in *The Observer* in 1938, a reader of *The Hobbit* asked Tolkien to provide some information about the name *Hobbit* and the origins of Bilbo Baggins, because "it would save so many research students so very much trouble in the generations to come." I should like to thank Professor Tolkien for the foresight and consideration of his response, which was that giving an answer would be "rather unfair to research students," because "to save them the trouble, is to rob them of any excuse for existing" (L.30). If Tolkien had been more forthcoming with his response, I should undoubtedly have found another excuse for existing, but I wonder if it would have been as entertaining as Tolkienology.

Since Middle-earth is located—to paraphrase Rod Serling's introduction to *The Twilight Zone*—'in another dimension, not of sight and sound, but of mind,' its artifacts are the products of the mind; words and names, rather than skeletons, pottery shards and flint tools. The *literary baggage* of each word and name in a language is built up out of all the usages of that word or name that a reader has ever been exposed to. Tolkien called this "the leaf mold" of one's mind (*Carpenter* 140-141). The purpose of this study is to offer the reader a glimpse into the literary baggage that I carry around for the words that make up Tolkien's Legendarium.

It is hoped that the explanations presented here will, to some extent, coincide with Tolkien's literary baggage and/or motivation for creating a word, but, at the same time, I recognize that Tolkien was correct when he said: "there is no substitute for me, while I am alive" (L.380). Tolkien's notes and papers are all that are left now. The publication of this volume was, therefore, understandably delayed, when *The Lord of the Rings: A Reader's Companion* (*Companion*), which draws heavily on previously unpublished materials, finally went into print in December 2005, so that I could consult this new authoritative source for a review and update of the articles contained herein.

Tolkien said that the linguistic invention that became Middle-earth was an idiosyncratic enterprise, which he undertook to satisfy his own private linguistic taste. He was not surprised that most analyses of his work went awry because "linguistic invention" is a "comparatively rare" art form, and most analysts had little understanding "of how a philologist would go about it" (L.380).

I am a linguist who laughs at Tolkien's low philological jests, and plays the same kind of word games himself. It should also be pointed out to my credit that I correctly analyzed the place name *Dwaling* as a first name plus the ending *-ing* (descendants of), before the appearance of Tolkien's note on this name to the Dutch translator in *Companion* (lviii). (Q.V. "The Linguistic Landscape of The Shire," MythCon XXXV [2004].) To my discredit, however, I did not correctly analyze the origin of the name *Smaug*.

Tolkiennymy is an art rather than a science, and Tolkien's assessment of it remains the best. It "appear[s] to be unauthentic embroideries on my work, throwing light only on the state of mind of [its] contrivers, not on me or on my actual intention and procedure" (L.380). With that in mind, come with me now on a "journey into a wondrous land," as Rod Serling called it, "whose boundaries are that of imagination." In Tolkien's case, that covers a lot of territory.

Foreword to the *Mathomium*

When I flew to London in the summer of 2000, it was to catch the westbound train at Paddington Station for Wales. There *Cymdeithas Madog*, an organization sworn to aid, assist and abet North Americans in their acquisition of the Welsh language, had scheduled its year 2000 Millennial Course [*Cwrs y Mileniwm*] of *Cwrs Cymraeg* in the little town of *Caerfyrddin*, in tradition not far from the very spot where Merlin the wizard was washed up out of the sea into a sea-cave. An auspicious beginning!

Most North Americans have no idea that the Welsh have a native language as foreign to English as is Russian. But we Cymric language lunatics and culture vultures descended en masse upon *Coleg y Drindod*, Trinity College, *Caerfyrddin* for a week of intensive immersion in Welsh language and cultural studies. Perhaps the second day during a break between classes, I met a certain Mark T. Hooker. I just walked right up and introduced myself. He told me his consuming interest was the works of J.R.R. Tolkien, and that's why he was there learning some Welsh. Mark added that most people, when he told them he was into Tolkien, displayed blank, bewildered looks: *which planet did you say you were from?*

But I nodded with enthusiasm, and told him I understood, because Tolkien the author molded me as a young person during the 1960's. I may not have told Mark there on the spot, but Tolkien was one reason I also was at the Cwrs in Caerfyrddin. For the initiated know that *Cymraeg*, "the senior language of the men of Britain,"[1] inspired Tolkien's Elven language *Sindarin*.

Mark and I remained in touch ever since that summer both on line and in the post, chattering our fond theories and bantering our inside jokes about J.R.R.T. and his legacy. I found much to like in my newfound friend. Mark and I are language nuts. Perhaps our brains were similarly twisted and denatured from too many happy hours in the labyrinths of Germanic and Slavic verbs. But no, it goes much deeper than that. It is a matter of wiring: there is some complex in the speech center, exalted to a rare degree in certain brains, which can open the door to a chamber "within the very heart of language, in the white-hot furnace of essential speech."[2]

In Tolkien this primordial speech complex was exalted beyond the measure allowed to most mortals. Mark and I have enough glimmer of activity in this complex to recognize its activity when we see it, and to exalt and honor it where we find it.

It was I who suggested the prospect of this book to Mark Hooker. Why would one wish, then, to read what Hooker has to say? There are at least two important reasons.

Primus, the *Mathomium* is a kind of linguistic compendium for language nuts who love Tolkien. Not all Tolkien-fanciers are language nuts (alas!), but we're out there! If one would sit entranced like Lewis's Ransom, witness the descent of a Viritrilbia, Mercury or Thoth, and receive his revelations on the essence of language and its message to humankind, Mark Hooker is an excellent place to start. He knows and loves Tolkien's elemental mindset on places and their names. He has probed and configured Tolkien's

---

[1] Tolkien's words. See Janet Davies, *A Pocket Guide to the Welsh Language*, University of Wales Press, Western Mail, 1999, p. 9.

[2] From the descent of Viritrilbia, or Mercury and Thoth, lord of meaning and the archetype of language. See C.S. Lewis, "That Hideous Strength," The Macmillan Company, New York, Paperback Edition, 1969, p. 322.

linguistic landscapes and documented his findings with a dizzying body of research, in light of larger European traditions, even prehistoric material, including the archaeological record.

Secundus, it would appear that scholarship on J.R.R. Tolkien is becoming ever more *"pointed."* The avatar arrives: his message is first ignored, then derided, then tested, then enthusiastically praised, and finally *adopted*. But once the avatar *himself* is no longer among us, a fraternal order of High Priests and Scribes is lurking in wait to shove him up the eternal stairway of apotheosis, and to petrify his vital message in rigid stone (*"You belong to US now, baby!"*). Similarly, criteria defining what constitutes Tolkien scholarship are becoming ever narrower, more *exclusive*. A threatening body of scholarship notarized as *orthodox* by the fraternal order, like the rigid bronzing of baby shoes once soft and pliable, has enshrined and sealed the warm, living Tolkien, as Shakespeare, Goethe and Tolstoy before him, within a ponderous, impermeable shell of cold statuary bronze.

But deep within his *apotheotic* metallic prison I can hear the ringing of fists banging, the muffled cries from the *actual* Tolkien: **"Let me out!"** Who was this Tolkien of human flesh and brain? I believe that Mark Hooker, from insightful analysis of Tolkien's work, has some good ideas. If there *are* those to whom Hooker may not constitute orthodox Tolkien scholarship, these folks I would ask plainly: just how *"orthodox"* was our beloved Professor and hobbit-fancier himself in the beginning?

In the *Mathomium* one can glimpse Tolkien from another side much less frequented: the *real* dilatory Tolkien, who in between grading papers in Anglo-Saxon in his garage-study, cobbled together his linguistic landscapes of Middle-earth. Mark lets us hear Tolkien chuckling many a chuckle. Here is the mercurial jokester in "low linguistic jest," blowing linguistic smoke-rings fond or satirical, the man who loved beer and ribaldry, who *certainly did* read Buchan or Haggard, or Charles Dickens, perhaps even *Boys' Life*, wherein he might find an inkling of Aragorn; the man who wrote imaginative Christmas letters to his children. Statuary bronze, indeed!

In ascending my soapbox with thunder rumbling from the mustard bowl,[3] I almost forgot to mention *Tertius*, the *third* reason:

Hooker is proficient in a number of the exotic languages into which Tolkien has been translated, and has conducted a systematic study of these translations. For this reason, Mark mans an insightful observation post, from which he provides a rare and entertaining view of how Tolkien's text has been translated, transfigured, abridged, twisted, botched, fractured, or even mutilated. Frequently the translator even *succeeds*, with a hilarious twist! Those who have ever had to translate will both cringe frightfully and chuckle unmercifully at some of Hooker's revelations.

Mark T. Hooker, as the Germans say, is someone with whom one can steal horses. I am not slandering Mark (or myself) as a horse-thief. What this phrase means is that Mark is ready and able to warm to any task, enterprising, and most of all, fun. Language enthusiasts who love Tolkien will learn (and enjoy learning) a great deal from the *Mathomium*. In its pages one finds a wealth of offbeat factual knowledge and genuine scholarship, but also a spirit of linguistic fun, tongue dryly-however-firmly in cheek. I am proud to introduce and (in part) to illuminate the *Mathomium* manuscript: what is certainly Mark T. Hooker's *Red Book of Tref-y-Blodau* (Welsh for Bloomington).

James Dunning
Marietta, Georgia, USA
April, 2006

---

[3] Humblest apologies to Alexander Pope.

Contents

Preface	iii
Foreword	v
Contents	ix
Acknowledgments	xii
Abbreviations	xiii
What Is a Mathom?	1
previously unpublished	
The Linguistic Landscape of Bree	7
previously published in English in *Beyond Bree,* May 2002 and in Russian as «Лингвистический пейсаж Брийской округи», *Palantir* (the journal of the St. Petersburg Tolkien Society), No. 31, 2002.	
Esgaroth	15
previously unpublished	
The Linguistic Landscape of Tolkien's Shire	19
presented at MythCon XXXV (2004). The article on "Dwaling" was originally published in Russian as "Dwaling" in *Palantir*, No. 42, 2004.	
The Water	65
previously unpublished	

Contents

Stock   69
    previously unpublished
"And why is it called the Carrock?"   79
    previously published in *Beyond Bree*, November 2001, and in Russian as «А почему это называют именно Каррок?», *Palantir*, No. 34, 2002.
In Search of the Origin of the River Lune   83
    previously published in *Beyond Bree*, April 2002, and in Dutch as "Op zoek naar de oorsprong van de rivier Lune," *Lembas* (The journal of the Dutch Tolkien Society), No. 104, 2002.
In League with Miles   93
    previously unpublished
Fractured Fairy Tales from Middle-earth   101
    previously published in *Beyond Bree*, June 2004, in Dutch as "Verwarde Feeënverhalen van Midden-aarde," *Lembas*, No. 117, and in Russian as «Сломанные сказки Средиземья» in *Palantir*, No. 43, 2004.
Tolkien's Use of the Word "Garn!"   105
    previously published in *Translation Journal*, volume 9, No. 2, 2005, and in Dutch as "Garn!," *Lembas* No. 120, 2005.
Spit, Spat, Spittle: Those Whom Tolkien Wouldst Belittle   113
    previously published in *Beyond Bree*, May 2005.
The Leaf Mold of Tolkien's Mind   117
    previously published in *Beyond Bree*, April 2005.
Frodo Quatermain   123
    previously published in *Para Nölé*, No. 13, 2005.
Tolkien and Haggard: Immortality   133
    previously unpublished
Tolkien and Haggard: The Dead Marshes   147
    previously unpublished
The Feigned-manuscript Topos   153
    previously unpublished
In a Hole in the Ground There Lived a …   179
    previously published in *Beyond Bree*, November 2002, and in Russian as «В норе под землей жил-был …», in *Palantir*, No. 35, 2002.
In a Fogou in the Ground There Lived a Cornish Hobbit   189
    previously unpublished
A Tale of Tolkien's Woods   191
    previously unpublished
The Bounders   203
    previously published in *Beyond Bree*, May 2006.

The Cinematographer of Waverly	207
performed at MythCon XXXV (2004), and published in *Beyond Bree*, October 2004.	
Estel	217
previously unpublished	
Bracegirdle	227
previously published in *Beyond Bree*, March 2006.	
Whence an Oliphaunt?	233
previously published in *Beyond Bree*, February 2006.	
Tolkien in Chinese: A Thesis Review	237
previously published in *Translation Journal,* volume 8, No. 3, 2004.	
Appendix '**A**': The 39 Historic Counties of England	247
Appendix '**B**': A Brief Guide to the Translations Cited	249
Illustration Credits	251
About the Artist	255
About the Art	256
Index	259
About the Author	275

Acknowledgments

I should like to thank James Dunning for suggesting this project, and for reading the manuscript for blunders.

Nancy Martsch (the editor of *Beyond Bree*) also deserves a word of thanks, not so much for publishing some of the articles herein, as for the pointed questions she asked before they went into print.

Nor should I forget David Doughan, whose comments on the drafts of many of these articles have been pointedly insightful and helpful; Ron Pirson, who offered a balanced perspective and encouraged me to have my articles translated into Dutch; and Alla Khananashvili, who did the Russian translations of my articles and asked endless, hard questions.

Thanks are likewise due to my wife Stella, who did the Dutch translations, and without whose encouragement and support, not to mention fine multilingual editing skills, this project would not have seen the light of day.

Abbreviations

Aa.xxx   Appendix A. The Appendices are found in volume III of *The Lord of the Rings*, and are identified by a letter designation '**A**' through '**F**.' Cites to the Appendices are given as an upper case letter '**A**' for Appendix, followed by a lower case letter that identifies which Appendix (a-f).

NOTE: The page numbers given after the period (.) for *The Lord of the Rings* and *The Hobbit* are those in the 1965 Ballantine edition, the pre-movie standard for citations. These are the page numbers cited in Foster's *The Complete Guide to Middle-earth*. For readers with post-movie editions of *LotR*, which have a different pagination than the Ballantine paperback, in addition to the page-number cite for the Ballantine edition, there is also a cite to the Book and chapter, using Roman numerals for the Book (I-VI) and Arabic numerals for the chapter. For example, the citation III.5 refers to the chapter entitled "The White Rider," which is chapter 5 of Book III. For readers with post-movie editions, references to *The Hobbit* give the chapter number in Roman numerals.

Carpenter   Humphrey Carpenter, *Tolkien: A Biography*, New York: Ballantine Books, 1977.

Abbreviations

Companion	Wayne G. Hammond and Christina Scull. *The Lord of the Rings: A Reader's Companion*, Boston: Houghton Mifflin, 2005.
D	Dutch
DQ	The Ormsby translation of *Don Quixote* being rather difficult to find in print, readers are referred to the on-line edition (in two parts) below.

<http://www.csdl.tamu.edu/cervantes/english/ctxt/DQ_Ormsby/part1_DQ_Ormsby.html>. LVO 2/23/2006.

<http://www.csdl.tamu.edu/cervantes/english/ctxt/DQ_Ormsby/part2_DQ_Ormsby.html>. LVO 2/23/2006.

This eText is fully searchable, and, therefore, cites to the novel will only indicate the part and the chapter from which the quote is taken: "(DQ#/##)".

Etymologies	"The Etymologies," *HoMe*, volume V, New York: Ballantine Books, 1996, pp. 377-448.
F.xxx	*The Fellowship of the Ring*
G	German
G&G	The Grushetskij and Grigor'eva Russian translation
H.xxx	*The Hobbit*
HoMe	*The History of Middle-earth* (in 12 volumes), edited by Christopher Tolkien, Boston: Houghton Mifflin, 1983-1996. The individual volumes are identified in the text using Roman numerals i-xii.
KSM	Since there are so many different editions of Haggard's *King Solomon's Mines*, readers who wish to see the quotes from the book in full context are referred to the Project Gutenberg eText edition, which can be found at:

<www.gutenberg.org/etext/2166>. LVO 2/17/2006. This eText is fully searchable, and, therefore, cites to the novel will only indicate the chapter from which the quote is taken: "(KSM ##)".

K&K	The Karrik and Kamenkovich Russian translation
L	Latin
L.xxx	*The Letters of J.R.R. Tolkien.*, selected and edited by Humphry Carpenter with the assistance of Christopher Tolkien, Boston: Houghton Mifflin, 1981. Cites are to the page number.
LotR	*The Lord of the Rings*
LT.xxx	*The Book of Lost Tales* (in two parts), edited by Christopher Tolkien, Boston: Houghton Mifflin, 1983.

LVO	Last viewed on
M&K	The Murav'ev and Kistyakovskij Russian translation.
OE	Old English
OED	*The Oxford English Dictionary*
Nomenclature	J.R.R. Tolkien. "Guide to the Names in *The Lord of the Rings*," in *A Tolkien Compass* (Jared Lobdell ed.), New York: Ballantine Books, 1975, pp. 168-216. Also in *Companion*, as "Nomenclature of *The Lord of the Rings*," pp. 750-782.
P.xxx	The "Prologue" to *LotR*.
PG vx.xxx	*The Parliamentary Gazetteer of England and Wales, Adapted to the Most Recent Statistical Arrangements, and Lines of Railroad and Canal Communications, with a Complete Country Atlas of England, Four Large Maps of Wales and an Appendix Containing the Results, in Detail, of the Census of 1841*, in four volumes, London: A. Fullerton & Co, 1854.
PP	Since there are so many different editions of Dickens' *The Pickwick Papers*, readers who would like to see the quote in full context are encouraged to avail themselves of the eText of *The Pickwick Papers*, which is available from *Project Gutenberg* at: <www.gutenberg.org/dirs/etext96/pwprs10.txt>. LVO 2/17/2006. It is fully searchable, and, therefore, cites to the novel will only indicate the chapter from which the quote taken: "(PP ##)".
Q	Quenya
Q.V.	quod vide (Latin): see the article in this text.
R.xxx	*The Return of the King*
S	Sindarin
S.xxx	*The Silmarillion*, Boston: Houghton Mifflin, 1977.
SHE	Because there are a number of different editions of Haggard's novel *She*, readers who would like to see the quote in full context are encouraged to avail themselves of the eText of *She*, which is available from *Project Gutenberg* at <http://www.gutenberg.org/etext/3155>. LVO 2/17/2006. It is fully searchable, and, therefore, cites to the novel will only indicate the chapter from which the quote is taken: "(SHE ##)".
T.xxx	*The Two Towers*
UT.xxx	*Unfinished Tales of Númenor and Middle-earth*, Boston: Houghton Mifflin, 1980.
W	Welsh

THE REDBOOK OF TREF·Y·BLODAU

What Is a Mathom?

Mathom is an extinct Anglo-Saxon word that Tolkien brought back to life with a new meaning in the form that it would have had, if it had survived the transition from Anglo-Saxon to English. The new (March 2001) article on the word *Mathom* in the *Oxford English Dictionary On-line* (*OED*)[4] lists a number of examples of its use with Tolkien's new meaning in modern English, demonstrating Tolkien's direct impact on the vocabulary of the English language. The article also points to the word's Anglo-Saxon antecedents.

Most commentators—including the *OED* and *Companion*—limit themselves to a brief gloss of the meaning of the Anglo-Saxon *mathum* ("a precious thing, a treasure, a valuable gift"), spelled here with a '**U**', following Christopher Tolkien's lead in *HoMe*, to distinguish it from the modern meaning his father created, spelled with an '**O**'. This gloss, however, would hardly have been satisfactory to Tolkien, who loved the stories that words tell, and undoubtedly knew the story behind the word *mathum* well, as it is used numerous times in *Beowulf*, a work with which Tolkien was very familiar. In a letter to *The Observer* in 1938,

---

[4] <http://dictionary.oed.com> LVO 12/15/2005.

Tolkien listed *Beowulf* as being "among [his] most valued sources" (L.31). He would have wanted the story to be told in addition to the gloss. A reader without an understanding of the context of the Anglo-Saxon tradition of Gift Giving (*mathum-gifu*, *Beowulf*, line 1301), which was bound up in the culture of the time in which the word *mathum* was actively used, misses the comic irony that Tolkien planted in his story by redefining the word *mathom* in Hobbit terms. It is only in contrasting the two meanings that the humor of Tolkien's 'low philological jest' becomes apparent.

In his article entitled "The Social Context of Warfare in Anglo-Saxon England,"[5] Dr. Richard Underwood explains the significance of *mathums*, which in his modern text are referred to as *gifts*.

> [W]arriors were rewarded for their service with gifts, particularly of weapons and armour, and, after long service, with grants of land. These warriors were in no way mercenaries, however; the relationship between lord and his warband was long term and was considered to be honourable for both parties. Personal prestige was considered extremely important. The value of gifts given by the lord therefore lay not only in their monetary worth but also in the prestige they brought. Gift Giving was both public and formal, and reflected well on both the lord, who demonstrated his ability to provide gifts and the warrior who earned them.
>
> In return for their lord's generosity the warriors accepted a number of social obligations. The most important of which was the duty to fight in the warband and, if their lord was killed, to avenge him or die in the attempt.

Tolkien's knowledge of the Anglo-Saxon tradition of Gift Giving is clearly present in *The Lord of the Rings*. Christopher Tolkien points to the ancient horn given to Meriadoc by the Lady

---

[5] <www.millennia.demon.co.uk/ravens/context.htm>. This is the web site of *Ravens Warband*, a re-enactment society of the early Anglo-Saxon period (circa 500 A.D.). LVO 12/15/2005.

Eowyn as an example of "the word *mathum* used in Rohan for a 'treasure' or a 'rich gift'" (HoMe XII p. 39, p. 53). In the scene that Christopher Tolkien is referencing, Éomer also uses the modern word *gift(s)* in his address to Meriadoc.

> Kings of old would have laden you with **gifts** that a wain could not bear for your deeds upon the fields of Mundburg; and yet you will take naught, you say, but the arms that were given to you. This I suffer, for indeed I have no **gift** that is worthy; but my sister begs you to receive this small thing, as a memorial of Dernhelm and of the horns of the Mark at the coming of the morning (R.316; VI.6, **emphasis** added).

The reason that Éomer is prepared to shower gifts (mathums) on Merry is that Merry had fulfilled the social obligation placed upon him by entering into King Theoden's service (R.59; V.2), and by the previous bestowal of mathums of war gear (R.90; V.3). When all the other King's men had been killed or carried away by their terrified steeds, Merry had indeed come forward to fight with Eowyn as she stood between the Nazgûl and his prey, prepared to avenge Theoden's death, or die in the attempt (R.142-143; V.6). Merry's steadfastness in the fulfillment of his duty to the King had increased his honor and prestige beyond Éomer's ability to bestow a gift worthy of it.

The narrator concludes Tolkien's exposition on the tradition of Gift Giving in this scene, with the explanation that "Merry took the horn, for it could not be refused" (R.316; VI.6). The gift was not merely a kindness, but a traditionalized obligation that bound the bestower to present it and the recipient to take it.

In *Beowulf*, the hero's defeat of Grendel is followed by a mathum-giving (mathum-gifu, line 1301). The four mathums given to Beowulf (lines 1021-1023) are worked with gold and silver (lines 1030-1031). They are echoed in Tolkien's tales in the gifts (mathums) that the members of the Fellowship received.

- The first mathum was a golden standard (segen gyldenne), that in Tolkien's epic is represented by the great standard

given to Aragorn by Arwen, The Lady of Rivendell (R.56; V.2). It displayed the signs of Elendil: The White Tree, with seven stars about it, and a crown above it. The stars were made of gems, and the crown of gold and mithril (R.150; V.6).
- The second was a helmet (helm), which is reflected in the mathum war gear that Pippin received from Denethor. Pippin's helmet was high-crowned "with small raven wings on either side, set with a silver star in the center of the circlet" (R.96; V.4).
- The third was a corslet of ring-mail (byrnan), which is echoed most prominently in Thorin's gift of a corslet of mithril-rings to Bilbo (H.228; XII), a gift the worth of which was more than the value of The Shire and everything in it (F.414; II.4). Gimli called it "a kingly gift" (F.414; II.4), which is a translation of the Anglo-Saxon word *Theodenmathum*[6] attested in the Bosworth-Toller Anglo-Saxon Dictionary.[7]
- The fourth was a mathum-sword (mathum-sweord). It is most closely resembled in *The Lord of the Rings* by the scabbard given to Aragorn by Celeborn and Galadriel. It was ornamented with patterns of flowers and leaves "wrought of silver and gold," adorned with "elven-runes formed of many gems" that spelled out the sword's name and related its lineage (F.485; II.8).

The "white gem like a star" hanging upon a silver chain that Queen Arwen took from around her own neck to give to Frodo as he departs to return to The Shire (R.312; VI.6) is another example of a mathum in the Anglo-Saxon sense. This gift is recalled in *Beowulf* (line 2757) in the word *mathum-sigla* (mathum + carcanet[8]).

---

[6] In Anglo-Saxon, *Theoden* is the King or Leader of a *theod* (a nation or people).

[7] *An Anglo-Saxon Dictionary*: Based on the Manuscript Collections of the late Joseph Bosworth, D.D. F.R.S, edited by T. Northcote Toller, M.A., Oxford: At The Clarendon Press. 1898.

[8] See Tolkien's "Eärendil, the Mariner" for a use of *carcanet* in context (F.309 II.1).

All the mathums described above are of inestimable monetary value, but, as Underwood pointed out, that is not where their true worth lies. They are not symbols of wealth, but rather symbols of honor, prestige and respect; and herein lies Tolkien's subtle comic irony. In olden days ("beyond living memory"), the Hobbits, "though they have never been warlike or fought among themselves" (P.25), had once considered mathums tokens of esteem for feats of arms and valor. This is suggested by Tolkien's comment that the Hobbits had "been often obliged to fight to maintain themselves in a hard world" and by the fact that a relative of the word *mathum* had survived in the vocabulary of the 'modern' Hobbits. To the Hobbits of the end of the Third Age mathoms were things that they "had no immediate use for, but were unwilling to throw away" (P.25). Weapons "were used mostly as trophies, hanging above hearths or on walls," or collected in the Mathom-house (P.25), a word that is another Anglo-Saxon revival. In Anglo-Saxon *mathum-hus* meant 'treasure house' or 'treasury.' In The Shire, it is only a museum.

The 'low philological jest' contained in Tolkien's re-definition of the word *mathum* into *mathom* is, therefore, a subtle variant of Bilbo's throw-away line in *The Hobbit*: "We are plain quiet folk and have no use for adventures. Nasty disturbing uncomfortable things! Make you late for dinner! I can't think what anybody sees in them" (H.18; I). The *mathums* of old, earned by being late for dinner because of nasty disturbing things, had turned into *mathoms,* that modern Hobbits had no use for, except as dust catchers in the Hobbit Museum in Michel Delving (F.414; II.4).

Mr. Bilbo Baggins, esq. and the corslet of chain mail he is donating to Mathom House: courtesy of *The Hobbiton Daily News*: Drawn by JWD

The Linguistic Landscape of Bree

Bree, a town of both Men and Hobbits, was located at the intersection of the Great East Road and the North Road. It was built against Bree Hill, and was the principal town of Bree-Land, which consisted of the villages of Archet, Bree, Combe, and Staddle.

The name Bree Hill is one of Tolkien's philological jests, a joke only a linguist could love. It is what toponymists refer to as a tautology, a bilingual place name that repeats its meaning in both of its languages. Tolkien himself pointed this out in his "Notes on Nomenclature" (*Nomenclature*) where he specifically refers to the place name Brill (north-east of Oxford[9]), which is composed of the elements Bre (Welsh) + hill (English) (*Nomenclature* "Archet"). This type of construction shows up all across the linguistic landscape of England. There is another Brill, for example, in Cornwall (between Helston and Falmouth). This construction can be seen in the place names Breedon and Bredon, which also contain two elements that both mean "hill:" the Welsh

---

[9] For those who do not have an atlas of the United Kingdom at hand, I recommend <http://www.multimap.com/>. LVO 12/15/2005.

bre and the Old English (OE) *don*. Bredon Hill (north-north-east of Bredon, see the map on page 12) goes it one further with three elements that mean "hill."

The same tautology seen in Tolkien's Bree Hill is also present in Tolkien's name for the wood near Bree: *Chetwood*. In Old Celtic, *chet* means "wood." On the real-world map, this tautological construction shows up in the names Chetwode (south-west of Buckingham) and the Chute Forest in Wiltshire. The element *chet* also shows up in one of the other villages of Bree-Land: Archet. The prefix *Ar-* in the name Archet can be found in a number of Welsh place names, where it means 'nearby.' Tolkien's name, therefore, means 'near the woods,' which is exactly where he placed Archet in his description of Bree-Land: "on the edge of the Chetwood" (F.205; I.9). Compare: the Welsh place name Argoed [literally: 'by a wood', in Welsh, *coed* means 'wood,' and the '**C**' changes to '**G**' through the process of lenition].

A similar tautology can be seen in Tolkien's name *Combe* in combination with its location. Tolkien's description of Bree-Land placed Combe "in a deep valley" (F.205; I.9). The Old Celtic *kumb*, meaning 'valley' (compare the Welsh: *cwm*, which means 'hollow') was used so extensively that it was adopted into OE as *cumb* and has yielded numerous place names based on this root, such as Combe (Oxfordshire, Powys and West Berkshire), Coomb (Cornwall and Devon), Combwich (north-north-west of Bridgwater), derived from the combination of the OE *cumb* + *wic*, meaning "valley dwelling or hamlet," Compton (Devon, Hampshire, Surrey, West Berkshire, West Sussex), from the OE *comb* + *tun*, which means 'valley village'. Tolkien shows the same process that brought the Celtic *kumb* into OE, when *kumb* shows up in the Rohirric (Anglo-Saxon) place name *Deeping Coomb*, the valley in front of Helms Deep.

Linguistically, *Staddle* is the odd-man-out in Bree-Land. *Archet*, *Bree* and *Combe* share a certain Celtic ancestry, while Staddle has a Germanic origin. This should not be unexpected, because Bree-Land is a border area, inhabited by both Hobbits and Men. It is quite logical, therefore, that the place names in Bree-Land should reflect a similar linguistic mix. A linguistic mix of this type is, after all, merely a reflection of the linguistic landscape of England, where Celtic, Germanic, Latin and Norman elements dot the linguistic countryside, reflecting the history of the comings and goings of the peoples who spoke these languages. Stratford—ford (OE) on the *stratum* (L) or 'Roman road'—is on the banks of the river Avon (W). Bewdley—a corruption of the French *beau lieu*, which means "beautiful spot"—is located in Worcestershire on the edge of what remains of the once great Wyre Forest (W) on the banks of the river Severn (pre-Celtic).

Staddle shows up in British toponymy as Staddle Bridge in north Yorkshire, and as the place name Staddlethorpe in the East Riding of Yorkshire, near Goole. The toponymic element *-thorpe* is very rare in OE and place names with this ending are almost always Norse in origin. It can be seen reflected in the modern Dutch and German words for "village" *dorp* (D) and *Dorf* (G). The combination of *staddle* with *-thorpe* underscores the place name's Germanic origin.

Staddle can also be found in the vocabulary of architecture, in which a *staddle stone* is a mushroom-shaped stone used to raise the floors of barns, granaries and the like off the level of the earthen ground, to keep vermin from gaining access to the grain and fodder stored there. A barn built on staddle stones looks like it is on stilts.[10] The concept of *Staddle Barn* is so much a part of the linguistic landscape that it is the only street address necessary for The Danebury Trust in Cholderton. In modern German, *Stadel* is a dialectical word for *barn*.

Staddle was inhabited mostly by Hobbits (F.206; I.9). If its name was given to it by the Hobbits, Staddle should not be the sole member of this linguistic family in the Hobbits' dialect of Westron, which Tolkien describes as marked by their adherence "to old-fashioned local names of their own, which they seemed to have picked up in antiquity from the Men of the vales of Anduin" (Ad.483). The original language of the Hobbits "was evidently a Mannish language of the upper Anduin, akin to that of the Rohirrim" (Af.509). When Hobbits heard Rohirric, they recognized many words and could feel that there were similarities

---

[10] See a picture of an old barn on staddle stones at: <http://members.tripod.com/Chris_Breeze/favourable/barn.htm>. LVO 12/15/2005.

between the two languages (Af.517). Rohirric—and consequently the place name Staddle— should have a certain Germanic feel to it, because Tolkien created it from Anglo-Saxon, noting that Anglo-Saxon is "the sole field in which to look for the origin and meaning of words or names" in Rohirric (L.381).

The linguistic boundary line between "Germanic" culture and "Celtic" culture that passes through Bree is, however, not a reflection of the cultural boundary between Hobbits and Men, but rather of the boundary between Northerners and Southerners, be they Hobbits or Men. The older language of the southern Stoors and the Bree-men, reflected in his "translation" of *The Red Book of Westmarch* by Celtic elements common in England, like *bree* and *chet* (Af.516), represents the culture of the Southerners.

In a note to the Dutch translator, Tolkien commented that Celtic elements were also to be found in the place names of Buckland and the East Farthing, like *Crickhollow* (*Companion* 93). Another reflection of this is the honorific given to the Head of the Oldbuck family, who started the construction of Brandy Hall and changed the family name to Brandybuck. He was called *Gorhendad* (F.141; I.5, Ac.476). This title is simply the modern Welsh word for *great-grandfather*.

On the other hand, the Staddle Hobbits, who "claimed to be the oldest settlement of Hobbits in the world" (F.206; I.9), represent the other two breeds of Hobbits, whose migration from "the upper vales of Anduin, between the eaves of Greenwood the Great and the Misty Mountains" (P.21), did not take them into the southern realms visited by the Stoors before the Stoors moved north again (P.22). The name *Shire* (Q.V.) reflects their origin. This name can be traced to the word *scir*, the Anglo-Saxon territorial administrative unit, which was governed by a *scir-gerefa* [*Shire-reeve*, later *Sheriff*]. In choosing the name *Staddle*, Tolkien was adding to the depth and realism of his linguistic tour de force. Without it, his linguistic landscape would have been flat.

In a letter Tolkien pointed out that the invention of his toponyms was an idiosyncratic enterprise, which he undertook to satisfy his own private linguistic taste. "The 'source', if any," said Tolkien, "provided solely the sound-sequence (or suggestions for its stimulus) and its purport *in the source* is totally irrelevant" (L.380).

I can well empathize with Tolkien's statement, because I, too, play word games in which the sound envelope of a word or phrase suggests an improbable, and therefore, funny meaning, if the envelope is slightly rearranged. In Russian, for example, the ubiquitous expression of agreement очень хорошо [ochen' khorosho] (very good) becomes the title of a movie starring the world-famous actor of faux-Russian descent Boris Karloff: 'Ocean Horror Show.' In Dutch, to the dismay of native speakers, the word for *errands* (*boodschappen*) becomes a flock of 'boat sheep' (**bootschapen*), and 'a little present not worth mentioning' (*kleinigheidje*) becomes 'a small goat' (*klein geitje*). Those who do not speak Russian or Dutch, might appreciate an evening at the opera with the Muppets, where they could hear *Placido Flamingo* sing an aria from **La Travi Otter.* Rocky and Bullwinkle fans will recognize the infamous Boris Badunov as the evil counterpart of Boris Godunov (*good enough), the title character of Pushkin's play and Moussorgsky's famous opera based on it. Another excellent example can be found in Victor Borge's "Inflationary Language," in which *before* [be-4] becomes *be-five*, *benign* [be-9] becomes *be-ten* and *beaten* [be-10] becomes *be-eleven*. The temptation to look for real-life parallels to Tolkien's names on the map of England is, therefore, irresistible.

There are a number of Breedon-s, but only one Bredon. It was made famous by Alfred Edward Housman (1859-1936) in his poem "A Shropshire Lad." There is even a "Bredon Hill" pattern available from Royal Doulton China. Bredon and Bredon Hill are located in the Vale of Evesham.

This suspiciously Tolkienian Bredon is north-west of Oxford, in Worcestershire. The area is bounded by the Malvern Hills (rising to about 1,400 feet) and the Cotswold Hills (just over 1,000 feet) and bisected by the river Avon, which winds through the wooded Vale of Evesham. The countryside is beautiful and picturesque. The county is bordered by Gloucestershire in the south, Herefordshire in the west, Warwickshire in the east, and Staffordshire, West Midlands and Housman's Shropshire in the north. The hilly, wooded region in the north west is the remains of the once mighty Wyre Forest, which once extended all the way from Worcester to the Bristol Channel.

Bredon Hill (991 feet high), close to the south-western border of the county, is ringed by a number of small villages with evocative, Tolkienesque names, including:

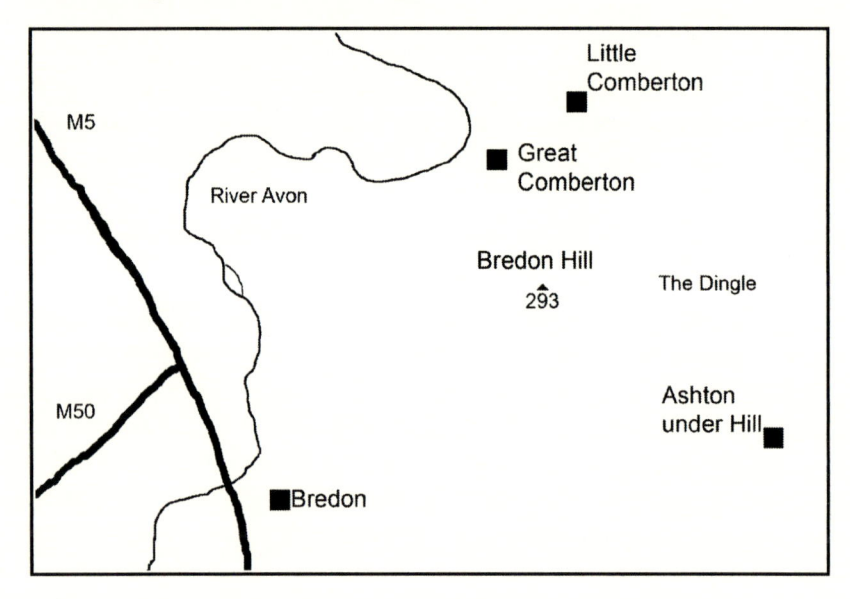

- Ashton under Hill, which carries a nice Tolkienian echo of Frodo's traveling name in Bree,
- Great Comberton and Little Comberton, which are suggestive of Tolkien's Combe in Bree-Land in the same way that Bree is suggested by Bre(don),
- Bredon, a village on the river Avon with a mill pond, tithe barn (132 feet long), and of course, a pub, which is, unfortunately called *The Fox And Hounds*.

As if this were not enough, *The Dingle* is located east of Bredon Hill. This topographical feature can only be seen on the 1:25,000 map of the area, and because of this, it is, to a certain extent, hidden, a characteristic that calls up visions of Entmoot in Dern Dingle, a "hidden," "deep (tree-shadowed) dell" (*Nomenclature*).

Another thing that makes this particular Bre(don) especially Tolkienian is the presence of the village of Pershore, at the end of the Vale of Evesham, to the north of Bredon Hill. Pershore plays an important role in the misunderstanding in *Roverandom* that kept Old Artaxerxes from finding his way back to Persia so that he eventually crossed paths with the little dog hero of the story.[11] If Tolkien knew where Pershore is, he would have known where Bredon is.

When the scale of the map is expanded to include Pershore and Evesham, the region of Buckland then falls within its bound-

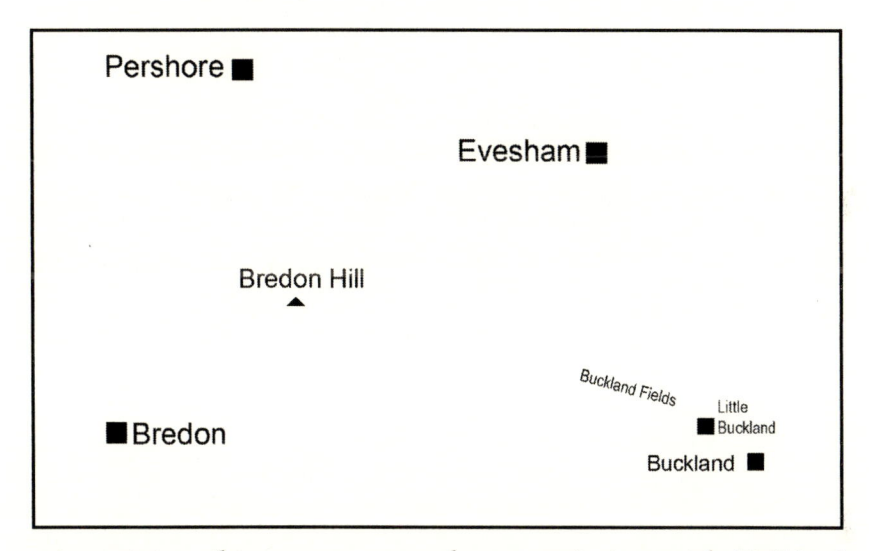

```
Pershore ■

                        Evesham ■



            Bredon Hill
                ▲

                              Buckland Fields
                                               Little
■ Bredon                                       ■ Buckland
                                        Buckland ■
```

aries, giving this area yet another association with Tolkien's toponymy. The region consists of the village of Buckland, plus Little Buckland and Buckland fields north-west of the village.

The Avon river valley has been the site of tobacco farming since the mid-sixteen hundreds. Eckington, Pensham and Upton Snodsbury were noted for their tobacco. This is a very Tolkienesque detail for this area, given that in the Prologue Meriadoc Brandybuck speculates that Tobold Hornblower of Longbottom in the Southfarthing, who was the first to grow true pipeweed in his garden, brought it back with him from Bree, where it, at any rate, grew well on the south slopes of Bree Hill (P.28-29). The Vale of Evesham is conducive to agriculture, because it sits in a pocket of warmth, created by the Gulf Stream, which is funneled up the Severn and Avon valleys by the hills on either side. This fits

---

[11] *Roverandom*, p. 14.

precisely with Tolkien's description of where pipe-weed grew best. "[It] flourishes only in warm sheltered places like Longbottom" (P.29).

Bredon sits near the intersection of the M5 (north-south) and the M50 (east-west) motorways, but that is probably not what Tolkien had in mind when he placed Bree at the intersection of the Great East Road and the North Road. The (in)famous "M" motorways are much too modern for that. It is more likely that he was thinking of medieval times when Evesham was on one of the great highways leading to Wales. The reader with a modern map and a desire to get to Wales from Evesham can follow the M50 west until it turns into the A40 before entering Wales. Conversely, that is the road that the Hobbits would have followed east on the way to Bree. The suggestion is intriguing, and certainly begs to be followed up on, but that is another story.

Esgaroth

Esgaroth is a city called "Lake Town" in the common speech. It was built on piles driven into the bed of Long Lake. Most of the mentions of Esgaroth are in *The Hobbit* (H.172. 185-93, 234-38, 239, 286; IX, X, XIV, XIX), but it is also mentioned in Bilbo's birthday speech in *LotR* (F.55; I.1). It is not glossed in *Nomenclature*, but it is glossed in the *Etymologies* under ESEK-, as 'Reedlake,' because of the reed banks in the west,' pointing to the Ilkorin word *esgar* (reed-bed) (HoMe v.396).

The name, however, does yield to a more prosaic Celtic etymology. Celtic elements in Tolkien's place names should come as no surprise to any reader. Bree-Land has its share in names like *Archet* and *Bree*. The Westron translation for *Esgaroth* is "Lake Town," which is the same as the translation that would be produced if the name is assumed to contain Celtic roots: *es* [water, river] + *garth* [protected enclosure].

The first element (*es*) is derived from the Celtic root for *water*. This root has even made its way into English in the word *whiskey*, which is really a borrowing of the Irish term *uisge*. This spelling of the Irish root is reflected in the English name for the

Welsh river on which Casnewydd-ar-Wysg [Newport] is situated: *The Usk*.

In Welsh, this root is seen as *(g)wy*, where it shows up in a number of hydronyms (river names) like Conwy [the great river], Elwy [gliding water], Gwy [The Wye in English], Llugwy [clear water] and Mynwy [small water], with shortening of the vowel and lenition of the initial consonant, as is normal in Welsh compounds. In Welsh, the same root shows up in the words for a number of water fowl, such as *hwyad* [duck], *gwydd* [goose], *gwylan* [sea gull], *gwylog* [guillemot], and in the word for *seaweed*, *gwymon*.

This element shows up on the map of England in a number of orthographic variations as the names *Eskdale* (Cumbria), *Easebourn* (West Sussex), the *Is* and the *Isbourne* (a tautology), the river *Esk*, and the river *Exe*. The Welsh name for Exeter [derived from Exceastre: Army camp on the river Exe] is *Caerwysg* [Army camp on the water, river]. The use of the Celtic element *es* in the place names and hydronyms above is suggestive of the linguistic forces behind Tolkien's choice of the name for the river that flowed east through The Shire, *The Water* [Q.V.].

The second element, *garth*, is derived from a root that shows up in English as *garden*, and as a part of the name of Lancelot's castle (*Joyous* **Gard**), and as an element in the name of Saruman's castle (*Isen***gard**). In Russian, it can be found in the word *city* город [gorod]. In Modern Welsh, it survives as *garth* and *gardd* [garden, the 'th' and the 'dd' both having similar pronunciations], and, in archaic Welsh as *garthan* [encampment] and *lluarth* [army camp, llu = army, host. The initial '**G**' is lost to lenition.]. In Cornish it is *garth* and *lowarth* [garden]. In Gaelic, the liquid '**R**' has preserved both its vowels, as is the case with the Russian *gorod* [city] and Tolkien's *garoth*. There, it is *garadh*. The double vowel around the liquid '**R**' gives Tolkien's creation a feeling of antiquity. The presence of vowels on both sides of a liquid '**R**' suggests an older form of the word. The meaning of this root is 'a guarded and protected place,' usually surrounded by a wall. This is a good logical match for Tolkien's description.

Tolkien says that Esgaroth was "built out on bridges far into the water as protection against enemies of all sorts" (H.172;

IX). When Thorin and Co. arrived there after their escape from the Wood-elves, they were taken across the great bridge and through the gate by the captain of the guard and six of his men (H.188-189; X). Though the guard was lax, and the threat to the town small when Thorin and Co. arrived, that was certainly not the case when the town earned the name *Esgaroth*. As the Celtic elements in the name say, Esgaroth was then 'a water guarded enclosure.'

If *Lake Town* is the English translation of the Celtic *Esgaroth*, then *Long Lake* must have also have another name, but Tolkien does not give one. The hypothetical Welsh translation of *Long Lake*, **Llyn Hir*, does indeed exist in the Cambrian Mountains of Powys, in Wales. It is on Mynydd Waun Fawr [Mountain of the Great Moor] at the 390-meter contour line, about two-thirds of the way from Talerddig to Four Crosses, north-north-east of Newton. There is, however, nothing around it on the map to suggest other Tolkien place names.

The discovery of Celtic elements in *Esgaroth* provides a unique insight into the history of the people who inhabited Lake Town, in the same way that the Celtic place names of Bree-Land reflect the origin of Bree-Land's inhabitants (Af.414). The commonality of place name elements in Bree and Lake Town suggests a common linguistic ancestry for the Lake-men and the Bree-men.

Esgaroth

> [O]ne's mind is, of course, stored with a 'leaf-mould' of memories (submerged) of names, and these rise up to the surface at times, and may provide with modification the bases of 'invented' names.
> • J.R.R. Tolkien (L.409)

The Linguistic Landscape of Tolkien's Shire

Tolkien's famous letter to Rayner Unwin (L.249-251) about the translation of the toponymy of The Shire is often quoted in serious analyses of Tolkiennymy, but one of the points in Tolkien's letter that is seldom, if ever, quoted is the one that says that "the toponymy of The Shire ... is a 'parody' of that of rural England" (L.250). Most serious analysts take themselves too seriously, forgetting that Tolkien had a marvelous sense of humor. This study will place a bit more accent on that aspect of 'parody,' while keeping in mind that The Shire map is "based on some acquaintance with English toponymical history" (L.250).

The hallmark of parody is that it takes as its target something familiar to the audience and transforms it subtly to defeat the audience's expectations about the target of the parody. The best-known parody of *Lord of the Rings* is, of course, *Bored of the Rings*. It takes the sound envelope of Tolkien's title and only changes one sound, but the result is funny because it is simultaneously something familiar and something new.

Tolkien's work is full of this kind of humor. His parody for the name of the central administrative building for The Shire is based on exactly the same linguistic sleight of hand that produced *Bored of the Rings*. He only changed one sound in the sound envelope of *The Town Hall*, and the result was the delightful *The Town Hole*, playing on the opening line of *The Hobbit*: "In a hole in the ground there lived a Hobbit."

Town Hall, Barnard Castle

It is the interaction of the two elements of a parody—the target and the foil—that makes it funny. Without its target, a parody-foil is not funny at all. One of the goals of this study is to find the target of Tolkien's parody-names.

While the modern reader can appreciate the kind of linguistic humor contained in *Town Hole*, that is not always the case. Tolkien plays a variation on the game of "sounds like" in the poem (F.276-8 I.12) that Sam recites about a troll in chapter 12 of Book I ("A Flight to the Ford"). In the final stanza, Tom—the man confronting the troll—has kicked the troll and hurt his foot, and Tolkien offers up a homonym-pun that may fall a bit flat for modern readers whose Shakespearean English is a bit rusty.

> Tom's leg is game, since home he came,
> And his bootless foot is lasting lame.

To appreciate this joke, one has to know that *bootless* can mean both 'without a piece of footwear' and 'without any use.' The second use is clearly visible in Shakespeare's *King Henry the Sixth*, part 3, scene iii (A field of battle) when George enters and says:

Our hap is loss, our hope but sad despair;
Our ranks are broke, and ruin follows us:
What counsel give you? Whither shall we fly?

To which Edward replies:

Bootless is flight, they follow us with wings;
And weak we are and cannot shun pursuit.

Both meanings of *bootless* are supported by the context of Tolkien's poem, and that is what makes it funny. Unfortunately, if the audience has to have the relationship between the two elements of the parody explained, the joke is not funny, and this is the case with many of Tolkien's 'low philological jests,' which is what Tolkien called his explanation of the name *Smaug*.

Tolkien's explanation of the origin of the name *Smaug* must be regarded as authoritative, but before I read Tolkien's letter (L.31), I had developed a different derivation of the name on strictly linguistic grounds, forgetting that Tolkien liked history and was moved by it, especially such history as "throws light on words and names" (L.264). My linguistic etymology was based on the Proto-Indo-European root for *smoke* *smeug(h)-/smeuqh-. It seemed to me that *Smaug* (Smoke) would be a particularly picturesque name for a fire-breathing dragon. In old Lithuanian *smoke* is *smáugiu*; in Teutonic it is *smauk. In Middle-high German it is *smouch* and in old Dutch it is *smooc*. An excursion into the Slavic languages adds an even more interesting twist to an etymological study of the name. In Old Church Slavonic, смокъ (smok" [the silent vowel ъ is transliterated in English as a quote mark ") is the word for *dragon*, and in old Czech it is *smok*. In modern Polish the word for *dragon* still is *smok*, which is pronounced almost exactly like the English word *smoke*.

Tolkien says that the name Smaug is a "pseudonym—the past tense of the primitive Germanic verb *Smugan*, to squeeze through a hole: a low philological jest" (L.31), referring to the passage in which the company is looking at the map of the Mountain, and Gandalf explains that Smaug could not possibly have used the hidden passage to the lower halls, "because it is too small."

> 'Five feet high the door and three may walk abreast' say the runes, but Smaug could not creep into a hole that size, not even when he was a young dragon, certainly not after devouring so many of the dwarves and men of Dale" (H.32; I).

This study is an attempt to find the history behind the names of The Shire, but readers are cautioned—remember the etymology of *Smaug*—that Tolkien's literary efforts were an attempt to "create a world in which a form of language agreeable to [his] personal aesthetic might seem real" (L.264). Tolkien's 'personal aesthetic' and mine may not always coincide, but I do like his linguistic sense of humor, and hope that if the explanations of the parodies of the map of England herein are not his, then at least they are as funny or as interesting as his, and can give the reader "some acquaintance with English toponymical history."

The Shire. In *Nomenclature*, Tolkien comments that *Shire* is derived from the OE *scir*, which "seems very early to have replaced the ancient Germanic word for a 'district'," that survives today in the Dutch *gouw* and the German *Gau*, and can be attested in the earlier Gothic form *gawi*.

In the president's opening address to the Historical section of the Archeological Institute at Taunton on August 7, 1879, entitled "The Shire and the Gá,"[12] Edward Freeman explores the difference between these two terms. He contrasts the names of the counties in England that contain the element *shire* with those that do not, pointing out that "to many counties of England the ending *shire* is never added. Some of us may have heard the phrase of going into 'the shires,' as distinguished from those parts of England which are not shires. No one ever adds the word to Kent, Cornwall, Sussex, Essex, Middlesex, Norfolk, Suffolk, Northumberland, Cumberland, or Westmoreland." Only

---

[12] Edward Freeman, *English Towns and Districts*, London: Macmillan, 1883, pp. 103-133.

23 of the names of the 39 "historical" counties of England contain the element *shire*. (See the Appendix 'A' for a full list.)

Using *Somerset* and *Northamptonshire* as his main examples, Freeman convincingly argues that *Somerset* represents a class of counties that "are undoubted tribal settlements," bearing "undoubted tribal names," and that *Northamptonshire*, "whose name is not heard of till the eleventh century," represents a class of counties that are "a land gathered round a town," named after the town that is "the natural head and centre" of that land. This is the result, he concludes, of the fact "that West-Saxon England was made only once, while Mercian England had to be made twice. The Mercian *shire* is another thing from the West-Saxon *gá*, because Mercia, or the greater part of it, was conquered and divided by the Danes in 877, while the Danes tried in vain to conquer and divide Wessex in 878." The original names of the lands that fell under Danelaw were replaced by new ones, reflecting the new political reality of the time. "When Ædward the Unconquered[13] [ruled 900-924] and his sister the Lady of Mercia won the land back for England and for Christendom, when they founded many towns and fortresses, they seem to have mapped out the recovered land afresh," says Freeman (p. 124).

While Freeman's analysis of the historic significance of the two terms may suggest a historical and political subtext to Tolkien's choice of the name for the land inhabited by the Hobbits, Tolkien could have hardly chosen *Gá* for the name of the homeland of the Hobbits, because it would not have been recognized by non-specialist English-speaking readers. The word *Gá* has disappeared from the map of England, but, to a toponymist, its footprints can still be seen—primarily in Essex and in Kent—in such place names as *Surrey* (Southern Gá), *Eastry* (Eastern Gá), *Sturry* (river-Stour Gá) and *Ely* (Eel Gá). On the map of Holland and Germany, *Gá* can still be seen in such place names as *Follega*

---

[13] Edward "the Unconquered King," also known as Edward the Elder, was the son of Alfred the Great and Ælhswith. He was born in 869, and died in 924. He is buried at Winchester Cathedral, Winchester, England. Assisted by his sister Æthelflæd the "Lady of Mercia," who headed her own troops, he won back the lands that had fallen under Danelaw, extending his sway over Mercia, East Anglia, and Northumbria.

(Folle's Gá) and *Wolvega* (Wolf's Gá) in Holland (both in the province of Friesland) and in *Schwangau* (Swan Gau) and *Oberammergau* (the Gau above the Ammer river) in Germany (both in Bavaria).

The term *scir* was also used for districts smaller than the county names that are the most commonly recognized modern usage. Sometimes the term *shire* (*scir*) was used for the names of Hundreds or Wapentakes. Sometimes it was used to designate special districts known as an *Honour* or a *Liberty*. These were districts in which there was a separate jurisdiction from that of the county in which the district was located. The Liberties of the Bishop of Durham, for example, were called Allertonshire, Howdenshire and Islandshire. The Honour of Richmond was known as Richmondshire and the Liberty of Ripon was Ripeshire.[14]

An *Honour* and a *Liberty* were types of charters granted by the king which conferred a kind of independence with regard to the maintenance of law and order. These were only abolished in 1888 when the County Council was established. The Honour of Richmond was, for example, granted to Alan the Red of Brittany by William the Conqueror for his services in the campaign against King Harold. The Liberty of Ripon dates to Saxon times, when it was granted to the Archbishop of York.

The independent nature of Tolkien's Shire seems to indicate that perhaps The Shire was previously a Liberty granted by the high king at Fornost, or Norbury, as the Hobbits called it (P.30).

The Dutch translations[15] use *Gouw*—a simple dictionary look-up for the reader—as the translation of *The Shire*, while both the German translations[16] use *Auenland* (land of meadows). Carroux agreed with Tolkien's comment in *Nomenclature* that the "recent" use of *Gau* "in regional reorganization under Hitler has spoilt this very old word," and Krege did not change the name. The most successful Russian translations[17] are the imaginative

---

[14] A.H. Smith, *English Place Name Elements: Part II, The Elements JAFN-YTRI*, Cambridge at the University Press, 1956, p. 110.

[15] For more information on the Dutch translations, see Appendix 'B', and "Bilbo Balings Turns 50."

[16] For more on the German translations, see Appendix 'B'.

Хоббитания [Hobbitania], by Murav'ev and Kistyakovskij, and the insightful Хоббитшир [Hobbitshire] by Matorina. *Hobbitania* mirrors one of the forms that Freeman attests for Somerset (*Somersetania* [p. 122]), while *Hobbitshire* resembles the model for English county names ending in *-shire* represented by Northamptonshire in Freeman's presentation.

Taken to the illogical extreme of a purely historical analysis, *Hobbitania* would seem to be the land (Gá) of the tribe of the Hobbits, that never fell under Danelaw, while *Hobbitshire* would seem to be a political subdivision (Shire) of the kingdom, like a Liberty, and Honour or a County.

From the point of view of the modern reader, unaware of the historical background presented here, *Hobbitshire* is more clearly recognizable as an English toponym, while *Hobbitania* is not necessarily marked as to its location and could fit in anywhere. The ending *-ania* is Latin and shows up in the names of countries like: Lithuania, Mauritania, Pennsylvania and Transylvania. In translating a Mythology for England, *Hobbitshire* should have been the winner, because it preserves the 'local colour,' but *Hobbitania* is the more widely recognized form in Russia.

The river **Shirebourn**, which rises in Green-Hill Country, is a tributary of the Brandywine. In its lower reaches, it forms the border between the East- and the Southfarthing. It is not mentioned in *Nomenclature*, but in his notes to the Dutch translator (*Companion* lix), Tolkien commented that the name "has nothing to do with 'The Shire.'" He told Schuchart that it was derived from an actual hydronym with the meaning of "bright spring," or "bright stream," and in Dutch, *Shirebourn* became *Klaarbeek* (*clear stream*).

In the German translations, *Shirebourn* is recorded as *Auenbronn* (meadow spring), repeating the same element used in the German translation of *The Shire* (*Auenland*) for the first part of the name, and using an element common to German place names such as *Heiligenbronn* (holy spring) and *Heilbronn* (healing spring), for the second. The differences between the German and the Dutch translations point clearly to the ambiguities involved

---

[17] For more on the Russian translations, see Appendix '**B**'.

in the purely linguistic interpretation of this name without an assist from Tolkien himself.

Tolkien's *Shirebourn* has a number of relatives on the map of England. The spelling varies, but the underlying elements are the same:

- Sherborne (Dorset, Gloucestershire)
- Sherbourne (Warwickshire)
- Sherburn (Durham, Yorkshire)
- Shirburn (Oxfordshire).

The ones in Dorset, Gloucestershire, Warwickshire and Durham are all attested as *Scireburne* in the Doomsday Book. Regardless of how the name is spelled today, the constituent elements are the OE *scir* and *burna*. The second element (*burna*) is commonly glossed as 'spring' or 'stream.' *The Cambridge Dictionary of English Place-Names* (2004, cited in *Companion* lix), comments that the OE word *bruna* was commonly used to name bodies of clear running water, emanating from springs, that flowed over gravelly beds, but which were not sufficiently large to be called a river. It is related to the German *Brunnen* and the Dutch *bron,* both meaning *spring*, as in 'water welling up out of the ground.'

The meaning of the first element (*scir*) is the one that contains the greater ambiguity. Glosses of place names and hydronyms containing this element frequently point to the difficulty of telling OE *scir* (*shire*) from OE *scir* (*clear, pure*). (Compare the modern English *shear* and *sheer*.) In modern studies of English place names, hydronyms and the names of places located on a stream or river are often glossed as 'bright,' 'clear' or 'pure' in reference to the quality of the water. This was Tolkien's instruction to the Dutch translator: *Klaarbeek* (*clear stream*). Ekwall (1940),[18] for example, glosses *Sherbourn* as "bright stream," while Cave (1976)[19] calls it "clear stream."

---

[18] Eilert Ekwall, *The Concise Oxford Dictionary of English Place Names*, Oxford at the Clarendon Press, 1940, p. 397.

[19] Lyndon F. Cave, *Warwickshire Villages*, London: Robert Hall, 1976, p. 21.

Johnson (1915),[20] however, glosses *Sherborne* and its variants as "shire or boundary brook," pointing specifically to Sherbourne brook in Warwickshire as the "boundary between the Hundreds of Barlichway and Kineton," apparently quoting Duignan (1912).[21] Cave, despite his gloss of Sherbourne as "clear stream," repeats Duignan's comment about the Sherbourne brook being the border between the Hundreds of Barlichway and Kineton. Duignan goes on to explain that the river 'Shirbourn,' which passes through Coventry, was a part of the boundary line between Allesley and Coventry, and between the old parishes of St. John's and St. Michael's, in Coventry.

Regardless of the fact that the gloss of Sherbourne as 'boundary brook' does not have wide currency in the modern etymological studies of English place names, and was not Tolkien's intended meaning, it is the definition to be implied from Tolkien's map, which shows the Shirebourn as the border between the East- and the Southfarthing. This is the meaning behind the name replacing *Sherbourn* on the map in the first Polish[22] translation: *Rzeka Graniczna* (rzeka = river, granica = border).

Smith (1956)[23] offers three possible explanations for *scir* when used as an adjective in the first element of a place name defining settlements and topographic features.

- common land available to all the men of the shire
- the place where the shire-moot is held
- places or object(s) on the border of the shire

These usages can be seen in the names:

- Sherwood Forest (Nottinghamshire, spelled Shirwood in the *Whatley Gazetteer*[24]) the wood belonging to the shire

---

[20] James Johnson, *Place Names of England and Wales*, London, John Murray, 1915, reprinted London: Bracken Books, 1994, pp. 440-441.

[21] W.H. Duignan, *Warwickshire Place Names*, Oxford University Press, 1912, p. 101.

[22] For more on the Polish translations, see Appendix '**B**'.

[23] A.H. Smith (ed.), *English Place Names Elements: Part II (JAFN-YTRI)*, Cambridge at the University Press, 1956, p. 110.

- Shireoaks (Nottinghamshire) the oaks of the shire, the location of the shire-moot, or the oaks at the border of the shire (analyses vary)
- Shireshead (Lancashire) the top of the shire, in this case, the northern border of the Amounderness Hundred
- Shireland (Derbyshire, spelled Shirland in the *Whatley Gazetteer*) the *lundr* (Old Norse: sacred grove) belonging to the shire
- Sherland (Kent) the common land belonging to the shire
- Shiremark (Surrey, Sussex) the mark (borderland) of the shire and
- Shireley (Derbyshire) the *leah* (meadow) where the shire-moot was held

Documentary evidence—hard or impossible to find for some names—is needed to conclusively prove any of Smith's usages. Scir boundaries were subject to change, and that change may have left some 'border' markers bereft of their original purpose, and the reason for their names.

The OE element *scir* (shire) shows up in *LotR* in other words that Tolkien used to give The Shire a feeling of more historical depth. It can be seen in *Shire-moot* (scir-gemot) [P.30] and *Shirriff* (scir-gerefa) [P.31]. Though Tolkien did not use it, the OE *scir-mann*, a *steward of the shire* was contemporary with *Shire-moot* and *Shirriff*.

On the map of England, the river Sherbourne flows through the city of Coventry. Coventry is famous for Lady Godiva, for its textile industry and for being a place to be sent to when people are mad at you (a linguistic artifact of the Civil War [1633-1642]). In the early part of the sixteenth century, Coventry's cloth and thread dyers became so famous for their ability to produce blue materials that did not fade, that the expression "as true as Coventry blue" became proverbial, giving Coventry's textile industry the kind of brand name recognition that many a modern company would be envious of. It survives today as a

---

[24] *England's Gazetteer* : or An Accurate Description of all the Cities, Towns and Villages of the Kingdom (in three volumes, Stephen Whatley, ed.), London: J. and P. Knapton, D. Browne, A. Miller, J. Whiston and B. White, 1751.

linguistic artifact to describe someone who is unswervingly true to his/her principles; sometimes shortened to 'true blue.'

The tale is told that, at the height of the popularity of true Coventry blue, the river Sherbourne used to run blue from the effluents of the dyers along the river, a problem that "concerned the rest of the community very closely."[25] Gorton (1833)[26] comments that "the water of the river Sherbourn is famed for its excellence as medium for dying blue." If Tolkien heard the story, then it could have been the impetus for the name of the river Lhûn. (Noldorin lhûn = blue, compare: Lhúnorotni = Blue Mountains, Lhúndirien = Blue Towers, HoMe v.412)

Newbury is a village in Buckland. It is not mentioned in *Nomenclature*, but Tolkien does discuss *Norbury*, indicating that *Norbury* means 'north (fortified) town.' *Newbury* is clearly OE, a combination of *niwe* + *burh* (dative: *byrig*), which means 'new (fortified) town.' In the German translation, *Newbury* became *Neuburg*, retaining the same linguistic elements Tolkien used. In Dutch, it became *Nieburg*, using an old form of the word *new* that is common in Dutch place names.

There is only one Newbury in the *Shell Touring Atlas of Great Britain*,[27] and it is the only town with that name in the *Parliamentary Gazetteer* of 1854.[28] This Newbury is located in Berkshire, which is south of Oxfordshire and separated from it

---

[25] Smith, Frederick, Coventry; *Six Hundred Years of Municipal Life*, Coventry: Corporation of Coventry in association with the *Coventry Evening Telegraph*, 1946 (revised ed).

[26] John Gorton, *A Topographical Dictionary of Great Britain and Ireland* (in three volumes), London: Chapman and Hall, 1833, vol.1, p. 521)

[27] *Shell Touring Atlas of Great Britain*, London: Book Club Associates, 1981, p. 16 G 5.

[28] *The Parliamentary Gazetteer of England and Wales, Adapted to the Most Recent Statistical Arrangements, and Lines of Railroad and Canal Communications, with a Complete Country Atlas of England, Four Large Maps of Wales and an Appendix Containing the Results, in Detail, of the Census of 1841*, in four volumes, London: A. Fullerton & Co, 1854.

by the Thames. The town is situated on the river Kennet at the intersection of the A4 and the A34. While there is only one well-known place named *Newbury*, place names with this general meaning are relatively common, indirectly reflecting the historical processes which caused the 'old' walled town—after which the new town was named—to become uninhabitable: war, plague, fire and other such calamities. Many of the names of these 'new walled towns' are linguistically closely related to *Newbury*. Newburgh (Yorkshire) is also derived from OE *niwe* + *burh*, as are Newbrough (Northumberland) and Newborough (Staffordshire). There is also a Newtown located just to the south of Newbury.

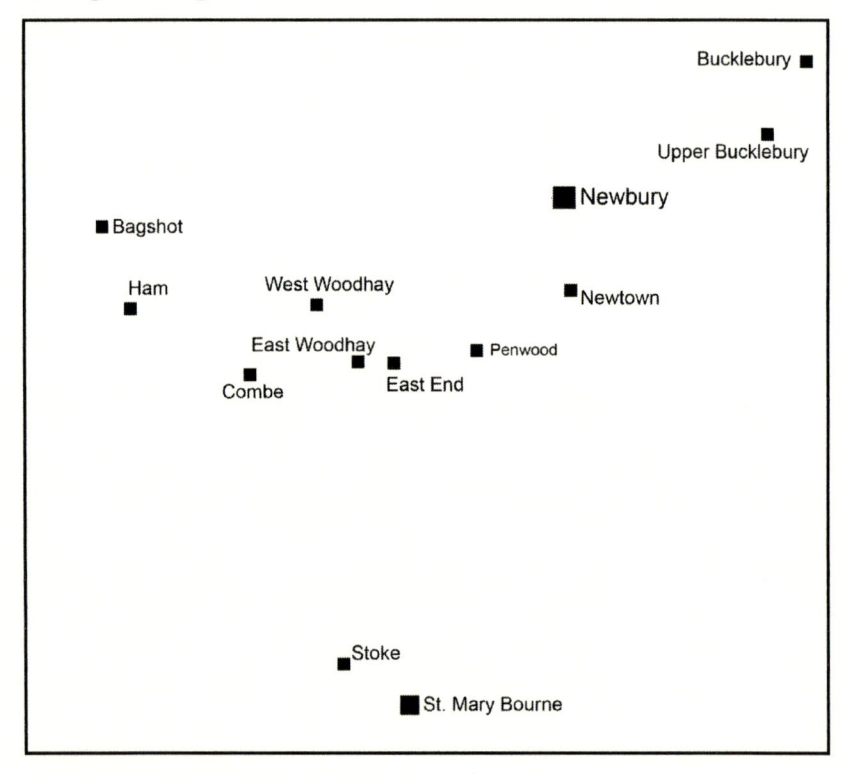

Newbury should have been known to Tolkien, in part, because of the prominence of John Winchcombe, better perhaps known as Jack O'Newbury, a fourteenth century textile magnate, and, in part, because Newbury was the site of two famous battles during the English Civil War in the 1600-s, the first in 1643 and the second in 1644. Both the battles and Jack O'Newbury are mentioned in a popular children's history of Britain,[29] and Tolkien would certainly have been at least that well read in British history.

Because this *Newbury* is so well known, it suggests itself as a starting point to look for other Shirish place names, and the search quickly pays off, locating no less than nine Tolkienesque place names in the vicinity. Bucklebury and Upper Bucklebury are north-east of Newbury. Bagshot is west of Newbury, and north of Ham (as in *Farmer Giles of*) and Combe (in East Breeland). There are two towns south-west of Newbury that suggest The High Hay (defensive hedge) of Buckland: West Woodhay, East Woodhay. Slightly to the east of East Woodhay is East End, which recalls *Haysend* in The Shire. To the reader with a knowledge of Welsh, like Tolkien, Penwood, north-east of East End, and south of Newbury is suggestive of *Woody End* of The Shire, because, in Welsh, *pen* means *head* or *end*. Stoke—a close linguistic relative of Tolkien's *Stock*—is south-south-west of Newbury, near St. Mary Bourne.

Newbury is mentioned in Ditchfield's book on OE Customs[30] in his section on *Fairs*, as one of the towns in which the institution of "Mock Mayor" could still be found "until recent years" (his book was published in 1896). His presentation of this custom calls to mind Tolkien's description of "the Mayor of Michel Delving (or of the Shire)", who was elected "at the Free Fair ... at the Lithe, that is at Mid-summer " for a period of seven years. (P.31)

In Newbury, there was an annual election "with burlesque formalities" for "the Mayor of the City" (or, as he was more correctly known, "of Barthelmas") held on St. Anne's Day, July 26th (p. 246).[31] The election was followed by an "official banquet,

---

[29] *Hamlyn's Children's History of Britain: From the Stone Age to the Present Day*, London: The Hamlyn Publishing Group, 1977, pp. 118, 138, 139.

[30] P.H. Ditchfield. *Old English Customs Extant at the Present Time: An Account of Local Observances, Festival Customs, and Ancient Ceremonies yet Surviving in Great Britain*, London: George Redway, 1896.

[31] St. Anne is the mother of the Virgin Mary, and the

at which beans and bacon formed the principal dish" (p. 247).[32] After the banquet, the Mayor marched around the town in procession, accompanied by a "band of music," carrying "a cabbage on a stick" (instead of a scepter) and other similar items of mock civic dignity (p. 247). The primary duties of Tolkien's mayor had a similarly unofficious air about them. They consisted of presiding at banquets given on The Shire's numerous holidays (P.31).

Ditchfield quotes the historian of Newbury, Mr. Walter Money, who thinks that the mayor's 'titles' are connected with "the limits of the fair granted by King John (1215 A.D.) to the Hospital of St. Bartholomew" (p. 246).

As Ditchfield points out, the word *fair* is derived from the "ecclesiastical term *feria*, a holiday." Originally religious festivals held to honor a saint, fairs were an occasion for people to come from the neighboring towns and villages, which enterprising tradespeople took advantage of to display and sell their wares. As the religious elements passed away, the *feria* became what we think of today as a *fair*. (p. 138)

Bucklebury—6 miles east-north-east of Newbury—stands out just like Newbury does by being the only town with that name in the *Parliamentary Gazetteer*. Earlier attested forms of the name show that it means *Burghild's fortified town*. Some place name studies point to the daughter of Coenwulf (Anglo-Saxon king of Mercia 796-821) as the possible namesake of the city.

Tolkien offered an alternative explanation in *Nomenclature*, advising translators to use the same element that was used in translating *Buckland, Buck Hill, Brandybuck* and *Oldenbuck*. He

---

grandmother of Jesus. She is the patron saint of housewives and grandmothers.

[32] The Fairlop **Fair** was held on the **first Friday in July**. It was initiated by Daniel Day of Wapping (born 1683), who visited his estate at Hainault on that day to collect the rent from his tenants. The event was held under the shade of the huge branches of the great oak in Hainault Forest, known as the Fairlop Oak, where a feast of **beans and bacon** was served. This oak was 36 feet in diameter, measured at a point a yard above the ground. It was, unfortunately, blown down in 1820.

said that the element *-le* was to be considered either an alteration of *Buckenbury* or a contraction of the element *-land* in *Buckland*. For the element *-bury*, he wanted translators to use a variant of the OE *burg* (fortified town), recommending that they consult his explanation in *Nomenclature* for the name *Norbury*.

Bucklebury, from an old engraving

In the German translations, *Bucklebury* became *Bockenburg*, using the same initial element as was used in the translation of *Buckland*: *Bockland*. This is a good replication of the first of Tolkien's possible original forms: *Buckenbury*.

In his instruction to the Dutch translator (*Companion* 42), Tolkien offered another explanation of the element *-le*. He said that it was a contraction of the element *-hall* (mansion, great house) in the name *Buckhall*. In the Dutch translation, *Bucklebury* became *Bokkelburg*, following Tolkien's instructions perhaps a bit too literally for its language of adoption. In Dutch, *Buckland* is *Bokland*, but *Brandy Hall* is *Brandeburcht*, therefore **Buckhall* (unattested in *LotR*) should have been **Bokburcht*, which would not have been able to contract into *Bokkelburg*.

Schuchart's name does, however, sound very Dutch. The element *-el* is quite common in Dutch place names such as *Boekel*, *Borkel* and *Harpel*, where it is most commonly explained as the element *-lo* (woods), with its vowel shifted from one side of the liquid 'L' to the other. When read by a Dutch toponymist, Schuchart's name will, therefore, likely be read as 'the fortified town at Bok's woods,' a more than satisfactory solution.

Bagshot is not a terribly common name either. There are two places on the map with this name: the one near Newbury and the other in Surrey. The *Parliamentary Gazetteer* points out that the Bagshot in Surrey is famous for the fine flavor of its mutton. There was formerly an enclosed park there belonging to the King of England, and both James I (1603-1625) and Charles I (1625-1649) liked to go hunting there. The Civil War (1633-1642), however, saw an end to its status as a royal park. There are a number of stately homes in the area. Of particular note is Bagshot Park, to the west of Bagshot, which was the residence of George IV (1820-1830), when he was the Prince of Wales (PG v1.93).

The name *Bagshot* is commonly explained as *a corner of land* (sceat) *occupied by badgers* (bagga). The same element can be seen in place names like *Bagley*, which means *badger woods*. In *Nomenclature*, Tolkien explains that Bagshot Row is a row of small smials in the lane below Bag End. He conjectures that the name refers to the fact that "the earth removed in excavating Bag End was shot over the edge of the sudden fall in the hillside," later becoming the gardens and walls of the more modest dwellings located below.

In the German translations, Bagshot Row was rendered as *Beutelhaldenweg* (Beutel = bag, purse, wallet, Halde = heap, as in slagheap, Weg = way), keeping in step with *Bilbo Beutlin* (Bilbo Bag + diminutive ending) of *Beutelsend* (Bag-end). All-in-all, an excellent translation.

In Dutch, it was *Balingslaantje* (baal = [burlap] bag, bale + laantje = little lane), following the lead of *Bilbo Balings* (Bilbo [burlap] bag + ings) and *Balingshoek* (Bagend = [burlap] bag +

ings, hoek = corner). This is slightly less successful than the German translation in that it leaves out the element *shot*. In Dutch toponymy, the element *schot* is nearly identical with the element *shot* (*sceat*) as used in the real place name *Bagshot*. It can be found in such Dutch place names as *Oirschot*, *Baarschot* and *Voorschoten*. *Balingsschot would have sounded very Dutch, and, to take it even further, *Balingsoverschot could have even carried a part of Tolkien's original pun. The word *overschot* in Dutch means *excess*, thus *Balingsoverschot would be both the 'excess' from Bag End, and the 'corner of land on the other (over) side of Bag End.'

Woody End is not included in *Nomenclature*, which makes its interpretation somewhat problematic. There is no *Woody End* in the *Parliamentary Gazetteer* or, for that matter, any place names that contain the first element *woody*. *Woody End* does show up, however, in the addresses of the headquarters of Rugby Union Football (RUF) in Hertfordshire and a media company in Devon. The media company is at: Woody End, Darracott, Nr. Barunton, Barnstaple, North Devon EX33 1JY, and the RUF is at: Woody End, 9 Tall Trees, St. Ippolyts, Herts SG4 7SW, the latter seeming to be of modern contrivance, as all the street names in the vicinity are the names of trees. There is also a youth hostel in the Lincolnshire Wolds near Ruckland known as Woody's Top.[33]

A lack of real-world place names attested on maps and in gazetteers to match place names in The Shire is not uncommon for Tolkien, and no student of Tolkiennymy should stop looking when that proves to be the case. Tolkien was not an author, but rather the 'translator' (see Appendix F.II) of *The Red Book of Westmarch*, which today is more widely known under the titles of *The Hobbit* and *The Lord of the Rings*. Given Tolkien's predilection for Welsh, English translations of Welsh place name elements are an oft neglected possible source for Shire names. That may be the case with *Penwood*, which is just south of Newbury. For Tolkien's agile multilingual mind, the translation of *Penwood* to

---

[33] Thanks to Pat Reynolds for this name, as it does not show up on any map or gazetteer I have. You have to have been there to know about it.

Woody End would have been the kind of child's play that would tickle his linguistic sense of humor.

The normal translation for *Penwood*, however, would be *Wood End*, of which there are several in the Whatley *Gazetteer of Less Noted Villages* (1751).[34] If *Penwood* had been a monolingual Welsh place name, it would have been *Pencoed* (Glamorganshire, Wales), or Pencoyd (Herefordshire) (pen = head, or end, coed = woods).

As a surname, *Woody* is commonly explained as a condensation of the place name *Woodhay*, pointing to the two *Woodhay*-s in Berkshire as examples of the full form. The definition of *woodhay* normally given is that of a farmstead or settlement in the woods enclosed by a hedge (hay), not to be confused with Heywood (Wiltshire) or Haywood Oaks (Nottinghamshire), which is a wood near or bordered by a hedge. The surname *Woody* is, therefore, considered to mean someone who lives in the woods in a farmstead or settlement enclosed by a 'hay', or, in some interpretations, 'a wild man from the woods' (Compare Tolkien's Woses).

If the first element in the place name *Woody End* is the condensation (woody < woodhay), then *Woody End* would be 'the end of a wood hay,' that had had the woods removed from around it, judging from Tolkien's map. If the first element in *Woody End* is an adjective, used to distinguish one kind of *end* from another, then the Dutch translation is correct. It is *Houtenend*, an excellent calque of *Woody End*. (houten = wooden, woody) The Bobyr' Russian translation had the same solution: Лесной Конец [Lesnoj Konets]. The German translation, on the other hand, treated Woody End as if it was *Wood End / Pencoed*, rendering it as *Waldende*. (Wald = wood, forest)

The names *Ham*, *Combe* and *Stoke/Stock* are generously spread across the map of England, and their presence near Newbury is just as much an indication of the number of times that they

---

[34] *England's Gazetteer*. Volume 3, Being a New Index Villaris, or, Alphabetical Register of the Less Noted Villages; with their Distance, or Bearing, from the next Market-town, or Well-known Place (Stephen Whatley, ed.), London: J. and P. Knapton, D. Browne, A, Miller, J. Whiston and B. White, 1751.

appear on the map as it is of a Tolkienesque relationship to *Newbury*. Every good parody requires its share of easily recognizable elements to be truly effective.

Bindbale Wood is the spelling on the map in my 1965 Ballantine Books edition and the spelling listed in Fonstad (*An Atlas of Middle-earth*), Foster (*The Complete Guide to Middle-earth*), Strachey (*Journeys of Frodo: An Atlas of JRR Tolkien's The Lord of the Rings*) and Tyler (*The New Tolkien Companion*). Christopher Tolkien, on the one hand, asserts that the spelling is really **Bindbole Wood**, even though his father spelled it Bindbale Wood in a note on the Dutch translation (*Companion* lvii). Rather than enter into this controversy, this paper will offer an explanation for both spellings.

The name is not listed in *Nomenclature*, nor is there a similar place name to be found on the map of England, or in the *Parliamentary Gazetteer*, or in the *Whatley Gazetteer*, and this has left earlier investigators at a loss as to how to explain it. In the Dutch translation, following Tolkien's suggestion (*Companion* lvii), it is *Pakkebaal Bos*. The second element (*baal* = bag, sack, bale), perhaps unintentionally on Tolkien's part, offers yet another play on the Dutch version of Baggins (Balings), Bag End (Balingshoek) and Bagshot Row (Balingslaantje).[35] The third element (*bos*) is the most common translation of *wood*, as in 'a group of trees.'

Schuchart's initial translation of *Bindbale Wood* was *Het Boze Woud* ("The Evil Forest," not "The Devil's Wood," as glossed in *Companion* [lvii]).[36] This is the stuff of Dutch fairy tales, where Little Red Riding Hood and Hansel and Gretel are to be found, along with scary things like a *pakkeman*. Tolkien, however, rejected this solution (*Companion* lvii), and offered two suggestions for the first element: *pakke-* and *binde-* (*Companion* lvii). The element *binde-* does not appear in Dutch compounds. It is attested by itself as the common name for a climbing plant, the akkerwinde (Concolculus arvensis). In Dutch compounds, the element *bind-*

---

[35] The spelling convention in Dutch is that long vowel sounds are spelled with a double letter, unless the following syllable begins with a vowel. *Baal* (bag, sack, bale), for example, becomes *balen* in the plural.

[36] Compare: Het Zwarte Woud = The Black Forest of Germany.

(without the final 'e') is found in words like *bindbalk* (rafter, literally: connecting beam), *binddraad* (binding wire, compare: *packthread*), *bindtouw* (tying twine), *bindwerk* (flower arrangement). The verb *binden* corresponds to the English *to bind, to lash, to strap, to tie*.

The element *pakke-* is only found in the Dutch compound word *pakkeman* (1. a ranger, a sheriff; 2. a bogeyman). The Dutch verb *pakken* is roughly *to catch* (a thief, a train), *to understand, to grasp, to grab*, as well as *to pack* (a suitcase). In compounds, the element *pak* (package, bale) is used in such words as *pakdraad* (packing wire), *pakbon* (invoice), *pakdoek* (burlap, literally, 'packing cloth,' which is used to cover packages and bales, and is sewn closed with *pakgaren* [packing thread]), and *pakhuis* (warehouse).

Tolkien's instruction to Schuchart (*Companion* lvii) suggests that Tolkien was unaware of the subtleties of Dutch compounds described above, and was looking for two elements both having to do with *packaging* or *tying/binding*. The result (*pakkebaal bos*), however, could be read as 'ranger-bag wood' or as 'bogeyman-bag wood', which is not that far away from Schuchart's original suggestion.

Schuchart's original rendition of *Bindbale Wood* (*Het Boze Woud*) is not without some logical justification.

Beowulf—an undeniable favorite of Tolkien's—offers one possible explanation of the name *Bindbale* in lines 975-6, where it describes how the monster was tightly gripped by the "baleful bonds" (balwon bendum) of its wounds. This explanation is in the style of Tolkien's 'low philological jest' in his etymology of the name Smaug, where he says that the name was based on the past tense of the primitive Germanic verb *smugan*, 'to squeeze through a hole' (L.31). An implied reference to Beowulf gives the name *Bindbale Wood* a certain historical depth that would have appealed to Tolkien's sense of myth, hinting at the tale of the death of the wounded monster somewhere in the woods, just as the interpretation of the name *Smaug* hints at the historical segment in *The Hobbit*, in which Gandalf explains that Smaug could not use the hidden passage, because it is too small (H.32; I). In a letter to Christopher, Tolkien commented: "I like history, and am moved by it, but its finest moments for me are those in which it throws light on words and names! ... Nobody believes me when I say that my long book is an attempt to create a world in which a form of language agreeable to my personal aesthetic might seem real. But it is true" (L.264).

Dragons and other monsters are an undeniable part of Tolkien's Legendarium, and a hidden reference to one in a Shire place name would not be out of place. Dragons are mentioned numerous times in *LotR*. They are mentioned in the scene at *The Ivy Bush* (F.47; I.1), and in the scene at *The Green Dragon* (F.73; I.2), dragons are referred to again, as are the giant Tree-men, one of whom was seen recently beyond the North Moors. In Chapter 2 ("The Shadow of the Past"), the narrator hints at other monsters, saying "[a]nd there were murmured hints of creatures more terrible than all these [Orcs, Trolls], but they had no name." (F.72; I.2) The stories were there, but Tolkien only alludes to their presence. Another subtle hint, albeit an allusion to the "legends of the dark past, like a shadow in the background of [the Hobbits'] memories," would not be out of place in a story as finely layered as Tolkien's (F.72; I.2).

Popular nursery rhymes hide similarly disturbing tales. The rhyme "Ring-around-a-rosie" is widely held to refer to the Great Plague, while others associate "London Bridge is falling down" with the destruction of London Bridge in the eleventh century by King Olaf, following a battle with King Ethelred of England. Those who lack the ability to grant an author what Tolkien requested of the reader of a fairy tale—the suspension of disbelief—would do well to listen to Sam's reply to Ted Sandyman. Sam says: "and I daresay there's more truth in some of them than you reckon" (F.73; I.2).

Another, more prosaic, botanical explanation for the name *Bindbale* is also possible. This approach to the name is supported by Tolkien's rather large store of botanical knowledge, which can easily be seen in *Nomenclature*, where, in describing the meaning of the name *Butterbur*, Tolkien refers to the "generally botanical names of Bree," giving the Latin name of the butterbur plant: *Petasitis vulgaris*. The first element in the word **bindbale* (*bind*, now more commonly *bine*) is attested in the names of the varieties of hop-plants based on the characteristics of the bine or stem:

grey-bind, red-bind and white-bind (*OED*). *Woodbind* is attested in Chaucer, but is today more widely seen as *woodbine* (honeysuckle). Bindweed of the family *Convolvulaceae* (morning-glory family) is a climbing plant, as is bindwood, attested as both *ivy* (*hedera helix*) and as *honeysuckle* (Lonicera perclymenum). *Bind* is, in other words, a climbing plant that entwines the stems of other plants or the trunks of trees. The linguistic connection with *bind*, as in *to tie up*, suggests that vines were the predecessors to ropes.

The second element in **bindbale* (*bale*) is attested in a botanical context in the Middle-English word *balewort*, which is glossed as 'some sort of poisonous or narcotic plant, possibly the opium poppy (*Papaver somniferum*).' The antonym of *balewort* is *bonwort* (*bon* = *good*), which describes any of a number of medicinal plants. By itself, *bale/balo* is glossed as *evil, misfortune* or *calamity* (in Dutch, *boze*). This element also appears in *balewa*, which means 'the baleful or wicked one, Satan,' in *Bealowes gást*, glossed as 'the devil,' and in *balocraeft*, which means 'the evil arts.'

The compound **bindbale* would, therefore, mean 'entwining evil,' which is a not inappropriate sobriquet for the plant that is known in the dialect of Buckinghamshire as *Devil's Gut*,[37] the common bindweed. The bindweed is a very invasive nuisance that can cover fences or anything that stands still, causing tender garden plants that it climbs on to fall down just by the sheer weight of its vines and leaves. In America, it is on the Noxious-Weed lists for 42 States.

Bindbale Wood was created as a "form of language agreeable to [Tolkien's] personal aesthetic." My initial (before *Companion*) inclination in choosing between the two possible etymologies above was to the first of them, but, like the purely linguistic analysis that I once wrote for the name *Smaug*, that I later discovered to be incorrect when I read Tolkien's letter (L.31), the linguistic-botanical analysis of the name *Bindbale Wood* above is also not in keeping with the beauty defined by the eye of the original beholder, professor Tolkien.

If spelled *Bindbole Wood*, the second element of the name

---

[37] <http://met.open.ac.uk/genuki/big/eng/BKM/Vocabulary/index.html>. LVO 12/15/2005.

(*bole*) is likewise attested in Middle English. The first listed meaning for *bole* is *bull*. It is found in this meaning in the areas of animal husbandry (the male animals of the bovine family), heraldry (the figure of a bull on a coat-of-arms) and astronomy (the constellation Taurus). It appears in such compounds as *bolehorn* (bull's horn), *bolestirk* (strong as a bull) and *bolehed* (the head of a bull, bull-headed). If this was the intended meaning behind *Bindbole Wood*, then a Modern English translation of *Bindbole Wood* would be something like *Tethered-Bull Wood*. Another possible meaning is *Stud Wood*, because *binden* is a Middle English verb that describes what amorous bulls and cows do when they get together.

The second listed meaning for *bole* is *tree trunk; plank* or *beam*. Tolkien uses the word *bole* with the meaning of *tree trunk* no less than 12 times. The first time he uses it in Chapter 3 of Book I ("Three is Company"), it is connected to the word *tree* with a hyphen: *tree-bole*. "Sam and Pippin crouched behind a large tree-bole, ..." (F.116; I.3). The secondary usage (*plank* or *beam*) can be seen in the Modern German word *Bohle* (beam, railroad tie). Modern Dutch has an interesting compound word that suggests an appropriate meaning for the unattested Middle-English **bindbole*. In Dutch, the word for *rafter* is *bindbalk*. The first element (*bind*, sometimes spelled *bint*) is the same as in **bindbole*, and the second element (*balk*, not too distantly related linguistically[38] to *bole*) means *beam*;[39] literally: a *connecting beam*.

If this was the meaning that was intended, then *Bindbole Wood* would be the wood where the trees were good for making rafters. Bates points out that ash would have been the wood used for the rafters in a settlement such as the Anglo-Saxon village of West Stow in north Suffolk, which was occupied from

---

[38] Dutch *balk* [pronounced: balluk], compare: *bull* > *bullock*, *hill* > *hillock*, *bole* > **bollock*.

[39] The word *beam* has a parallel usage. Tolkien explains that *Quickbeam* is an alternate name for the Rowan-tree (Sorbus aucuparia). In OE *cwic bêam* means living tree. The use of the word *beam* in the meaning of *tree* is still preserved in other tree names like *hornbeam* (Carpinus betulus) and *whitebeam* (Sorbus aria). The word *beam*, as used in the construction industry, originated when buildings were not as tall as they are today, and beams were made of wood instead of iron or steel.

around 420 to 620 A.D..[40] The logical conclusion, therefore, is that Bindbole Wood would have been a stand of ash trees.

The Hobbits made use of wood in smials, as can be seen from the description of Bag End in *The Hobbit*: "The door opened on to a tube-shaped hall like a tunnel ... with panelled walls" (H.15; I). It is, therefore, logical to assume that they would need other wooden elements, like rafters, to build a smial.

On the other hand, Chapter 4 of Book III ("Treebeard") has a sentence, in which "dusk was twined about the boles of the trees" (T.91; III.4). In the context of this sentence, the element (*bind*) in *Bindbole* seems to suggest the meaning of 'a forest of tree trunks entwined (by dusk).'

Without older attested variants of the name or salient topographical features at the named site, it is impossible to tell which meaning of *bole* (*bull* or *stud* or *beam*) was intended. All three produce logical explanations of the name.

The place names *Bolham* (Nottinghamshire) and *Bolam* (Durham and Northumberland) are normally defined as "at the tree trunks," but could also be "at the bulls." Unless some new information is unearthed from Tolkien's papers, the ambiguity will remain to puzzle Tolkienists just like some real place names on the map of England puzzle toponymists. What could be more appropriate to a parody of the toponymy of rural England than a little ambiguity when there is plenty to be found on the real map? In a note to the Dutch translator, Tolkien said that not all names are meant to be "clear in etymology" (*Companion* lvii).

The Yale is only mentioned in Book I, where it is a region traversed by the road from Tuckborough to Stock: "At that point it [the road] bent left and went down into the lowlands of the Yale making for Stock; but a lane branched right, winding through a wood of ancient oak-trees on its way to Woodhall" (F.114; I.3). This context makes it clear that it is a region.

The Yale is not mentioned in *Nomenclature*, but it is locatable on the map, not of England, but of Wales. Llanarmon yn ial (the

---

[40] Brian Bates. *The Real Middle-earth: Exploring the Magic and Mystery of the Middle Ages, J.R.R. Tolkien and "The Lord of the Rings"*, New York: Palgrave Macmillan, 2003, p. 36.

church of St. Garmon in the Yale) is located between the river Alun and Offa's Dike. The appellation 'in the Yale' is used to distinguish it from Llanarmon Dyffryn Ceiriog (the church of St. Garmon of the Ceiriog river valley), further to the south in Denbigshire. The presence of the Yale region on the map can also be seen in the place names Llandysilio yn ial (the church of St. Tysilio in the Yale), Rhiw-ial farm (Rhiw = river name, just north of Llanarmon.)

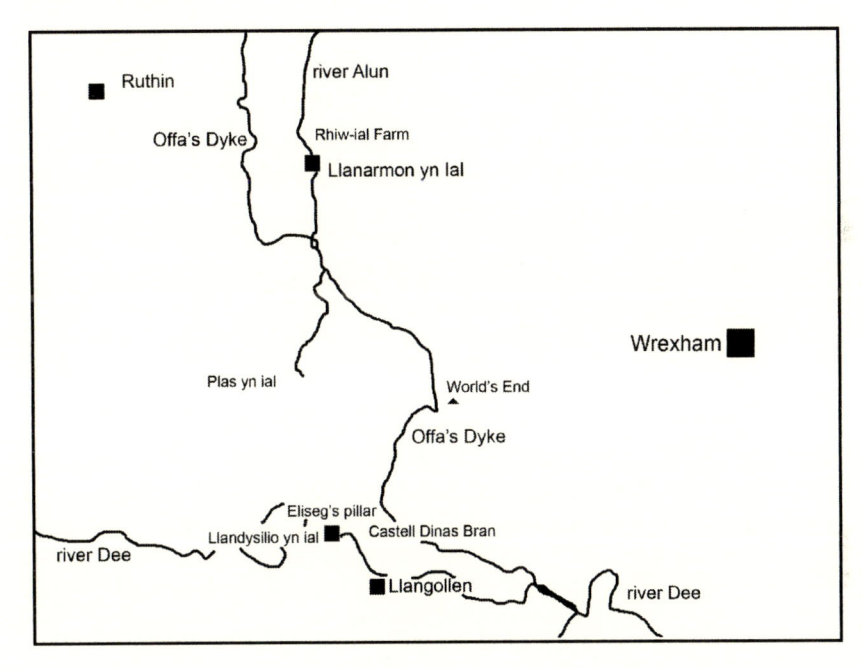

Llandysilio yn ial is the site of the Pillar of Eliseg,[41] erected by Cyngen in memory of his great-grandfather King Eliseg (or Elisedd) of Powys, who lived in the early eighth century. When first erected, the pillar stood over twelve feet high, and was a adorned with a Latin inscription[42] generally acknowledged to be one of the longest to survive from pre-Viking Wales. Though the inscription is today illegible, it survived due to the efforts of

---

[41] Chris Barber and John Godfrey Williams, *The Ancient Stones of Wales*, Abergaveny: Blorenge Books, 1989, p. 104.

[42] Read the text of the inscription at: <http://www.webexcel.ndirect.co.uk/gwarnant/hanes/genealogies/genealogieseliseg.htm>. LVO 12/15/2005.

Edward Llwyd, who transcribed it in 1696. It tells of Cyngen's grandfather's victories against the Saxons, and records the lineage of the lords of Powys, showing them to be the descendants of Vortigern and Magnus Maximus.

King Eliseg lived in nearby Castell Dinas Bran (Castle of the city of Bran). The word *bran* is attested in Welsh and Irish Gaelic with the meaning of a large black bird, either a raven (Irish) or a crow (Welsh). There are numerous personages named Bran in Celtic history and folklore: kings, heroes and gods. The best known of these are probably the Irish Bran (Bran mac Febail of the *Imran Brain* [*The Voyage of Bran*]) and the Welsh Bran (Benfigeidfran [Bran the Blessed] of the *Mabinogion*). Tolkien would have been familiar with the latter.

In his book[43] on the history of Wales, Lloyd describes the commote of Ial as "a long strip of upland which took in the western part of the valley of the [river] Alun and abutted upon the [river] Dee where it works its devious way through the gorges of Llangollen" (p. 244). According to Lloyd, this was "the ancient home of the kings of Powys" (p. 244), "the heart of northern Powys [which] remained in the possession of the Welsh as long as they retained their independence" (p. 245). The ancient kingdom of Powys took up most of central Wales, a region that "may be regarded as a broad table-land, through which rivers great and small furrow their way in winding courses to the sea, but which has few clearly marked mountain ranges or stretches of fertile plain" (p. 242). At its widest point, the kingdom of Powys extended "from the neighborhood of Mold to the river Wye, near Glasbury and Hay" (p. 242).

Though undoubtedly the most significant one, being the seat of the kings of Powys, this was not the only Yale on the map. To the trained linguistic eye, there are two more in Wiltshire. Ekwall[44] notes that the name *Deverill* is composed of the element

---

[43]John Edward Lloyd, *A History of Wales: From Earliest Times to the Edwardian Conquest*, second edition, in two volumes, London: Longmans, Green and Company, 1912, volume 1.

[44] Eilert Ekwall, "The Celtic Element" (pp. 15-35), in *Introduction to the Survey of English Place Names*, A. Mawer and F.M. Stenton (eds.), Cambridge at the University Press, 1924, p. 28.

ial and the common Celtic place name element *dever* (Welsh: *dwfr* = water, river). The shape of this Yale is generally defined on the map by what are known as *the Deverills*. The Deverills are a group of villages in the valley of the river Wylye, which probably corresponded to the original Yale. There were at least nine of them listed in the Doomsday Book, but today there are only five: *Brixton Deverill, Hill Deverill, Kingston Deverill, Longbridge Deverill* and *Monkton Deverill*. There are signs pointing to "The Deverills" on both the A303 and the A350. What makes this Yale so interesting in the context of Tolkien is that it happens to be near a village named *Newbury*. This Newbury, unlike its larger, better well-known namesake, is not in the *Parliamentary* or *Whatley Gazetteers* or in the *Shell Touring Atlas*.

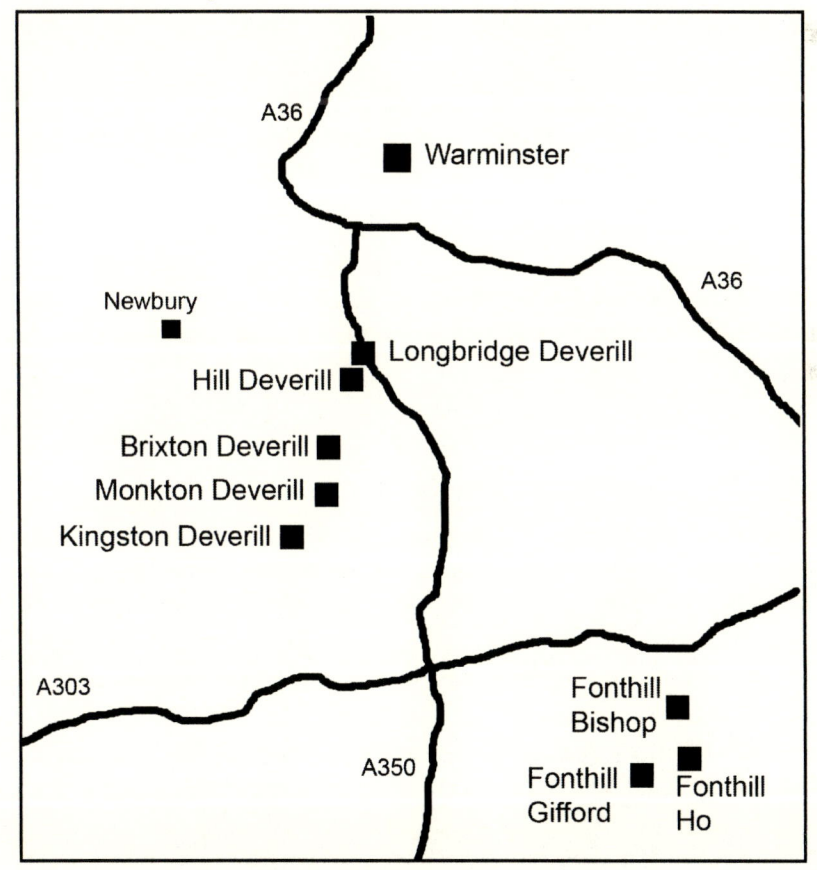

The neighboring Yale is visible in the place names *Fonthill Bishop*, *Fonthill Gifford* and *Fonthill Ho*, all located to the south-east of the Deverills. Ekwall explains the place name *Fonthill* as a combination of the element *ial*, and the element *Font* (spring, well), and these villages are indeed located near the source of the river Nadder. The spelling *Fonthill* appears to be a normalization for use on today's maps, as the names are also earlier attested as *Fontill*, which more clearly supports Ekwall's analysis.

To the more modern, less linguistic reader, *The Yale* is perhaps better recognized for its association with Elihu Yale, the benefactor of Yale University. The seat of the Yale family was Plas yn ial (the manor in the Yale, spelled Plas yn Yale on modern maps), which is located between Bryneglwys (the hill of the church) and Llandegla (the church of St. Tegla), just to the south of Llanarmon yn ial.

On the German map of The Shire, *The Yale* is *Das Luch* (a marsh), which seems more a reflection of the description of 'the lowlands' part of Tolkien's "the lowlands of the Yale," than a reflection of the 'toponymical history' of the name *The Yale*. Though the second German translator changed a number of names, the translation of *The Yale* remained the same in his version.

The Yale was not included on The Shire map until the second edition (1966) of *The Fellowship of the Ring* (*Companion* lx), which explains why it was not in the first version of the Dutch translation (p. 103). In the second version, Schuchart rendered it as *de Jaal*, a good phonetic representation of the name in Dutch. This is the same tactic that the second Polish, and most of those Russian translators who bothered to tackle the name (5 out of 9) used. The first Polish translator just left the name spelled *Yale*.

For the English-speaking reader of the Gruzberg Russian translation, the effect of this version of the place name *The Yale* is incredulously funny. There the road went down into the lowlands of Джейл [Dzhejl], which is pronounced 'jail.' It could only have been funnier, if this place name had been the location of the Lockholes in the Chapter "The Scouring of the Shire."

The Czech translator[45] had a none-of-the-above solution for *The Yale*. She turned it into a river. In her version, the road went down into the lowlands of the Člunkova řeka. (člunok = boat, shuttle) Apparently she went dictionary diving and

---

[45] For more on the Czech translation, see Appendix '**B**'.

discovered that *yale* is an alternate spelling of *yawl* (*OED*). Having reached that conclusion, it is obvious that a yawl needs something to float on, and a river would fit nicely in the context of Tolkien's "[the road] bent left and went down into the lowlands of the Yale [river valley] making for Stock."

In the unofficial Dutch translation, the road ran through *de lage landen van de Lips*. The first part of the phrase (*the low lands*) is clear enough, but the second is problematic. It appears to be drawn from the terms *lipssleutel* (a Yale key) and *lipsslot* (a Yale [cylinder] lock). *Yale* is the trade name of a company that produces cylinder locks of the type invented by an American locksmith Linus Yale, Jr. (1821-68). Dictionary diving can be fun, if you don't get the bends from finding the wrong word.

Woodhall is a village on the edge of the wood in the Eastfarthing at the end of a branch in the road from Tuckborough to Stock. It is not mentioned in *Nomenclature*, but it is an existing place name on the map of England. The name is commonly glossed as OE (*wudu* + *hall*) for 'a hall in or by a wood.' In the German translations, it was shown as *Waldhof*, a very serviceable calque, using the same element for *wood* as was used for the element *woody* in *Woody End*.

In his note to the Dutch translator (*Companion* 95), Tolkien said that the element *-hall* in *Woodhall* was not the same as the *Hall* in *Brandy Hall*, but rather a "recess, a piece of land half enclosed (by slopes, woods, or a river bend)." Schuchart, the official Dutch translator to whom the note was addressed, turned *Woodhall* into *Bosrode*, using a common element for *wood* (*bos*), combined with an element (*rode*) that is common in Dutch place names where it means a place in the woods that has been 'cleared' or 'developed.' It can be seen in place names like *Roden, Roderwolde* (wolde = woods), *Middelrode, Nistelrode* and *Amstelrade*. In general, *Bosrode* is a very successful calque of Tolkien's instruction.

The unofficial Dutch translation was *Bosburg*, which makes *Woodhall* sound a bit grander than a manor house (hall, compare Brandy Hall) in the woods (burg = castle, compare: *Valkenburg* in Limburg).

There is a Woodhall in Yorkshire and a Woodhall in Lincolnshire, but only the one in Lincolnshire is mentioned in the *Parliamentary Gazetteer*. Woodhall is now called "Old Woodhall" on the map to distinguish it from the nearby Woodhall Spa, which came to prominence in the nineteenth century as one of the great spas that were so popular in the Victorian era.

There is an association between Woodhall Spa and *a hole in the ground* that gives Woodhall Spa a certain Hobbitesque feeling. The establishment of the Spa was really the accidental result of prospecting for coal in the early 1800-s. John Parkinson sank a mine shaft on the moor near Woodhall, but his efforts to find an exploitable coalfield were in vain. At over 500 feet down, the miners encountered water, and the project was eventually stopped and the pit was capped. The water subsequently filled the pit and overflowed into the neighboring fields. Tales began to spread about the curative power that the water had for people who drank it. Thomas Hotchkin, the Lord of the Manor of Woodhall, had the water tested, and it was found to contain iodine and bromine, which proved effective in treating rheumatism and other ills. In the early 1830-s, Hotchkin built a Pump Room and Bath House and the famous, palatial Victoria Hotel. With the construction of a rail line with a station at Woodhall Spa in the mid-1850-s, the spa became even more popular, something that is reflected in the fact that this line was one of the most profitable in the country.

In its heyday (roughly the 1890-s and the Edwardian era), Woodhall Spa was famous throughout the country, even hosting England's Royals. It was included in the 1897 edition of Baedeker's *Guide to Great Britain*. By 1898, the Great Northern Railway (GNR) was running a direct service from King's Cross Station, London, to Woodhall Spa.

Tolkien could have hardly been unaware of Woodhall Spa, and, for me, the story behind the name *Woodhall* on the map of The Shire (whatever its derivation) suggests an elegant resort at which Hobbits could take the medicinal waters in a quiet, refined atmosphere.

Everything seemed to change in England after World War I, the spa included. The popularity of the spa began to decline and it attracted fewer and fewer visitors. The event that seems to have marked the end of Woodhall Spa's era of fame and prosperity was the fire that burnt down the Victoria Hotel on Easter Sunday 1920. The rail line quit running in 1954, and the well collapsed in 1983, bringing down the final curtain on the spa. Even though there is no longer a spa there, Woodhall Spa remains a popular tourist destination. Today, it is home to the English Golfing Union, and boasts one of the best golf courses in England.

The name **Dwaling** has caused a lot of consternation in Tolkienists circles because it seems to defy explanation. It is not explained in *Nomenclature*. There is nothing similar to it on the map of the United Kingdom, or in the *Parliamentary* or *Whatley Gazetteers*. The association with the name of the Dwarf Dwalin, which Jim Allan glosses as *Torpid*,[46] has been soundly rejected by numerous Tolkien scholars as an unsuitable basis for a Shire place name.

The German map of The Shire points the way to *Nachtschatten*. The name on this German map is the work of the first translator (Carroux), who looked up *dwale* in a rather large dictionary like the *OED*, and picked one of the meanings there. Her conclusion was that the meaning that Tolkien had in mind was 'Deadly Nightshade (*Atropa Belladonna*).' (Perhaps she thought that Belladonna Took kept a house there.) The name *Nachtschatten* is literally 'night shade,' the German word for *Atropa Belladonna*. The etymology for this meaning of *dwale* in the *OED* points to the Danish words *dvale* (dead sleep, trance, torpor; Compare Allan's gloss of the name *Dwalin* as *Torpid*.), *dvaledrik* (soporiferous draught), *dvalebær* (narcotic berry). The popular German name for *Atropa Belladonna* is *Tollkirsche* ('crazy cherry'), the first element of which (*toll*) is the same as the one in *Tolkien* < *tollkühn* = 'foolhardy.' (L.218)

The Czech map points the way to *Bludov*, a place name based on the Czech word *blud* (error, heresy), which produces derivatives like bludiště (maze), bludički (marsh lights, i.e. "tricksy lights, candles of corpses" T.296; IV.2) and bludař (heretic). It is also found in such phrases as bludný Holanďan (The Flying

---

[46] Jim Allan. *An Introduction to Elvish*, Frome, Somerset: Bran's Head Press, 1978, p. 222.

Dutchman), bludný rytíř (knight errant) and bludné střely (stray bullets).

This is the same sense as the modern Dutch word *dwaling* (mistake, fallacy, misapprehension), which shows up in compounds as *dwaaltuin* (maze), *dwaallicht* (marsh lights), *dwaalleer* (heretical teachings) and *dwaler* (heretic). In Dutch, however, *knight errant* is *dolende ridder*, derived from the verb (*dolen* = to wander, to be lost), a derivative of which can also be seen in the Dutch word *doolhof* (maze). In a figurative sense, the dictionary says that the verb *dolen* means 'to follow *dwaalleer* (heretical teachings).' In the southern dialect of Dutch, the verb *dolen* also means *to be delirious* and *to go insane*. This same meaning can be seen in the word *hondsdolheid* (hydrophobia, literally: dog's insanity), where the element *dol* is related to the first element in *Tolkien*.

On the first Polish map, the arrow leads to *Dwalin* (sic), but in a sense it is also an error, as the position it occupies on the map is the one held by the arrow pointing to Little Delving on the English map. *Michel Delving* remained *Michel Delving* on this Polish map. The arrow that should point to *Dwaling*, simply says: *do Miasteczka* ("to the little town"). This mislabeling is mirrored in the Karrik and Kamenkovich Russian translation, where the arrow pointing to what should be *Dwaling* shows the way to Сельцо [Sel'tso] ("the little village").

Most attempts at finding an etymology for the name *Dwaling* have concentrated on its first element without success, primarily stumbling over its meaning in OE and a number of other Germanic languages, like Dutch. Beginning at the other end, however, puts the name in a different light. In British toponymy, the ending -*ing* is commonly indicative of a place name derived from a personal name. It names a place occupied by the descendants (-*ing*) of some founding ancestor-hero (personal name). Doddington (Cambridgeshire, Kent, Lincolnshire, Northumberland, Shropshire) for example, are the towns (tun/dun) where the descendants of Dodda lived; Woking (Surrey) is the place where Wocca's people lived; Buckingham (Buckinghamshire) is the home (ham) of Bucca's people; Billingham (Stockton-on-Tees) is the home of Billa's people. (Tolkien's note to the Dutch translator confirms this hypothesis as the correct approach [*Companion* lviii].)

Tolkien loved to play with names. He is, after all, the man who described the etymology of the name *Smaug* as 'a low philological jest' (L.31). He told his children stories with characters like Bill Stickers and Major Road Ahead (*Carpenter* 180), and said that "names always generate a story in my mind" (Carpenter, 193). It is reasonable to assume that the story behind the name *Dwaling* would play on the name elements immediately recognizable to Tolkien that would tickle his philological sense of humor, like his own surname in Gothic. In a letter, Tolkien says that he sometimes used the Gothic translation of his surname—Dwalakoneis—for 'Gothic' inscriptions in books that he had read (L.357). *Dwaling*, therefore, would be the ancestral estate of the family Dwala(koneis).

A Bill Sticker

The Dutch map shows the traveler the way to *Dullingen*. This spelling is attested as a street name in the town of Brasschaat, north of Antwerpen in the Flemish-speaking part of Belgium, and as the name of a familial estate in Liebenwerda Kreis in Germany. In the Brandenburger Land of Germany, it is found as *Döllingen*, and there are a number of *Dolling*-s in Oberbayern and a *Dolling* in Kärnten, in Austria. There is a *Dollinghausen* in Land Niedersachsen, Germany. In his *Surname Book*,[47] Naumann points to the same first element as the one in *Tolkien* as the basis for the place names that the surname *Döllinger* is derived from. On the map of England, there is a *Dullingham*, attested in older documents as both *Dullingeham* and as *Dollingeham*. Ekwall[48] says that the meaning of this name is attributable to the same

---

[47] Naumann, Horst (Hrsg.): *Familiennamenbuch*. Leipzig: Bibliographisches Institut, 1987.

[48] Eilert Ekwall, *English Place-Names in -ING* (second edition), Lund: Gleerup, 1962, p. 128.

root as the first element in *Tolkien*. Schuchart seems to have found the perfect linguistic match for *Dwaling* as the ancestral home of the Dwala(koneis) family, the ancestral home of the descendants of *Toll*.

Pincup is another of Tolkien's names that has puzzled Tolkiennymists for years. Tolkien's note to the Dutch translator (*Companion* lvii-lix), however, finally makes it clear. Tolkien explained that, while a modern English speaker would not be able to break this contraction down into its component parts, it was a "well-known pattern," consisting of an animal name plus the element *hop* (a recess or retreat). *Oxenhope* and *Oxnop*, for example, can be found in Yorkshire, and *Swinhope* in Lincolnshire. The animal in the case of *Pincup* is the pinnuc, better-known to modern readers as "a finch or sparrow" (*Companion* lix).

In *Beowulf*, the element *hop* can be seen in the words *fen-hop* [fen = marsh] (line 764) and *mōr-hop* [*mōr* = lake] (line 449), pointing to a meaning of dry land in a marsh, and the element *hop* is indeed common in field names in the marshlands of Essex.[49] The place name *Hopton* (town on a hop) is a relatively common one. The same pattern can be seen on the map of Holland, which, like Essex, has its share or marshlands. In Dutch place names, the element *hop* is almost identical in meaning to the English place-name element *hop*. For example, it can be seen in place names like *Gorp* (goor = smelly marshland + *hop*, compare *fen-hop* in *Beowulf*), *Teckop* (Teke (name of a person) + *hop*), *Haps* (more than one *hop*), and *Wezup* & *Wezep* (both '*hop* on the wide stream').

The Dutch Shire map shows the reader the location of *Vinkop*, a skillfully constructed contraction of the combination of the Dutch words *vink* (finch) and *hop*. Without Tolkien's help, however, other translators took the place name Pincup further afield. In German, *Pincup* is *Felsmulde* (*Fels* = rock, bolder, *Mulde* = hollow). In the first Polish translation *Pincup* is, *Igielniczka* (pin cushion). In the second Polish translation, it is *Naparstek* (thimble). In the Czech translation, it is also related to *thimble*: *Naprstkov*.

---

[49] A.H. Smith, *English Place Name Elements: Part II, The Elements A-IW*, Cambridge at the University Press, 1956, p. 260.

In the academic, annotated K&K Russian translation, the name on the map is simply a transliteration: Пинкап [Pinkap]. In the Matorina Russian translation, it is Бочковый Овраг [Bochkovyj Ovrag] "Barrel Gulley." The maps in the other Russian editions did not include it.

Nobottle, located in the Westfarthing, has a comic sound to it for the modern reader, evoking an image of a Hobbit household where there were no bottles to be found, and Tolkien, undoubtedly enjoyed the playful sound of this place name himself. *Nobottle* is in *Nomenclature*, in the article on *Hardbottle*, where Tolkien points to the OE element *botl*, meaning a (large) dwelling.

The element *bod* (*dwelling*, compare the English *abode*) also appears in many Welsh and Cornish place names, such as Bodedern (W: Edern's house), Bottwnog (W: Gwynog's house), Bodnant (W: house by the stream, nant = stream), Bodwin (C: white house, gwyn = white), Bodrigan (C: the house of Rigan) and Bodmin (C: house of the monks).

In his book on the origin of Welsh place names, Morgan[50] notes that *bod* originally "meant a lord's residence." Welsh place names with the element *bod* are commonly a combination of that element with the name of the lord of the manor, as can be seen above. When the lord had two residences, continues Morgan, the summer residence was *Hafod* (haf = summer, *bod* > *fod* in compounds because of Welsh lenition), and the winter residence was *Gauafod* (gaeaf = winter, *bod* > *fod*). The element *hafod* can be seen in place names like *Pont yr hafod* (Pembrokeshire: bridge at the summer dwelling), Hafod y coed (coed = woods, in Blaenau Gwent) and the house *Nant yr Hafod* (nant = stream, near Offa's Dike in Denbigshire). "In the course of time," notes Morgan, "*bod* was used to designate any house or dwelling-place."

The *Parliamentary Gazetteer* lists *Nobottle* (Northhamptonshire), glossing the name as a variant of *Newbottle*. Despite this, *Nobottle* is what is shown on modern-day maps. There are many

---

[50] Thomas Morgan, *Handbook of the Origin of Place-Names in Wales and Monmouthshire*, Merthyr Tydfil, 1887, p. 12.

more *Newbottle*-s than *Nobottle*-s, in fact there is only one *Nobottle* attested. The *Whatley Gazetteer* lists four *Newbottle*-s: two in Northhamptonshire, one in Durham and one in Rutland; but no *Nobottle*-s. It also lists six *Newbold*-s, which Christopher Tolkien points out as having the same underlying root as *Nobottle* (HoMe VII.424). The difference in the first elements of *Nobottle* and *Newbottle* reflects a passage of some time between the founding of Nobottle and Newbottle. By the time Newbottle was built, Nobottle was not so new any more. This change can be seen in the various attested forms of the place name *Newbald*, of which there are several, also a relative of *Newbold*. *Newbald-on-Stour* is attested as *Niowebolda* in a charter from 991, but in the thirteenth century it is attested as *Newebold* (Johnson p. 379).

The only place name with a silhouette close to Tolkien's **Hardbottle** is *Harbottle* (Northumberland). The element *har* is troublesome to gloss in place names as it is not always possible to tell the difference between names formed from:[51]

- *h a r* (OE: 'grey, hoar.' This usage is especially common of objects like trees and stones that were covered with lichen.)
- *h a r* (OE: 'boundary.')
- **haer* (OE: 'a rock, a stone.' This root is only observed in place names. It is cognate with the Swedish *h a r*, meaning 'stony ground.')

What is troublesome to the toponymologist is grist for the mill of the writer of a parody. The more ambiguity, the better. Choosing **haer* as the original first element of the name *Harbottle* produces a gloss to match Tolkien's: 'rock, stone + building.' This is essentially the same as the Cornish place name *Boscarne* = stone house, *bos* being a form of *bod*, common in Cornish place names. As far as the spelling is concerned, Tolkien could easily have normalized the name to a modern spelling, as he did with names like *Entwade* (*Entwaed*) and *Stoning-land* (*Staning* [*land*]) (See *Nomenclature*).

The fact that Harbottle is in **North**umberland and that

---

[51] A.H. Smith (ed.), *English Place Names Elements: Part I (A-IW)*, Cambridge at the University Press, 1956, p. 234.

Hardbottle was located in the **North**farthing (off the map), only serves to tighten the bond between the two names. The parody can be taken even further by looking at the names of the families who held Harbottle Castle. The Taillebois family took over the castle in the early 1400s. While their name actually means something like 'wood cutter,' what parodist could resist the temptation to add one syllable to the name when it would produce the phrase *taille aux abois*, which means 'a waist at bay'? This faux-French name suggests itself as a synonym for *Bracegirdle*, the name of the Hobbit family that made its home in Hardbottle. The French phrase *être aux abois* is a part of the OED definition of the word *bay* [sb.4], and it is, therefore, reasonable to assume that Tolkien might have been familiar with it.

As to the other choices for glossing the element *har* in *Harbottle*: choosing *har* (boundary) as the original first element of the name *Harbottle* fits with the location of Harbottle Castle to the north of Hadrian's Wall and on the border with the Scotts, where it saw considerable fighting over the course of its history. In his book[52] on the region, Dixon says that Harbottle Castle was "the extreme outpost of the English over against Scotland in that part of the borderland."

Choosing the element *har* (grey) as the original first element of the name *Harbottle* could imply that the stone of the castle was grey, or that the castle took its name from the Harwood ('grey wood') Forest which is located to the south of the castle. The later definition points interestingly at Tolkien's *Greywood* under Amon Din, where the people of Ghân-buri-Ghân lived (R.313; VI.6).

Christopher Tolkien explains how the name *Nobottle* came to be on the map of The Shire. His father allowed him to add it to the map of The Shire that he made in 1943 and the name was

---

[52] D.D. Dixon, *Upper Coquetdale, Northumberland*, New-Castle-upon-Tyne: Robert Redpath, 1903, p. 178.

left on the map that was published in *The Lord of the Rings*. At the time, though, he "was under the impression that the name meant that the village was so poor and remote that it did not even possess an inn" (HoMe VII.424). The first Polish translation had a similar rendition. There *Nobottle* was *Bezpiwie*, literally: 'beerless.'

As a pair to *Nobottle*, the name *Hardbottle* suggests a hidden philological jest that hard liquor was served in Hardbottle, as opposed to the *tea*-totaling hospitality of Nobottle. This point of view is supported by the Volkovskij Russian translation, which renders Hardbottle as Подпивайлы [Podpivajly]. This name suggests that everybody there is drunk. In English, it would sound something like *Drunkenley*.

In *Nomenclature*, Tolkien pointed to *büttel*, as "the equivalent and related element in German place names." On the German map of The Shire, *Nobottle* was rendered as *Ohnbüttel*, literally: 'without a büttel.' This would at first seem a good solution, the German word for *bottle* (glass container) being *Flasche*. There are indeed some German place names that begin with the element *ohn* in this sense: *Ohnheim* (no home) and *Ohnholz* (no wood), for example. The place name *Offenbüttel* (open büttel) clearly shows that *büttel* is also a viable place name element. The problem arises from the fact that *Büttel* is also a slang word for *policeman*. Both the German translations use *büttel* as a part of their translation of Shirriff, *Landbüttel*. The philological jest in German, therefore, is not that there is nothing to drink (no bottle), but that there is 'no policeman,' which, given the Hobbit sense of law-and-order, was probably not such a bad thing.

The Dutch translation of *Nobottle* took an interesting turn, in that it recognized the meaning of *bottle* in *Nobottle* as 'building,' but that it did not recognize the meaning of *no* in *Nobottle* as 'new.' In Dutch, *Nobottle* ('new building') is rendered as *Geenhuijzen*, which is literally 'no houses.' The result is intriguingly funny. The official translation (Schuchart) of *Hardbottle* was a much less comical: Hardhuijzen (hard houses). The unofficial Dutch translation (Mensink-van Warmelo) was much more literal: *Hardfles* (hard glass container).

The Carroux German translation of *Hardbottle* was *Steinbüttel* (stone house or policeman), but Krege changed it to the marvelous pun *Hartbuddel,* which is a play on the German *Buddel* (slang in Northern Germany for *bottle*) and *buddeln* (to dig), *Buddelei* (digging [in sand], constantly digging up the roads for utility repairs) and *Buddelkasten* (sandbox). It is an interesting addition to Tolkien's family of 'hole' names. The existing *Hardthausen* (hard houses) would have been a more prosaic alternative. Much as I hate to admit it, I like Krege's version best.

The Ruins of Harbottle Castle

Sarn Ford on the southern border of The Shire, is where the road from Michel Delving to the Greenway crosses the Brandywine. In *Nomenclature*, Tolkien said that Sarn Ford was a 'half translation'—a process common in the formation of place names (compare: Penwood)—of the original Elvish name Sarn-athrad ('stony ford').

In the German translations, *Sarn Ford* became *Sarnfurt,* and in the Dutch translation, it was *Sarnvoorde*, both following Tolkien's instructions to the letter; keeping *sarn*, and translating *-ford*. Both the Polish translators did the same, their maps pointing to Brod Sarn (brod = ford). Most of the Russian translators did essentially the same thing. The main difference being that they added a Russian adjective suffix to *sarn*, creating Сарнский Брод [Sarnskij Brod]. The Czech translator, however, converted both elements to Czech. In her version Sarn Ford became **Kamenný Brod**. (Kamenný = stony) This was the same approach used in the Matorina and Nemirova Russian translations (Каменный Брод [Kamennyj Brod]). Two other Russian translators—Karrik & Kamenkovich and Gruzberg—transliterated the name: Сарнфорд.

Sarn is an element found in Welsh place names, where it can mean *a causeway* or *a paved road*. There is a village named Sarn in Dyffryn Ceri (The Vale of Kerry). It is located on the A489 between Yr Ystog (Churchstoke, another Shirish-sounding name: Stock) and Y Drenewydd (Newtown). The element *sarn* can also be found in such place names as *Pontsarn*, which is a contraction of *Pont y Sarn Hir* (Bridge of the Long Road), the long road most likely being the Roman road from Cardiff to the fort at Y Gaer outside Brecon; and in *Rhyd y Sarn* (the ford of the road) in the Maentwrog valley, near Ely.

The most famous Welsh *Sarn* is Sarn Ellen, named for Ellen Lluyddog (Ellen of the Army), daughter of the British King, Eudaf "Hen" (Octavius) and the wife of one of the last rulers of Roman Britain, Magnus Clemens Maximus (Macsen Wledig, *gwledig* is Welsh for *lord* or *king*). "The Dream of Macsen Wledig" in the *Mabinogion* tells the story of how she and her husband came to be wed. After her husband's death, she took the throne herself. She was a warrior-queen, leading her people into battle against the Picts, the Saxons, and the Irish. It was her military prowess that earned her the epithet "Lluyddog", which means "owner of an army." Legend credits her with building a network of roads to link militarily strategic locations, and a number of Roman-era roads and some old mountain tracks in Wales are still frequently known as "Sarn Ellen." The less romantically inclined point to a more prosaic etymology, positing that Sarn Ellen is derived from *Sarn Lleng* [the legion's road].

Logically, *Sarn Ford* could also just as easily be a half translation of *Rhyd y Sarn* [the ford of the road] as it is of *Sarn-athrad*, and Tolkien could have been playing with this existing Welsh place name to see what he could make out of it. The association of stones with the word *sarn* is implicit in its definition, as can be seen from the definition in the Webster's Revised Unabridged Dictionary of 1913: "Sarn n. [W. sarn a causeway, paving.] A pavement or stepping-stone." The Welsh-English dictionary also lists the meaning of stepping-stones for crossing a river (cerrig i groesi afon). Stepping stones used to be an integral part of a ford, not only to mark the path across the water, but also so that people on foot and those driving a cart while walking alongside would not get their feet wet while crossing. There is a good illustration of this in the movie *The Quiet Man*. In the sense of stepping stones, *sarn* is, therefore, also a type of ford. This would make Tolkien's name seem more like a bilingual tautology, similar to *Bree Hill* or *Creech Hill*. (Q.V.)

The closest thing to *Sarn Ford* on the map of the United Kingdom is *Sharnford* (Leicestershire). The name *Sharnford* is attested in the *Doomsday Book* as *Scerneford*, normally explained as 'dirty or muddy ford,' from the OE *scearn* + *ford*. The water at a 'muddy ford' could well be expected to be of a color that would make it a good match for the translation of the Sindarin name of the river that one could cross at Sarn Ford. The name *Baranduin* translates to 'golden brown river.'

This is not, however, the story that the name suggested to Tolkien. Tolkien's story is recorded in the manuscript for *Nomenclature*, which only just became available in *Companion* (163). The ancient crossing of the river Baranduin at this point took its name from the fact that the river passed over a large patch of shingles (small rounded pebbles). The Númenoreans named it after the legendary ford on the river Gelion that was in the lost land of Beleriand.

Rushey (spelled Rushy on Tolkien's map) is a village on the causeway in the Marish. In *Nomenclature*, Tolkien glosses this name as "rush isle," explaining that it is a 'hard' out in the fens of the Marish. The first element is obviously the rush plant (Latin: *Juncus*), and Tolkien felt no need to pay particular attention to it in *Nomenclature*. He clearly felt that the second element (*-ey*) might be problematic, and glossed it specifically as 'small island.' This element is common in English place names, like *Longney* ('Long Island', Gloucestershire), *Sandy* ('Sandy Island', Bedfordshire), *Thorney* ('Island overgrown with thorn bushes', Cambridgeshire), and *Horsey* ('Horse Island', Norfolk).

Tolkien's first (map) spelling matches the spelling of the real place name *Rushy Wier* (Oxfordshire near Bampton). The gloss given by Gelling[53] for *Rushy* in this place name is "rush island," showing the two spellings to be essentially the same. Since both spellings are possible, Tolkien's second (text) spelling simply seems to have been done to highlight the presence of the second element.

Tolkien likewise notes in *Nomenclature* that the German equivalent of *-ey* is *Aue* ('river-side land, water meadow'), pointing to it as a potential solution for this name in German. Though *Rohrau* (*Rohr* = reed; Latin: *Arundo*) is a real place name to be found in both Germany and Austria, neither of the German translators followed Tolkien's advice. Their solution was *Rohrholm*, which does not exist on the map. There is a whole herd of *Rohrbach*-s ('reed stream'), some *Rhordorf*-s ('reed village'), a *Rohrsee* ('reed lake') and a *Rohrbronn* ('reed spring, well'), but no *Rohrholm*.

The element *holm(e)* ('river meadow') is a common place-name element, in England. There are seven listings for *Holme* in the *Parliamentary Gazetteer*, and in Oxfordshire there are twelve different parishes where the element *holm(e)* appears in modern field names.[54] There is even a *Rusholme* on the map of England, now a part of the greater Manchester urban sprawl. The element *holm(e)* commonly replaced the element *-ey* in lands that fell under Danelaw (Compare: *Stockholm*, the capital of Sweden).

There are place names in England based on the element *reed*. These include *Redbridge* (Hamptonshire), which is attested in earlier documents as *Hreutford* or *Hreodford*, and glossed as "the Ford of Reeds' in *Bede*. Redbridge has been devoured by the Southhampton conurbation. There is also a *Redbourn* (compare the German *Rohrbach*) in Hertfordshire, located on the river Ver. There is also a *Reedmire* ('reed lake') in Yorkshire.

The official Dutch translation is *Lisse*, which is a real place

---

[53] Margaret Gelling (based on material collected by Doris Mary Stenton), *The Place Names of Oxfordshire*, Cambridge at the University Press, 1954, p. 304.

[54] Gelling, p. 453.

name on the map of Holland. The name is derived from *lis* of the family *Iridaceae*, of which the iris and the crocus are the most familiar varieties. This is not as strange a solution as it first seems. The Dutch translation of the botanical name *cat's tail* (Latin: *Typhia latifolia*) is **lis**dodde, which in German is **Rohr**kolben.

The most interesting thing about this choice is, however, that Lisse is a rather famous town in Holland. It is a town in the middle of the tulip fields which—when they bloom in the spring—are a major tourist destination.[55] Foreign tourists are perhaps more familiar with the name *Keukenhof* ('kitchen gardens'), because the tour buses take them right to the entrance of this famous garden. The Dutch bus driver, on the other hand, knows that he has to follow the signs to Lisse to get there. A Dutch tourist reading *The Lord of the Rings* on the train—trains remain a well-used form of public transportation in Europe—on the way to the Keukenhof, knows that (s)he has to get off at Lisse, where (s)he can catch the bus to the Keukenhof. When following the adventures of The Fellowship in Dutch, therefore, the reader is invited to visualize the splendor of the tulip fields in bloom in the spring on the west bank of the Brandywine, rather than a rush-covered 'hard' in the fens or the Marish. Perhaps this solution was to make up for not being able to find a notorious place name as the solution to *Woodhall (Spa)*. Transference of a pun from one element to another similar element is nothing more than good translation technique.

In her alternative, unofficial translation, Mensink-van Warmelo, chose a different rendition of the name *Rushey* to avoid this notoriety. Her version of the name is *Bieze*. This is a variant of the word *bies* (bulrush, Latin: *Scirpus*). There is a real place called *Biezen* in Zeeland on the map of Holland. The primary failing of the two Dutch translations is that they both disregard the second element (island) in Tolkien's name, and concentrate on its botanical component. They are, however not the only ones.

The first Polish translator also took this approach, and rendered *Rush(e)y* as *Łozina* (wicker). This obviously did not appeal to the second Polish translator whose name, interestingly, is Łoziński. The approach of the second Polish translator was to

---

[55] <www.keukenhof.nl> LVO 2/14/2006.

translate *Rush(e)y* as *Kępa* (pronounced [kempa], the Polish 'hooked' Ę being a nasal vowel). The dictionary definitions for kępa are exactly what Tolkien wanted. In the translating dictionary, it is defined as 'an islet,' with a pointer to the British 'holm.' In the defining dictionary, it is glossed as "a slightly elevated piece of terrain, especially in a marsh." It also has the meaning of an island on a river or a lake, overgrown with brush and trees.

Having lived in Warsaw for two years, however, the first thing that came to mind upon reading this name was the beautiful district of Warsaw called Saska Kępa. It is on the opposite side (the east side) of the Wisła river from the center of town, right on the river bank as its name suggests. It is one of the most desirable districts to live in, and home to many diplomats, embassies and international schools. Tolkien might have been pleased at seeing this place name. The adjective *saski* means *Saxon*, and the name Saska Kępa could, therefore, be read as 'Saxon Islet,' even though it is no longer an island, and the only remotely 'Saxon' inhabitants are probably attached either to the German (Saxony) or to the British (Anglo-Saxon) Embassies. From my point of view, the new Polish name for *Rushey* is an excellent pun, the match of Tolkien's hint of *Woodhall (Spa)*.

The Saska-Kępa side of the Wisła river is known as *Praga*, which is clearly recognizable as the 'Polish' spelling of the name of the capital of the Czech Republic, *Praha* (Prague), a fact that takes on some added significance in the discussion of the meaning of *Kępa*, because Prague has its own famous island on the Vltava river. *Kampa* is separated from the 'mainland' by a narrow stream called the Čertovka ('Devil's Brook'), and is reached by a stair that drops down from the Charles Bridge. It is popular with romantically inclined couples, dread-locked frisbee fliers and expat (as well as local) hippies, many of whom seem to be musically challenged. Visitors can stroll, feed the ducks or enjoy the people-watching, while taking a refreshment at any of several cafes.

The Czech translator—I would say wisely—chose not to translate *Rush(e)y* as *Kampa*, which many unwisely try to associate with the English word *camp*. Her version was *Rákosiny*, which is a place-name-like plural, derived from *rākos* (common reed, Latin: *Phragmites australis*).

The Bulgarian and most of the Russian versions of the name *Rush(e)y* were some variant of камыш [kamysh] (reed, Latin: *Arundo*). The ones that stood out were the Karrik and Kamenkovich (K&K) translation, which was Бугорок [Bugorok = little knoll] and the Matorina translation, which was Ямки [Yamki = holes]. The K&K translation could have been more imaginative, as were the other translations that were plays on *reed*. The Matorina translation, however, was not as far afield as it first seems. The name *Rushey* only appears once in the text, where the narrator is explaining that the authority of Brandy Hall was still acknowledged between Stock and Rushey (F.142; I.5). Matorina just extended that authority a little bit. In her list of names at the end of the book, she glosses Ямки [Yamki] not as *Rushey*, but as *Deephallow*, which, on Tolkien's map, was just across the Brandywine from Haysend. On her map, *Rushey* is rendered as a variant of камыш [kamysh].

No discussion of the Russian translations of *Rush(e)y* would be complete without an examination of the origin of three field names in the area of Aston Bampton in the Bampton Hundred of Oxfordshire that inexorably catch the eye of anyone connected with Russian Studies. The names of the fields are: *Aston Russia*, *Great Russia* and *Home Russia*. The element *Russia* in these field names is really a 'normalization' of Tolkien's *Rush(e)y*, which Gelling[56] shows attested as *Russeya*, *Russeye* and *Russhey*. Normalizations occur when the people who use the name no longer recognize its component elements and shift the name to a word in their active vocabulary that sounds like one they do not recognize. This phenomenon is an oft overlooked force in the study of place names, especially in the study of Tolkiennymy.

---

[56] Gelling, p. 303.

LINGUISTIC FOSSILS

The Water

The Water is Tolkien's name for the river that flowed to the east past the foot of The Hill from Needlehole to where it joined the Brandywine just above the bridge for the Great East Road that led to Bree. While it may seem somewhat strange to the modern reader, who is used to rivers and streams having a proper name, instead of simply being referred to as the liquid that flows in them, Tolkien was merely demonstrating his command of the nuances of toponymy. Isaac Taylor (1829-1901) offers an excellent explanation of the significance of Tolkien's name in his book entitled *Words and Places*,[57] in the Chapter "River Names."[58]

River names, says Taylor, especially "the names of important rivers, posses an almost indestructible vitality." They can survive when all other toponyms around them change. Because of this, they can be viewed as a type of linguistic fossil, preserving, as it

---

[57] Isaac Taylor. *Words and Places: Etymological Illustrations of History, Ethnology and Geography*, London: Macmillan and Co., 1885.

[58] Taylor, pp. 130-144.

were, the linguistic foot prints of the people who gave the rivers their names.

Taylor's study focuses on the predominance of Celtic river names across Europe. The river names of England are—almost without exception—Celtic in origin. Taylor divides Celtic river names into two classes. The first is made up of names that mean simply *water* or *river*. The second is made up of names based on adjectives. Tolkien's *The Water* represents a name of the first class. Taylor explains that:

> At a time when no great intercommunication existed, and when books and maps were unknown, geographical knowledge must have been very slender. Hence whole tribes were acquainted with only one considerable river, and it sufficed, therefore, to call it "The Water," of "The River" (p. 131).

Taylor goes on to explain that these appellations only became proper names, disconnected from their original meaning, when the original inhabitants were driven out by immigrants from the east, as the Gadhelic Celts were replaced by the Cymric Celts, who were crowded out by the Anglo-Saxons, who were supplanted by the Normans. The river Avon of Shakespearean fame, for example, is simply the Welsh word for *river*, *afon* [think *avon*]. There are no less than 15 rivers Avon in England, notes Taylor. In Welsh, the word for *water* is *dwr* [pronounced dur]. It shows up no less than 44 times by Taylor's count. The river Dover is nothing less than a corruption of "The Water." The Gadhelic Celts had another word for *water*. In Irish, *water* is *uisge*. This shows up in modern English as *Whiskey*, and in numerous mutations on the map of England as the name of rivers like *the Esk*, *the Ex*, *the Thames* [tem-ese: "broad water"], *the Usk* (known as the Wysg [pronounced uisg] in Wales).

By naming the river that ran through The Shire *The Water*, Tolkien is recreating a sense of the primordial time when the names of many of the rivers across England still meant what they said, and had not yet been stripped of their meaning by the arrival of a new wave of settlers, to whom the names were just so much alphabet soup.

The same thing can be seen in the *Etymologies*, where in the article for the root *KEL-* ("go, run [especially of water]"), Tolkien glosses the Noldorin and Ilkorin word *celon* as *river* (HoMe V.403). While the name of the river that ran through Long Lake ('The river Running') is glossed as Celduin (Aa.405), another look in the *Etymolgies* shows that in Ilkorin *duin* means *water, river* (HoMe V.394). The name *Celduin* could then perhaps be better literally translated as 'running water,' which would bring it more into line with the name of the primary river of The Shire (*The Water*), and with all the other river names that are some variation of the word for *water*.

Tolkien's village of Bywater, home to the Green Dragon Inn, located on The Water, at first seems to have no corollary on the map of England. There are no Bywaters to be found. The construction of Tolkien's name is not without precedent, however. There are a number of place names that are constructed out of the elements *by* (near, close to) and an easily identifiable topographic feature like a river, a ford, a hill or a wood. Byfleet, for example, is OE for "by the river." Though modern English speakers are more inclined to say "on the river," as in Stratford on Avon, this construction is still viable in Dutch. In the name Beeford, the first element of the name records an alternate pronunciation for *by*. Older sources show it spelled as Biford ["by the ford"]. The place name Beal shows the same pronunciation. It is a corruption of bi + hil ["by the hill"]. In Welsh, Argoed is literally "by the wood" [*ar* = by, close to; and *coed* = wood, with lenition of the initial consonant as is common in Welsh compounds]. Tolkien himself had a nice parallel construction in his Welsh/Celtic name Archet ["by the wood"], derived from the Welsh *ar* and the Old Celtic *chet*, which means wood.

Tolkien only had to look as far as the Welsh place names of which he was so fond to find place names that literally meant "The Water" and "By [The] Water". This can be seen in the Welsh river name Wysg and the appellation of a number of towns along the Wysg, like Caerlleon ar Wysg (Caerleon [literally:

"the Roman Legion fort on the Usk"]), Castellnewydd ar Wysg (Newport [literally: New Castle on the Usk]) and Tal y bont ar Wysg (Talybont-on-Usk [literally: "end of the bridge on the Usk]).

While Tolkien expressly avoids explicit Celtic (Welsh) elements in his Shire names, the second element in the name Bywater Pool is almost bilingual: English and Welsh. Tolkien's spelling shows it to be English, which prompts the modern reader to think of Blackpool and Liverpool. This same element can also be found in Pulford ["ford by the pool"], Bradpole ["broad pool"] and Withypool ["willow-tree pool"], which recalls Tolkien's Withywindle that flowed into the Brandywine at the south end of Buckland. At the same time, it is only a short linguistic step for Tolkien, with his knowledge of Welsh, to place names like Pwll ["pool"], Llan y pwll ["church of the pool"], Glaspwll, ["green pool"], Pont y pwll ["bridge by the pool"] and Pwllheli ["brine pool"] to name but a few.

Stock

Stock is such a very common element in British toponymy that it is not surprising that Tolkien included it on the map of The Shire. It can be seen spelled as *Stock* in place names like *Stock* (Essex), *Radstock* (Bath & North East Somerset), *Tavistock* (Devonshire) and *Woodstock* (Oxfordshire). It is also seen spelled as *Stoke* in place names like *Stoke Bruerne* (Northamptonshire), *Stoke-by-Nayland* (Suffolk), *Stoke Ferry* (Norfolk), *Stoke on Trent* (Staffordshire), and *Basingstoke* (Hants).

In names like *Stockbridge* (found in several counties), it is clear that it is derived from the OE *stocc*: *log*. *Stockbridge* is a combination of the OE *stocc* + *brycg* (*log bridge*). *Stockton* is another common place name found in several counties based on this meaning. It is a combination of the OE *stocc* + *tun*, literally *log town*. Before it came to mean *town*, the element *-ton* in *Stockton* meant *enclosure*. It is sometimes attributed a relationship with the Celtic word *dún*, *a fort*. *Stockton*, therefore, actually means *log enclosure*, in other words, *a stockade*. In some sources in the XVIII and XIX centuries, *stockade* was even spelled *stoccade*. This type of protection for villages was common in pre-Roman England. The same meaning can be found in the Dutch place name *Stokkum*.

In other place names, the meaning of the element *Stock* is less clear. Etymologies of these names frequently note that the name carries a sense of "a religious site," "a holy place," "a church." Toponymologists note that earlier variants of the place names *Stockwood* (Dorsetshire) and *Stoke in Hartland* (Devonshire) were *Stokes sancti Edwoldi* (1238) and *Nectanstock* (1086: a reference to Saint Nectan). *Stoke St. Milborough* (Shropshire) was *Godestock* [God's Stock] in 1086. *Stoke Gabriel* (Devonshire) derives its name from a church dedicated to Saint Gabriel. Many contemporary authors also point to the presence of religious establishments in the towns in question. There was an Anglo-Saxon monastery in Stoke by Nayland, an early abbey in Tavistock, and an Old English *hiwan* [religious order] in Hinstock (Shropshire), 'Stock of the Monks.' Stoke Priory (Worcester) belonged to the Worcester Priory.

All these interpretations of the meanings of place names based on *stock* fail, however, to offer a convincing linguistic explanation of the reason for the use of the element *stock* in the names. The reason for this is that the explanations are too modern. They are based on historical data from the Christian period. The origin of the names is older than that. Before the Christian saints, there were the old gods, whose association with *stock* can be found in the archaic expression "stocks and stones," a phrase that was applied by Christian-era writers contemptuously to the wooden and stone images of the old gods. The first example for this expression in the OED—dated circa 1000—is in Old English: "fremdum godum, stoccum and stanum" [foreign gods, trees and stones] (Ælfric Deut. xxviii. 36). The OE *stocc*—with a double 'C'—is clearly evident in this example.

The Irish King Cormac mac Airt (ruled approximately 254-277 A.D.), who supposedly died of a druid curse placed on him for turning his back on the old gods and accepting Christianity, is quoted by later bards as saying: "I will offer no adoration to any **stock** or image shaped by my own mechanic. It were more rational to offer adoration to the mechanic himself."[59]

Charles R. Beard devotes a whole chapter[60] to "Stocks" in his book *Lucks and Talismans* (1934), in which he examines the use of trees as royal, tribal talismans. Irish kings were elected to their office under the ancient "inauguration trees" that represented "the tutelary deity of the tribe" (p. 136). The king's scepter—the symbol of his power—was crafted from a branch of the tree.[61] In Irish, the word for such a tree is "bile," and, though the trees may now be gone, their presence can still be felt in place names like *Lisnabilla* in Antrim and *Rathvilly* in Carlow, both of which mean "the fortress of the Ancient Tree."[62] In his *Traces of the Elder Faiths of Ireland* (1902), Wood-Martin uses the place name *Billatinny* as an example, which he glosses as "the old" or "sacred tree of the fire" (vol. 2, p. 158).

Beard comments that "it would seem to have been accepted that the life of the king and possibly, by an easily understood extension, the survival of his line was bound up in that of the tree" (p. 136). When a tribe was defeated in battle, the conquerors of the tribe would chop down the tribe's tree and hack it to pieces. Since these trees were considered the *Crann Bethadh* (Tree of Life), says Ellis in his *Dictionary of Irish Mythology*,[63] destroying an enemy's tree would have been a way to ensure that a vanquished enemy remained vanquished.

Saint Boniface is famous for doing exactly that. In 723 A.D., at Geismar, near Fritzlar in Germany, he chopped down an oak

---

[59] James Bonwick, *Irish Druids and Old Irish Religions*, Sampson Low, Marston and Company, London, 1894, p. 164. (**Emphasis** added.)

[60] Charles R. Beard, *Lucks and Talismans*, London: Sampson Low, Marston, 1934, pp. 130-149.

[61] Patricia Monaghan. *The Encyclopedia of Celtic Mythology and Folklore*, New York: Facts on File, 2004. p. 45.

[62] Beard, p. 136. See also P.W. Joyce. *The Origin and History of Irish Place Names*, Dublin: McGlashan and Gill, 1871, whom Beard seems to be quoting, pp. 481-483.

[63] Peter Beresford Ellis. *A Dictionary of Irish Mythology*, Santa Barbara, CA: ABC-CLIO, 1987, p. 186.

of extraordinary size that was sacred to the pagan thunder-god. The pagans who had gathered to see Boniface get his comeuppance from Donar (compare the modern German word for *thunder*: *Donner*) were dumbfounded when no thunderbolt descended from the heavens to strike down the blasphemer who had dared to take an ax to the sacred tree, and many converted to Christianity on the spot. To press his point with his audience still further, Boniface used the wood from the oak to build a Christian chapel.

If the map contains Irish place-name elements with the meaning of sacred or ancient tree, there should also be a similar element in Welsh and English, but none has yet been identified. There is no Welsh word with the consonant envelope b*l that carries meanings to match the Irish *bile*. There is, however, one with an initial '**P**'. (The shift from initial '**P**' to '**B**' is one of the soft mutations in Welsh.) The meanings that the modern Welsh dictionary lists for the archaic word *pill* ("strength, tree trunk, branch and place of refuge") all fit comfortably within the logical valance for a tree of religious significance. The consonant envelope *p*ll-* can be found in a number of place names, such as:

- Y Pîl (Bridgend and Isle of Wight) spelled Pyle in English, Y = 'the,' compare Stock
- Pilley (Yorkshire, Gloucestershire and Hampshire) '*Pill* Meadow,' compare *Stockley* [Wiltshire]
- Pileford (Yorkshire, near Cottingham, from Doomsday) '*Pill* Ford,' compare *Stokeford* [Dorset]
- *Pyle Bridge* (Devonshire) compare *Stockbridge*,
- *Pilton* (Rutland, Northamptonshire, Somerset and Devon[64]) '*Pill* Town,' compare *Stockton*
- *Pilkington* (Prestwich) 'The Pill at King Town," compare *Kingston* (numerous occurrence)
- *Pilerdton* (Warwickshire) earlier attested as *Pylardynton* (1327), Pill [G]ardd yn ton = 'Pill Garden [enclosure] in the uncultivated land[65],' compare *Penarth* [Glamorganshire])

---

[64] The Pilton in Devon near Barnstapole (< OE *Beardan Stapol* = 'Bearda's standing pole') was a hill-top fort (dun). Compare *Stockton*.

[65] Ton (Welsh) = a piece of uncultivated land. Thomas Morgan. *Handbook of the Origin of Place Names in Wales and*

Toponymists point to a number of possible other solutions to the source of the element *p*ll-* in these place names. Some point to English words with the same consonant envelope and similar meanings, remarking all the while that, in many instances, it is difficult to tell one from another. *Peel* is an obsolete word that originally (first recorded circa 1330) meant "a palisade or fence of stakes" and then later "a castle." The OED reports that *peel* (also spelled *peil*) is the historical name of the enclosed park surrounding the Linlithgow palace in Scotland, and the OED remarks repeatedly that the use of *p*ll-* as a castle or fortified building is associated with Scotland or the Scottish-English boarder. Pointing to another source (1679) with yet another spelling, the OED quotes the definition that a "pele or pile, is a fort built for defence of any place." In MacKenzie's book on mediaeval Scottish castles,[66] the *peel* or *pele* is specified to be a timbered enclosure, a similar enclosure of stone and lime, being known as a *barmkin*.

Other potential solutions for the consonant envelope *p*ll-* in place names are:

- pile - a sharp, pointed stake, compare the Dutch word *pijl* = arrow pronounced [pile]. In later use "a large and heavy beam of timber or trunk of a tree, usually sharpened at the lower end," driven into lake or river beds or into marshy ground to support a building. Lake Town, for example, was built on piles. OED.
- *pill* - A local name found in the estuary of the river Severn and in Cornwall "for a tidal creek on the coast, or a pool in a creek or at the confluence of a tributary stream" OED. The OED suggests that this is a corruption of the Welsh *pwl*.
- *pale* - "a pointed piece of wood intended to be driven into the ground, especially as used with others to form a fence ... a paling, palisade" (OED). Compare the Latin *palus* (stake).

None of the currently available research, however, considers the hypothetical **pile* (ancient tree). The gloss given by Morgan[67]

Monmouthshire, Merthyr Tydfil, 1997, p. 25.

[66] W. M. MacKenzie. *The Mediaeval Castle in Scotland*, New York: Benjamin Blom, 1972 (reprint of the 1927 original), p. 197.

for the place names *Black Pill* (Glamorganshire) explains the name as a reflection of "the blackened stumps [*pill*] of a submerged forest, which are to be seen all along the shore." This gloss and the association of forms of *p*ll-* with enclosures fashioned of wood (stakes) noted above support the case for the hypothetical Welsh **pile* (ancient tree). This hypothesis is further strengthened by a recent archeological discovery.

In 1998, a pre-Christian religious site was discovered in Norfolk, near the village of Holme. Dendrochronology and radio carbon dating techniques place the date of its construction at 2049 B.C. It consists of a ring of 55 oak posts approximately 21 feet in diameter with the inverted stump of a huge oak tree at its center. It has been dubbed 'Seahenge' because of its location on the coast and its similarity to the great stone rings of Stonehenge.

To the modern reader, the size (21 feet in diameter) of the 'replica' of a sacred tree found at Seahenge may seem larger than life, but English history records a number of trees of prodigious size. The *Ceubren yr Ellyll* ('The Goblin's Hollow Tree') was located in Nannau Park in North Wales. It measured more than 27 feet in girth.[68] *Owen Glendower's Oak* near Shrewsbury could accommodate six or eight persons in the hollow of its trunk. It was over 40 feet in girth.[69] *William the Conqueror's Oak*, in Windsor Great Park, measured 38 feet around (Brewer). The girth of *Fairlop Oak*, in Hainault Forest, measured at a point up a yard from the ground was 36 feet (Brewer). *Cowthorpe Oak* in Yorkshire could accommodate seventy people in its hollow (Brewer). The hollow of *Major Oak* in Sherwood Forest could hold 15 people, the circumference of the trunk being approximately 37 feet. Nine people are reputed to have dined in the hollow of *Meavy Oak*, near Yelverton in Devon, which measured 25 feet in girth (Brewer).

---

[67] Thomas Morgan. *Handbook of the Origin of Place Names in Wales and Monmouthshire*, Merthyr Tydfil, 1997, p. 123.

[68] George Agar Hansard. *The Book of Archery*, London: Longman, Orme, Brown Green and Lomgmans, 1840, p. 194.

[69] E. Cobham Brewer. *The Dictionary of Phrase and Fable* (fifteenth revised edition, revised by Adrian Room, first printed in 1894), New York: Harper Collins, 1995, pp. 761-762.

Compared to these real-life giants, the timber circle at Seahenge is just a scale model.

Owen Glendower's Oak

The inverted tree at the center of Seahenge immediately calls to mind a number of religious traditions in which a tree grows upside down, with its roots in heaven, where the Creator resides, and its branches spread out on the Earth. It can be found in the *Bhagavad Gita*, and in the *Kabala*, and in the legends of Micronesia.

In the South Pacific, one of the creation myths is that in the beginning the earth was a vast, primordial sea. A great tree, rooted in the sky, grew upside down until its branches touched the sea. A woman was born in the branches of the tree and the sky-deity Yelefaz gave her sand, which she spread upon the sea to create the land.[70]

---

[70] Roland B. Dixon, *Oceanic* (volume IX of *The Mythology of All Races*, Louis Herbert Gray ed., in thirteen volumes), Boston: Marshall Jones Comapny, 1916, p. 249.

In his *The Legends of the Jews*,[71] Ginzberg says: "In Paradise stands the tree of life and the tree of knowledge, the latter forming a hedge around the former." This description seems to be replicated in the Seahenge site. The oak logs that formed the outer posts were split lengthways, and were set vertically in a trench with the bark side facing out and the split side in. This would have made the structure look like a huge tree from the outside, and like the inside of a tree from the inside, where the "Tree of Life" stood at the center.

Nature is not without its own version of an upside-down tree. The appearance of the baobab tree of Africa (*Adansonia digitata*) has earned it the nickname of "the upside down tree." It only puts out leaves for a few weeks at a time, during the rainy season, and for the rest of the year looks as if its gnarled roots were stuck up in the air. Legend has it that after the baobab had been planted by God, it kept walking, so God plucked it up and threw it back down to earth crown-first to make it stand still, and it has grown that way ever since. Baobabs can grow to be as much as 30 feet in girth and are often hollow. Particularly large baobabs are commonly given names beginning with 'mother.'

Evidence of timber circles has been found at various locations throughout the United Kingdom, including the Kilmartin Valley in Argyll (Scotland), Sarn-y-bryn-caled (Wales, south of Welshpool), Moel-y-Gaer (Wales, south west of Flint), Pont-ar-daf (Wales, south west of Brecon), Withybush (Wales, Pembrokeshire, north-west of St. Clears) and Arminghall (south of Norwich), which is, incidentally, just north of Upper Stoke and Stoke Holly Cross. These earlier known timber circles had large pits in the center, but researchers had no idea what had been in them because the stump that the pits had held had rotted away long before the circles were discovered. The discovery of Seahenge is the first time that the actual posts and center piece have been recovered. The timber elements of Seahenge were preserved because the site

---

[71] Louis Ginzberg (1873-1953). *The legends of the Jews* (in 7 volumes), translated from the German manuscript by Henrietta Szold, Philadelphia : Jewish Publication Society of America, c1910-c1938, vol. I, p. 70.

was located in marshy ground, and had been covered by layers of peat, clay and sand. The resulting acidic environment below the surface of the bog is inhospitable to the bacteria that make wood rot.

The identification of the center piece—the inverted stump of an oak—and description of the outer ring offer an interesting insight into the probable etymology of the place-name elements *stoke/stock bile/*pile*. The OE word for *tree stump/tree trunk* was *stocc*. It can also be seen in German in the famous *Stock im Eisen* ('tree in iron') in Vienna, directly across from St. Stephen's Cathedral (Stephansdom). *Stock im Eisen* is an old (first mentioned in 1533) tree trunk, encircled with an iron band and studded with handmade iron nails. Morgan's gloss of the place name *Black Pill* relates it to *tree stumps*. Johnson's gloss of *Peel* relates it to a *palisade*, which it what Seahenge looks like. The place names *Stokes sancti Edwoldi*, *Nistenstoch* (a reference to Saint Nectan) and *Godestock* point out the religious character of the site that these place names identify, and the Christian church was all too ready to co-opt old religious sites for its own use. All these facts taken together suggest that at the time when religious circles built of timber like Seahenge were in use, they would have been known as *stocc*, *bile*, or **pile*, depending on which language the speaker was using. This leads logically to the assumption that place names containing *stoke/stock* are common for the same reason that place names containing the element *Church* are common.

The map of England is dotted with place names based on *church*: Whitchurch (in several counties), Newchurch (Kent, Isle of Wight), Baschurch (Shrewsbury: 'Church of a man named Bassa'), Offchurch (Warwickshire: 'Church of a man called Offa'), Peterchurch (Herefordshire & Worcestershire), Pucklechurch (South Gloucestershire: 'Church of the goblin'), Southchurch (Essex), Stokenchurch (Buckinghamshire: 'Church made of logs'), Woodchurch (Kent: 'church of the wood'). Wales is likewise full of place names based on the place-name element *llan* [church]. It is indeed perhaps one of the most productive. Compare: *Llangoed* ('church of the wood'), *Henllan* ('Old Church') and Llanbedr ('St. Peter's').

Stocc would, therefore, appear to be the OE name applied

in pre-Christian times to a religious site. A *stocc* was, in other words, the pre-Christian predecessor of a church, either a real hollow tree of prodigious size, or a timber structure built to look like a tree within a tree.

An artist's concept of Stonehenge restored

"And why is it called the Carrock?"
• Bilbo Baggins

Gandalf's answer to Bilbo's question is: "He called it the Carrock, because carrock is his word for it. He calls things like that carrocks, and this one is *the* Carrock because it is the only one near his home and he knows it well" (H.117; VII). This answer makes it clear that carrock is the general name of a topographic feature. In the narration preceding the question, Tolkien describes the Carrock as: "a great rock, almost a hill of stone, like a last outpost of the distant mountains, or a huge piece cast miles into the plain by some giant among giants" (H.116; VII). (The last phrase in the description is an obvious hint at one of the origin legends for Stonehenge.)

The Welsh word *carreg* (stone, rock, escarpment) has the same consonant silhouette as Tolkien's carrock, and a meaning that matches as well. The coincidence of the meaning and silhouette suggests that carrock is simply a more modern, Common Speech (English) form of the older Welsh word. The three translations offered above for the meaning of the word *carreg* do little to convey the reality of the topographical feature that this word represents in the Welsh landscape. To really appreciate what a *carreg* is, you have to see one. Among the foothills of the Carmarthenshire Black Mountains (Dyfed), 4 miles (6.4 kilometers) south-east of Llandeilo, is a precipitous limestone *carreg* that towers almost 300 feet (90 meters) above the floor of the valley of the river Cennen, which isolates it from the hills to the south and the west. Tolkien's map (H.12-13; I) shows the Misty Mountains to the west and the Grey Mountains to the north.

Tolkien describes the valley in which the Carrock sits as being situated in a landscape of "trees that looked like oaks and elms, and wide grass lands, and a river running through it all." The Carrock cropped "out of the ground, right in the path of the stream which looped itself about it" (H.116; VII). The river Cennen winds its way through the valley around the escarpment in much the same way. On Tolkien's map, the river is called the Great River (The Anduin). The Cennen is hardly a wide, raging river. It is, however, a very active spate river. In dry weather, when water levels are low, the average depth of the Cennen is less than half a meter (20 inches), but in very wet weather, it can rise another two meters (6 feet 8 inches).

Perched atop the escarpment is a castle that has a commanding view of the valley below.[72] It is the most impressive of the castles of the Welsh princes. It is said to have been built by one of King Arthur's knights.

Tolkien did not say anything about a castle, but there are other coincidences with Tolkien's description of *the* Carrock. Tolkien says: "Very few people live in these parts, unless they have come here since I was last down this way, which is some years ago" (H.117; VII). The only habitation near Castell Carreg Cennen is the farm at the base of the carreg, which doubles as a tourist gift shop and restaurant. The tourists outnumber the domestic animals in the surrounding fields, but not by much. In Tolkien's day, the cows and sheep probably had the upper hand.

Tolkien's description of the Carrock continues with "a little cave (a wholesome one with a pebbly floor) at the foot of the steps ..." (H.116; VII) There is also a cave at Castell Carreg Cennen. A vaulted passage leads down along the top of the rock

---

[72] A picture is worth a thousand words and pictures of Castell Carreg Cennen can be seen at:
<http://www.greatcastlesofwales.co.uk/carreg_foto.htm>. LVO 12/16/2005.

face to steps that descend into the cave, which has a long, narrow galley that extends back into the carreg for about 50 yards (46 meters). The cave has been a tourist attraction since at least the early 1800's and its walls are covered with graffiti.

Legend claims that there is a warrior (one of Arthur's knights, or Arthur himself, depending on who you listen to) asleep in the cave in the cliff face beneath the castle, awaiting a call from the Welsh to return to the outer world to become king of Britain. Perhaps Tolkien, too, heard this legend and worked it subtly into his tale of the Carrock as one of the philological jests of which he was so fond.

With only a little bit of mirthful linguistic imagination, of which Tolkien had plenty, it can be seen as the combination of the Welsh word for *bear* is *arth*, and the Welsh ending *-wr* [pronounced "-ur"], which forms nouns that name people with the quality of the underlying root. The ending *-wr* is derived from *gwr* "man", with shortening of the vowel and lenition of the initial consonant, as is normal in Welsh compounds. The Welsh word *henwr*, for example, means *old man*. It is made up of the root *hen* (*old*) plus *-(g)wr*. *Arth* + *-(g)wr* ("bear" + "man"], thereby becomes a hint that Beorn, the skin changer who took the shape of a bear, is the "he" who had named the escarpment *the Carrock*.

Another version of the tale of the sleeping hero in the cave at Castell Carreg Cennen says that it is the Welsh Hero Owain Llawgoch (Owain of the Red Hand), one of the last chieftains who fought against the English. In this version of the tale he and his men will sleep there until wakened by the sound of a horn and a clang of arms on Rhywgoch, when they will arise and conquer their Saxon foes, driving them from the land. The story of an army lying in wait in a cave for the call to arms is certainly reminiscent of the Deadmen of Dunharrow (R.64-65, 71-75, 186, 509; V.2, V.2, Appendix F).

Castell Carreg Cennen is the only Welsh castle—except, of course, Pembroke Castle—noted for its cave. That fact combined with the seeming appearance of the cave's legends in Tolkien's works suggest that Castell Carreg Cennen is the model for Tolkien's Carrock.

Mathum Sword
(with an expanded view of the engraving)

In Search of the Origin of the River Lune

The river Lhûn of western Middle-earth flowed south from the northern Ered Luin into the Gulf of Lhûn. It formed the boundary between Arnor [Land of the King] to the East and the Elvish and Dwarvish lands to the West.

The tidal river Lune of western England first flows north and west from its source in Ravenstone-dale in Westmoreland, but then turns sharply south through a deep dale, passing Kirkby Lonsdale and the Roman station at Overburrow, where it enters the Lunesdale Valley. Continuing west-south-west, it passes Lancaster before entering Morecambe Bay. The stretch of the river between the quaint town of Kirkby Lonsdale and the historic city of Lancaster is one of the most picturesque, with the idyllic Crook O' Lune, providing one of the best views in the country.

The Lune river valley is considered one of the highlights of England's North Country. In his popular *Guide to the Lakes*[73], the

---

[73] Wordsworth, William, *A Description of the Scenery of the Lakes in the North of England*, 5th ed., Kendal: Hudson and Nicholson, 1835, p. iii.

Poet William Wordsworth (1770-1850) recommended that his readers should not miss the Lune Valley on their way to the Lakes. Tolkien could hardly have been unfamiliar with it.

The coincidence of the Westron spelling of the name of the river *Lhûn* with the modern-day spelling of the Celtic hydronym (river name) *Lune* irresistibly invites the curious linguist to take a closer look at the origins of the name *Lune*. Hydronyms can, as Taylor noted (Q.V. "The Water"), be considered linguistic fossils because they change very little in the course of time, and can, therefore, offer some interesting insights into the prehistory of the country in which they are found.

Tolkien glosses *Lhûn* as *blue* (S.361). This form of the adjective is used with singular (sg.) nouns. For plural (pl.) nouns, the form is *luin* on the analogy of Old Welsh singular/plural adjective pairs. (Compare: llydan (sg.) llydain (pl.) [broad, wide], bychan (sg.) bychain (pl.) [little, small].) In creating the name of the mountain range where the river Lhûn found its source, Tolkien needed the plural adjective form to match the plural noun *ered* [mountains]. The singular of *ered* is *orod* [mountain], which is suggestive of the Celtic *ard*, meaning "high," "lofty." (Compare: *ard* (Cornish, Gaelic, Manx), *hardh* (Welsh), *arduus* (Latin).)[74] This root can still be seen in this meaning in the name Yr Arddu [*ardd* + *du*, where *ardd* means "high land," and *du* means "dark" or "black"], south-east of Mount Snowdon. The *Etymologies* show a similar relationship between the Noldorin *orod*, the liquid '**R**' in which has retained the vowel on both sides, and the Doriathrin *orth*, which has lost its right vowel (p. 423).

An earlier form of the hydronym that is now spelled *Lune* is *Lon*. This spelling can be seen in the place name Kirkby Lonsdale, which means "dwelling by the church in the valley of the river Lon". The place name Lancaster, which means "Roman fort or 'Caster' on the river Lon," was spelled *Loncastre* in the *Doomsday Book*. The '**O**' to '**U**' shift can be seen in the pronunciation of London as [lundon], and in the Welsh and Cornish names for London: LLundain (W), Loundrez (C).

---

[74] Robert Williams, *Lexicon Cornu-Britannicum: Dictionary of the Ancient Celtic Language of Cornwall*, London: Trubner & Co., 1865, p. 11.

The hydronym *Lune* is widely assumed to be Celtic in origin. The presence of Celtic hydronyms outside the areas that are now inhabited by the descendants of the Celtic tribes (the Welsh, the Irish, the Scots) should come as no surprise. The name of the river, upon which the city of Stratford of Shakespearean fame lies, is simply the modern Welsh word for river: *afon* (more familiar to English speakers as *avon*). The river name Dover, along which the city of Dover is to be found, is simply the Welsh word for water: *dwfr* [pronounced duvr].

The veneration of water—rivers and wells—was a key feature of Celtic society. Numerous votive offerings cast into rivers and wells by the Celts have been recovered by archeologists. It is, therefore, not surprising that Celtic hydronyms were selected to honor a hero or a deity, as is the case with the river Boyne, named after the Irish water goddess Boann [she of the white cattle; compare the old Welsh *bu*, which means *cow*, and the English *bovine*].

The name *Lon* belongs to a number of blacksmiths from Celtic lore who could qualify as a hero or deity. **Lon** mac Liomtha is the great mythical smith, who wrought Mac an Luin [The Son of the Spear], the famous enchanted sword of Fionn mac Cumhail. **Loan** Maclibhuin is the smith of Manx legend who made the sword Macabuin for King Olave II, Goddardson, of the Isle of Man. It could even cleave through a mountain of granite. Cu**lann**, the Ulster Smith, forged Conchobhar's weapons.

In "The Lay of the Smithy," a part of the *Duanaire Finn* [The Book of the Lays of Fin], a group of Irish heroes is compelled to follow the giant **Lon** mac Liomtha, the teacher of all smiths, to his forge in the north where one of the heroes— Daolghus—makes some weapons. When Daolghus finished his work, the giant gave the heroes a number of enchanted weapons, which—like all weapons of this type—had names of their own. One of these was Mac an **Luin**, which brings us back to Tolkien's adjective pair *Lhûn/luin*.

Welsh river names associated with weapons or tools are reasonably common. The names were meant to reflect the way the rivers cut through the earth. The Welsh name of Milford Haven, for example, is *Aber-dau-gleddau* [Estuary of the two swords]. It is at the confluence of the *Cleddau Fawr* and the *Cleddau Fach* [The Greater and Lesser Sword rivers]. Tolkien would certainly have been aware of this, and it may have had a limited influence on his name.

Mac an Luin is often translated as *Son of the Spear*, in reference to the mythical spear Luin, one of the most famous enchanted spears of early Irish literature. It belonged to the Red Branch hero Celthchair. Mac Cecht uses it to kill Cuscraid. Dubthach Doeltenga borrows it for the second battle of Magh Turieadh. A river name containing the element *spear* is not without precedent. In the Norse tales, all the rivers of the nine worlds spring from the cauldron Hvergelmir near Valahalla. One of them is *Geirvimul* [spear teeming].[75]

Water again comes to the fore in an alternate translation of Mac an Luin. This name is sometimes translated as *Son of the Waves*, but in the stories where this translation is applied, Mac an Luin was given to the hero by the Manx God of the sea, Manannan, who is older than the Tuatha de Danann. Culann is considered a later incarnation of Manannan Mac Lir.

Mac an Luin could equally well be understood as *Son of Lon*, because in Irish, *luin* is the genitive case form of *lon*. The name of the spear Luin could likewise simply be a possessive condensate of "Lon's (spear)." Archaic Welsh points to an even greater simplification. In Welsh, *llain* means *blade, sword*. This spelling brings us back to the spelling of *Lon* in the place name **Lan**caster, the "Roman fort or 'Caster' on the river Lon," and is echoed in the name of the Ulster smith Cu**lann**.

While the logical connection between a smith and water is not immediately obvious to the modern reader, there is one to the student of Celtic lore, a group of which Tolkien should certainly be considered a member. The principal attributes of a smithy are the forge, the anvil, the hammer and the water trough. Irish folklore attributes a great curative power to the forge water used by a blacksmith to cool his irons.[76] The cure for rickets, for example,

---

[75] Kevin Crossley-Holland, *The Norse Myths*, New York: Pantheon Books, 1980, p. 62.

[76] Ó Súilleabháin, Seán, *A Handbook of Irish Folklore*, Dublin: Published by the Educational Company of Ireland Ltd. for the Folklore

was to have the patient bathed in forge water and then placed on the anvil, where the smith would pass his hammer over the patient.[77] Rubbing your hands in forge water was a cure for warts. Drinking forge water was recommended for pregnant women to ensure the safe delivery of the baby. It was additionally potent, if it could be obtained without the smith's knowledge.[78] If the smith did know about it, no payment could be made for it, or it would lose its power. According to legend, a smith's vigor is renewed every time he washes his hands.[79]

The curative power of forge water completes the circle that begins with the commonly accepted etymology of the hydronym *Lune*. It derives from an Old Irish word meaning "Health Giving," exactly what Irish folk belief holds forge water to be. This connection implies that the lost mythic origin of the river Lune is to be found in the water trough in the smithy of **Lon** mac Liomtha in his various incarnations.

The river Lune is not the only river on the British isles named for a mythical smith. In addition to the numerous phonetic variations of Lune to be found on the map of England, there is also the river Gavenni in Wales. It is named for the mythic blacksmith Govannon. In Irish Govannon is known as Goibhniu. The word for *smith* in all the Celtic languages is derived from the same root. In Irish, it is *gabha*, in Scottish, *gobha*, in Manx, *gaave*, in Welsh, Cornish and Breton, *gof*. In Persian legend, the renowned blacksmith of Ispahan was called gava,[80] which points to a Persian-Celtic linguistic connection.

The difference between **Lon** mac Liomtha and Gobannion is that one represents the Gaelic tradition and the other represents

---

of Ireland Society, 1942; and Lady I.A.P. Gregory (1852-1932), *Visions and Beliefs in the West of Ireland*, New York and London: G. P. Putman's sons, 1920, p. 275.

[77] Iona Opie and Moira Tatem (ed.), *A Dictionary of Superstitions*, Oxford [England] and New York: Oxford University Press, 1989, p. 29.

[78] <http://members.aol.com/irllondon/olga.htm>. LVO 2/14/2006.

[79] Ó Súilleabháin.

[80] Williams, p. 174.

the Cymric tradition. **Lon** mac Liomtha is the mythic smith of Irish and Manx tradition, and Govannon is the smith god of Welsh tradition. This differentiation is also reflected in the divergence of Gaelic and Welsh languages. One of the key linguistic divergences is seen in place names denoting the confluence of two waters: either two rivers or a river and the sea. In the Gaelic-speaking area, these place names begin with *Inver-*, while in the Welsh-speaking areas, they begin with *Aber-*. Compare: *Inver*ness [estuary of the river Ness] and *Aber*gavenny [estuary of the river Gavenny].

The name *Lon* is commonly translated as "Blackbird," but it can also be translated as "ousel" (spelled ouzel in American English). The ousel's description in Shakespeare's *Midsummer Night's Dream* (Act 3, Scene I) shows why both are possible. In Shakespeare's words the ousel cock is very "black of hue", and has an "orange-tawny bill." In the Welsh tale of *Culhwch and Olwen*, the Ousel of Cilgwri has a role in the search for Mabon, the son of Modron. She is one of the oldest living creatures, but she has no news of Mabon. The logical connection between the smith Lon mac Liomtha and the ousel (Irish: lon) is a smith's anvil. In describing her age, the Ousel of Cilgwri explains that she is so old, that in the course of all the years that she has lived, she has worn an anvil down to less than the size of a nut by cleaning her beak on it each night as she went to bed. The image is an interesting one, because it not only points to the great antiquity of the Ousel of Cilgwri, but also to the great antiquity of those who use anvils, the smiths. The color associated with the blackbird/ousel is also not inappropriate for a **black**smith.

A blacksmith having been drawn into the equation, Tolkien's word for *mountain* [*orod*] in the name *The Blue Mountains* [ered Luin] deserves another look. The Irish and Welsh words for "smith's hammer" bear a striking resemblance: *ord* (I), *gordd* (W). A convincingly logical connection could be made between the word for *mountain* and the word for the *hammers* of the Dwarvish smiths who lived and worked under the mountain. The *Etymologies*, however, do not offer any support for this view (p. 423).

For the modern reader, there is likewise no immediately apparent logical connection between swords/spears and the color blue. Again, there is one to be found in Irish legend. When the work in his smithy was done, Lon mac Liomtha gave each of the heroes a spear and "a **blue** blade of true fierceness."[81] The Celts were early adopters of iron, which, when compared to the red hue of the earlier bronze weapons, could be considered to have a hue of blue. The real meaning of the blue blade of true fierceness from this tale may be that it was made of iron.

The blue blade of true fierceness from the legend of Lon mac Liomtha may find a reflection in Tolkien's tale in the sword Sting, which was crafted by Elvish smiths in the elder days and glowed coldly (F.404 II.4) **blue** (T.419, 421; IV.9, R.219; VI.1), if there were orcs nearby. It worked where others failed, and Tolkien called it "bitter" (T.421; IV.9, 429; IV.10), invoking the older meaning of the word, which is near to the sense of fierceness that was a quality of Lon mac Liomtha's blades.

There is another—less direct—connection between the Celts, the color blue and weapons of war. In his *Gallic Wars*, Julius Caesar made note of the fact that "all Britons stain themselves with woad, which produces a blue color, and gives them a more horrible appearance in battle." The Greek geographer Strabo of Amasia (Circa 64 B.C.-19 A.D.) called the Celts "war-mad," and it is easy to understand why, given the description of the spear Luin. When it smelled the blood of an enemy, it would turn and writhe in the hands of its owner, but if that blood was not spilled, the spear had to be dipped into a cauldron of black poison to quench its thirst for blood, or it would turn on the person wielding it.

The spear Luin is one incarnation of the spear of Destiny, one of the four gifts that the ancestors of the Celts who now inhabit Ireland received from the Tuatha De Danann, who built their capital on the hill (507 feet) known as Tara in County Meath. Before coming to Ireland, the Tuatha De Danann lived in the northern isles of the world (like Lon mac Liomtha), where they acquired knowledge, skills and cunning. Their gifts to the Irish were: a spear, a sword, a cauldron and a stone, each with

---

[81] *Duanaire Finn: The Book of the Lays of Fin*, Part II (Irish text, with translations into English), Gerard Murphy, London: Simpkin Marshall for the Irish Texts Society, 1933, v.28, p. 13.

powerful magical properties. The stone was the "Stone of Destiny", which can identify the rightful ruler of the land by giving out a loud cry. Dagda, the father of the Tuatha De Danann, was the owner of the cauldron from which no one departed hungry. The sword was the irresistible sword of Nuada, from which no one ever escaped. The spear was the spear of Lugh Lamfhota [the "long-armed"] against which no battle was ever won.

The connection between the color blue, the Celts and weapons of war takes an even more interesting turn in Dorothea Chaplin's book, *Matter, Myth, and Spirit: Keltic and Hindu Links*[82], in which she makes an interesting comparison of the name Tara in Celtic and Hindu Mythology. The Hindu Tara, whose appearance is horrible, is the Goddess of War. She is blue.[83] This Tara is the Morning Star (the Nila [Blue] Sarasvati of India),[84] the mother of Buddha, the Wise.[85] Chaplin continues her search for Celtic-Hindu parallels with the proverbial "Holy Cow," which is an integral feature of Hinduism. Chaplin connects this to the mound of the Grey Cow and the Well of the White Cow at the Irish Tara, traces of which can still be found there.[86] The translation of the name of the Irish water goddess Boann [she of the white cattle] only serves to reinforce Chaplin's point about Celtic-Hindu links. The holy cows of Hindu fame are indeed white.

The Irish Tara is one of the most famous sites of the early Celtic world. Remains at the site date back to 2000 B.C.. Much of early Irish literature either takes places at Tara or mentions it in some way or another. Tara's widespread fame is attested by its appearance as the name of Scarlett O'Hara's plantation in *Gone with the Wind*. The Irish Tara in County Meath was the seat of kings and the Stone of Destiny. It is home to the "Great Hall with a Thousand Soldiers,"[87] the name of which only serves to

---

[82] London: Rider & Co., 1935.

[83] Chaplin, p. 40.

[84] Chaplin, p. 62.

[85] Chaplin, p. 38.

[86] Chaplin, p. 53.

[87] Chaplin, p. 62; and Daragh Smyth, *A Guide to Irish*

underscore the importance of warfare among the Celts of that time.

Chaplin's association of Tara—the Hindu goddess of war—and the hill Tara—considered holy to the early Irish pagans—falls somewhat flat. The name of the hill—Tara—is the anglicized version of the name, generally considered to be derived from *Teamhrach* [Irish: "Tea's Hill(?)"]. Tea was the wife of Eremon, the first High King of the Milesians, the mythic people who defeated the Tuatha De Danann. Chaplin would have done better to point to the Celtic god *Taranis*. He is the god of thunder and lightning to whom, just like the Roman Jupiter and the Slavic Perun, the oak tree was sacred. His name is still reflected in the word for *thunder* in the vocabulary of Welsh and Cornish (taran), Irish (toran), Manx (taarnagh) and Gaelic (torrun),[88] the last of which displays some linguistic hints that it might be related to Perun and to Thor.

According to the Roman poet Lucan (1st century A.D.), Taranis was one of the three principal deities of Gaul and Britain. A ninth century commentary on Lucan describes Taranis as a "master of war."[89] Chaplin's work shows that the linguistic and logical registers for *Tara* and blue coincide quite closely in this context. Tara the Hindu goddess of war was blue, the same color that the Celts stained themselves before going into battle, presumably following the master of war, Taranis.

In a letter (L.380), Tolkien noted that the processes behind the creation of his toponyms was idiosyncratic. The result was intended to satisfy his own personal linguistic taste. "The 'source', if any," said Tolkien, "provided solely the sound-sequence (or suggestions for its stimulus) and its purport *in the source* is totally irrelevant." While only Tolkien can say for certain if the origin story of the river Lune was one of his "sources," there are clearly a number of linguistic and logical intersects between the story and his river name to support that conclusion.

Mythology, Dublin: Irish Academic Press, 1996, p. 168.

[88] Williams, p. 331.

[89] James MacKillop, *Dictionary of Celtic Mythology*, Oxford: Oxford University Press, 1998, p. 355.

A BRIEF MCLE IN DATE ENGLISH FEET

In League with Miles

In *The Hobbit*, Tolkien only uses the word *miles* (22X) to define long linear distances. In *The Lord of the Rings*, however, he has mixed metrics, using both *miles* and *leagues* to define distance. In "The Prologue" of the first edition, Tolkien describes The Shire as occupying an area that is 50 leagues square[90] (P.24). In reporting the location of Bree relative to The Shire, however, he says that Bree lay approximately 40 miles to the east of The Shire (P.23). This alternation continues throughout the three volumes.

At first glance, Tolkien appears to use the two terms interchangeably. The narrator and several of the characters use both *leagues* and *miles*: Gandalf, Frodo, Strider/Aragorn, Faramir, Gimli, Legolas, Pippin and Gollum. The first Dutch translator apparently thought that there was no difference, and simply converted all the *leagues* to *miles* on a 1:1 basis, which made The Shire much smaller: 50 miles square instead of 50 leagues square. The conversion error was corrected in the second Dutch translation,

---

[90] In Tolkien's first edition (1954), The Shire was 50 leagues east to west by nearly 50 north to south. With the fourth edition (1965), it changed to 40 by 50, omitting the "nearly."

but everything continued to be expressed in *miles* in Dutch. There is no better rendition of *leagues* into Dutch, where every child knows that *seven-league boots* are called zeven**mijls**laarzen.

The difference between *miles* and *leagues* does not become apparent until Sam's usage of units of measurement is considered. He only uses the word *miles*. Sam is quintessentially English, while the other characters are more cosmopolitan, or, at least, more widely travelled.

Tolkien also gives an indication that the further they get from The Shire, the less well-known distance measurements in miles are. When Merry asks how far it is from Weathertop to Rivendell, Strider replies that he is not sure if the road from one to the other "has ever been measured in miles" past the *Forsaken Inn*, which is a day's travel east of Bree (F.253; I.11). This statement places a certain sense of geographical limitation on the use of the word *mile*.

It suggests something similar to the dichotomy of *miles* and *leagues* to be found in literature. Although the French introduced the kilometer on the continent in the wake of the French revolution (1789-1799), the word *leagues* continued in literary use for some time afterward. In *A Tale of Two Cities*, Charles Dickens (1812-1870) uses *leagues* to describe the length of Charles Darnay's journey in France. In *The Count of Monte Cristo* by Alexandre Dumas (1802-1870), the traveler was hardly 3 leagues from Rome when night began to fall. In *White Lies* by Charles Reade (1814-1884), it is 45 leagues from Beaurepaire to Paris. In *The Scarlet Pimpernel* by Baroness Emmuska Orczy (1865-1947), the distance to Miquelon is 3 leagues. In *King Solomon's Mines* by H. Rider Haggard (1856-1925), the map prepared by da Silvestra shows the width of the desert to be forty leagues. In *The Crimes of England* by G.K. Chesterton (1874-1936) the prelude to the battle of the Marne (September 1914) contains a consideration of the defense of "the last desperate leagues" before Paris.

The differentiation that Tolkien would appear to be seeking to express with his use of both *leagues* and *miles* is, perhaps, best documented in an old dictionary definitions of the word *league*. The 1913 *Webster's Dictionary* says that *league* was "used (as a land measure) chiefly on the continent of Europe, and in the

Spanish parts of America." In these geographic areas today, the word *league* has largely been supplanted by the word *kilometer*. The definition in *Webster's* shows that the use of the word *league* had a geographic marking early in the twentieth century, similar to the geographic marking that Tolkien was hinting at with Strider's doubt about the road ever having been measured in miles past the *Forsaken Inn*.

The *OED* definition of *league* says: "never in regular use in England, but often occurring in poetical or rhetorical statements of distance." Tennyson (1809-1892) is a good example of this: "Half a league, half a league, half a league onward. Into the valley of death rode the six hundred." In other words, Tolkien might have wanted to lend a sense of grandiloquence to his tale with the use of the word *league*, which is marked for poetical or rhetorical style, while the word *mile* was in everyday use in England in Tolkien's time.

Most young modern-day English-speaking readers have no clear sense of how long a *league* is, and their most common association with the word *league* as a measure of linear distance is probably with the title of Jules Verne's famous *20,000 Leagues Under the Sea*, or with Tennyson's *Charge Light Brigade*, neither of which lends itself to creating a concrete perception of distance.

Readers with only these associations who want to know exactly how long a *league* is have to get out a dictionary and a calculator, and even then, they may not discover a satisfyingly clear-cut answer, as the length of a *league* and a *mile* given in reference sources varies from country to country and across time. The Irish mile, for example, up into the twentieth century, was equal to 6,720 feet. Tolkien was clearly aware of this variation, because his notes indicate that a "Bree mile" was equal to 6,912 feet (*Companion* 23).

Those who have read *King Solomon's Mines*, however, know what every child used to learn in school: "forty leagues is one hundred and twenty miles." This was the conversion factor that the second Dutch translator used.

A member of the Roman Legion in Britain would likewise not have had the difficulty of the modern reader. The word *mile* is a condensate of the Latin term *mille passuum* [a thousand paces]. The Roman pace was a double stride, measured from the print of the left heel to the toe of the next print of the left foot. The length of the stride prescribed in the U.S. Army's Manual of Drill and Ceremonies (FM 22-5) is 30 inches. A double stride is, therefore, 60 inches, or 5 feet. A thousand paces marched off by an army formation cover a distance of 5,000 feet, which is the measured distance between surviving milestones of Roman roads. The modern standard or statute mile is 5,280 feet. This hypothetical Roman soldier would undoubtedly have personally counted off more sets of a 1,000 paces than he cared to remember, and would have an excellent idea of how long a mile is.

For this hypothetical Roman infantryman, the word *league* would also have a much more concrete meaning than the definitions contained in modern dictionaries, where *league* is defined in terms of yards, miles or (kilo)meters. A *league* is the distance that can be covered by marching troops in one hour. The U.S. Army prescribes a marching cadence of 120 steps, or 60 paces per minute (FM 22-5). In one hour, therefore, a military formation marching at this cadence would count off 3,600 paces, or 3.6 Roman-Legion miles (18,000 feet), which fits well within the range of values normally given for the length of a *league*.

In *Unfinished Tales*, Tolkien explains that he used the word *league* as the translation of *lár*, a Númenorean linear measurement that was approximately equal to 3 statute miles. "Except in forced marches" (UT.285), this was the distance covered by marching Númenorean troops in one hour (UT.279). Tolkien continues that a lár was equal to "5,000 *rangar* (full paces)" (UT.285), but his definition of the Númenorean pace (*ranga* [singular]) does not coincide with that of the *Roman pace*. He clarifies that the Númenorean pace was "the length of the stride, from rear heel to front toe of a full-grown man marching swiftly but at ease" (UT.285-286). This is only half a Roman pace.

Tolkien notes, however, that the equivalence of the lár with the league is only a supposition based on the recorded lengths of various things that can be compared with similar things of the present time (UT.285). Stressing the great stature of the Númenoreans, Tolkien explains that they had a longer stride, which he specifies as 38 inches (UT.285). By making the length of the Númenorean marching stride 8 inches longer than the stride required by FM 22-5, but keeping the distance covered in one hour the same, Tolkien reduces the cadence of the march. He states that a lár is 5,000 strides (rangar), which equals a Númenorean marching cadence of 41.6 Roman paces (double strides) per minute, almost 18 paces per minute less than the cadence mandated by the FM 22-5. Tolkien's cadence is more that of a leisurely walk than of a march.

Increasing the length of the Númenorean stride without changing the distance covered by marching troops in one hour introduces a certain logical fault into Tolkien's discussion of the length of the *lár*. From a Hobbitish point of view, perhaps, a cadence of 42 paces per minute would seem more leisurely, more pleasant, and more sustainable, for Tolkien remarks that this was a "pace they could maintain for long periods with adequate provision" (UT.279). From a military point of view, however, it is simply inefficient.

Númenorean troops would certainly be no less physically fit than Roman troops, and should, therefore, be able to replicate the Roman (U.S. Army) cadence with no problem. Increasing the length of the Númenorean stride **without** decreasing the Númenorean cadence would have produced a Númenorean mile (1,000 double paces) of 6333.3 English feet, 1,333.3 feet longer than the Roman mile, and in the range of the length of the Irish mile (6,720 statute feet) and the Bree mile (6,912 feet). This would produce a *lár* that would range in length from 19,000 English feet (3 Númenorean miles) to 22,800 English feet (3,600 Númenorean paces). The shortest of these is more than half a mile (3,160 feet) greater than a Roman league, which Haggard and Tolkien both equate to 3 English miles (15,840 feet).

The definitions of *league* above add new perspective to Éomer's wonder at the distance that Strider, Legolas and Gimli traversed as they chased the Orcs who had taken Merry and Pippin prisoner. He finds *Strider* too poor a name for someone who has crossed forty-five leagues in less than four days, and would call Aragorn *Wingfoot* (T.47; III.2). Using Haggard's and Tolkien's conversion factor of 3 English miles to the league, they covered 135 English miles. The same calculation based on Númenorean miles would be at least 162 English miles.

In his book on the Roman military,[91] lieutenant-colonel S.G. Brady notes a particularly exceptional march found in Caesar's records that covered "48 miles [16 leagues] in 24 hours with only three hours' rest." Wingfoot and his companions would not have matched that pace, but they maintained their pace for four days, coming close to Tolkien's Númenorean marching pace "in haste" of 12 leagues a day (UT.279). According to Brady, an ordinary day's march (*iustum iter*) covered approximately 16 to 17 miles [slightly less than six leagues] in seven hours. The Romans only marched from sun-up until mid-day. The remainder of the day was used to fortify the new position that they had taken up for the night. Forced marches (*magna itera*) could cover up to 30 miles [10 leagues].

The difference between the distances covered on Roman and Númenorean marching days is obviously attributable to the day's schedule. According to Tolkien, an ordinary day's march for a Númenorean marching formation covered eight lár over the course of a ten and a half hour day. The day consisted of eight hours of marching, with short breaks at the end of each lár (a word that originally meant *break* or *pause*), plus an hour stop at about mid-day (UT.279). He makes no mention of the Númenoreans fortifying their bivouac position at the end of the day. Had the Romans marched for ten and a half hours instead

---

[91] Lt. Col. S.G. Brady. *The Military Affairs of Ancient Rome & Roman Art of War in Caesar's Time*, Harrisburg, PA: The Military Service Publishing Company, 1947.
<www.pvv.ntnu.no/~madsb/home/war/romanarmy/romanarmy03.php> and
<www.globalsecurity.org/military/library/report/other/romanarmy.htm>. Both LVO 12/19/ 2005.

of seven, and not had to fortify their new encampment, they could easily have covered eight leagues as well.

Using a Roman Legionnaire's definition of these distances gives the modern reader a more personal sense of the distances covered in *The Lord of the Rings*, where, indeed, much of the travel was on foot. The German translations give the reader a somewhat better sense of the Roman Legionnaire's perception of these distances than does the original. In German, The Shire is defined as occupying an area 40 by 50 *Wegstunden* [road-hours]. The main problem for modern German readers is recognizing that this is not an hour's drive by car, but rather the distance covered on foot in an hour (3 Roman-Legion miles). The old-fashioned stylistic marker that accompanies *Wegstunden* helps the German reader overcome this problem, but if it is missed, or not applied correctly, the 'German' Shire becomes a lot bigger than it is in the original.

The Faversham Moot Horn.
This horn served for the calling of local assemblies at
Faversham, Kent, circa 1300.

Fractured Fairy Tales from Middle-earth

Tolkien enjoys word histories (L.264) and is not loath to create his own. At the Prancing Pony, Frodo sings a song that Bilbo was "rather fond of (and indeed rather proud of, for he had made up the words himself)" (F.216-218 IX.9). It does not take long before the reader recognizes that the song is that old childhood favorite: "And the Cow Jumped over the Moon." In reciting the history of the Battle of Greenfields, Tolkien offers the reader an etymology of the name of the game of golf (H.30; I).

Tolkien attempts the same trick again somewhat less elaborately and somewhat less successfully in Chapter 11 ("A Knife in the Dark," F.239). The cry of alarm—placed on a line of its own and all in CAPITAL letters—that accompanies the sounding of the Horn-call of Buckland is:

FEAR! FIRE! FOES!

The alliterative alarm alerts the populace to the danger of the Black Riders. As an element in this sequence, *FEAR!* seems a bit forced logically, because it is an abstract concept, and the other two are concrete. This logical stumbling block makes the reader stop to consider why Tolkien unbalanced the three elements in his alarm cry by making one of them not like the other two. A reflection of this logical discomfort can be seen in the translations of the cry of alarm. Of the sixteen translations[92] that I looked at, only four—the two Dutch, the second Polish, and the Bulgarian—translated *FEAR!*, all the rest replaced this element with something concrete.

In both German translations, the element *FEAR!* became *DANGER!* (GEFAHR!). In the Russian translations, it variously became DISASTER! (БЕДА! [BEDA!]), MISFORTUNE! (НАПАСТЬ! [NAPAST'!]), ALARM! (ТРЕВОГА! [TREVOGA!]) and LOOK-OUT! (БЕРЕГИСЬ! [BEREGIS'!]). In the Czech translation, the first element in the series was HELP! (POMOC!). In the first Polish translation, *FIRE!* was simply repeated (*Gore! Gore!*). It is clear from this that most of the translators felt uncomfortable with *FEAR!* as the first element of the alarm cry, and sensed a need to replace it with something else to make the alarm cry more 'logical' from their point of view.

The logical imbalance in Tolkien's list prompts the reader to look for a reason to explain the lack of equilibrium. In the context of Tolkien and his love of word histories, this inquisitive reader is wont to recall the words of the Giant in another well-known childhood tale that seems to echo Tolkien's alliterative alarm:

> Fee Fi Fo Fum,
> I smell the blood of an Englishman.
> Be he alive, or be he dead,
> I'll grind his bones to make my bread.

In creating his alliterative alarm, Tolkien appears to be attempting to present the reader with an etymology of the giant's nonsense alliterative rhyme (*Fee Fi Fo*), the explanation of which has eluded scholars for centuries. (There is a version in act 3,

---

[92] German-2, Polish-2, Dutch-2, Czech-1, Bulgarian-1, Russian-8.

scene 4 of Shakespeare's *King Lear* [1605]: Fie, foh, and fum, I smell the blood of a British man.) In Tolkien's version, the giant's rhyme would seem to be a worn-down form of the original Buckland cry of alarm, which does make sense.

Tolkien referred to this linguistic process himself to explain the changes in the Hobbit names of the days of the week. "[T]he meanings of their translated names were soon forgotten, or no longer attended to, and the forms were much reduced, especially in everyday pronunciation" (Ad.484). In explaining how the names of The Shire were translated, Tolkien says that the names were usually made up of elements commonly found in English place names, "either words still current like *hill* or *field*; or a little worn down like *ton* beside *town*" (Af.515).

The apparent reason for the imbalance in the first element in the alarm-cry of Buckland, would seem to be that it was 'forced' into the series because it needed to sound like the first element in the giant's nonsense alliterative rhyme.

The ideal translation of *FEAR! FIRE! FOES!* would, therefore, seek to find what target-language-speaking giants say before they announce that they are going to grind up an intruder's bones to make bread. Unfortunately, most non-English-speaking giants also seem to use the well-known proto-Giantish formulation, making it essentially impossible to find modern words with a logical match in the target language. The same is lamentably true of the translations of *King Lear*.

Since being able to replicate a viable etymology for *Fee Fi Fo* is unlikely in the target language, the translation of the Buckland cry of alarm should at least be alliterative, given Tolkien's known fondness for alliterative Anglo-Saxon poetry. Only the Dutch translations managed that, and I suspect that it was more by luck than by contrivance, because Dutch and English are rather closely related linguistically, and the most common Dutch translations of the words *FEAR! FIRE! FOES!* all happen to begin with the letter **'V'**: VREES! VUUR! VIJANDEN! The only other translators to come close were the Germans with GEFAHR! FEUER! FEINDE! (Carroux) and GEFAHR! FEURIO! FEINDE! (Krege), which appears to owe more to contrivance than to luck. None of the other translators came close.

:IT:IS:SORROW:AND:GARN:THAT:
:KEEP:HER:IN:HER:PLACE:

Tolkien's Use of the Word "Garn!" to Typify a Motley Crew of Reprobates

Tolkien is an excellent stylist and applies his knowledge of dialectical usage to paint a picture of his characters by putting typifying words into the speaker's dialogue. The literary *baggage* that these words carry around with them helps the reader to understand who the speaker is. This *baggage* is built up of all the usages of each word that the reader has been exposed to. It varies from reader to reader, even among well-read, educated native-English-speaking readers. Modern readers whose literary baggage is, in general, markedly different from Tolkien's, will very likely, not get the point of Tolkien's subtle *typifying usage* of words like *garn*, and, therefore, may appreciate a look into the literary suitcase that the word *garn* carries around with it.

The word *garn* is a bit of Cockney dialect that Tolkien puts into the mouths of a number of characters of less than sterling repute. The renowned showman W.S. Gilbert has a sentence that is an excellent illustration of the type of person who might use *garn* in his *The Hooligan: A Character Study* (1911). In it, his character says: "Garn! I don't want no wash! Washin' never freshened a bloke yet." In G.B. Shaw's *Pygmalion* (1914), *garn* is the word that prompts Professor Higgins to say that Eliza speaks a sort of "kerbstone English" that is going to "keep her in the gutter to the end of her days."[93] The reaction of the lyrical Professor Higgins in Lerner's and Loewe's *My Fair Lady* is, perhaps, somewhat better known: "It's 'Aoooow' and 'Garn' that keep her in her place. Not her wretched clothes and dirty face."

The characters whom Tolkien is keeping in 'their place' are:

- the Orc Shagrat (T.444; IV.10),
- a nameless small Orc tracker (R.247, R.248; VI.2),
- the largest and most evil-looking ruffian of the crew that came out to meet Frodo and Company at *The Green Dragon* (R.350; VI.8), and
- Ted Sandyman, a character of undoubted ill repute (R.366; VI.8).

All in all, a motley crew of reprobates, if ever there was one. What they have in common is that they alone of all Tolkien's many other characters use the word *garn*. Ted Sandyman even resembles Gilbert's character, who "don't want no wash." Just before Sandyman says "Garn!," Sam Gamgee comments that Sandyman apparently has "no time for washing." (R.366; VI.8)

In his short commentary entitled "Garn!" (*Beyond Bree*, January 2005, p. 5), Dale Nelson speculates that Tolkien might have heard *garn*, in the wild, so to speak, during his war-time service. The probability of this hypothesis is easy enough to test with the perusal of some on-line texts[94] about World War I that substantiate the use of *garn* by "Tommies" like those with whom Tolkien served. These texts not only contain *garn*, but also *Gawd lumme!* which shows up in the Cockney-esque speech of the trolls in *The Hobbit* as *Lumme*. (H.47; II)

---

[93] 1 *The Works of Bernard Shaw*, London: Constable and Co. Ltd., 1930, vol. 14, p. 214.

[94] *A Yankee in the Trenches* (1918) by R. Derby Holmes, who served as a corporal of the 22nd London battalion of the Queen's Royal West Surrey Regiment <http://www.gutenberg.org/etext/13279>. LVO 12/18/2005.

The Best 500 Cockney War Stories edited and published by *The London Evening News* in 1921. <www.firstworldwar.com/diaries/cockney_intro.htm>. LVO 12/18/2005.

The theory of the possible military origin of Tolkien's use of *garn* is given an additional bit of support by a couple of other pieces of linguistic decoration in the dialogue where the nameless, small Orc tracker uses *garn* twice. Tolkien not only identifies the tracker's interlocutor as "the soldier," but also has him threaten the tracker with: "I'll give your name and number to the Nazgûl" (R.248; VI.2), which sounds very much like the way "name and number" is used in the definition of "C.S.M." in "Tommy's Dictionary of the Trenches," which is found in a book on World War I by Arthur Guy Empey entitled *Over the Top*.[95] There the *Company Sergeant-Major* is defined as "the head non-commissioned officer of a company, whose chief duty is to wear a crown on his arm, a couple of Boer War ribbons on his chest, and to put Tommy's name and number on the crime sheet." "Name and number" is a fixed word collocation for the military jargon of the period. It is the information to be found in Tommy's "identification disk," worn around the neck. In modern American military slang, this is known as a "dog tag."

It is not particularly easy to find a translation for *garn*. The *OED* lists *garn* as an interjection, expressing "disbelief or ridicule of a statement." It is marked as colloquial usage, representing the—chiefly Cockney—pronunciation of *go on!* says the *OED*. This explanation of its origin, however, belies its stylistic marking. One of the examples in the *OED* indicates that its use is vulgar, and this is the marking that is given in the usually thorough *Wildhagen* German translating dictionary.[96] The *OED* quotes the *Glasgow Herald* from 1925: "He complained that if he used such words as 'garn' or 'struth'[97] he was accused of vulgarity …"

Ideally, the successful translation of Tolkien's trick of grouping these four characters together by means of their common use of *Garn!* will use the same word for *Garn!*, each time that

---

[95] <http://www.militaryquotes.com/forum/showthread.php?t=7448&highlight=dictionary+trenches>. LVO 12/18/2005.

[96] *The New Wildhagen German Dictionary* (Dr. Karl Wildhagen and Dr. Will Heraucourt, compilers), Chicago: Follet Publishing, 1965.

[97] *OED*: Short for "God's truth," used as an oath.

Garn! was used in the original. There is no semantic shift due to context for any of Tolkien's uses of *Garn!*, therefore, there is no semantic reason to use different target language renditions in each of the repeats. Unfortunately, the two Dutch (Schuchart and Mensink-van Warmelo) and the two German (Carroux and Krege) translators had a variety of renditions for *Garn!*.

The *Van Dale* English-Dutch dictionary[98] offers the following translations of *garn*: *Kom nou! Nee toch! Loop heen!* The *Wildhagen* translating dictionary offers *Quatsch!* as its only translation of *Garn!*, which it marks as vulgar, showing it to be derived from *go on!*, though not indicating its Cockney origin. *Quatsch!* itself, however, is not marked socially. Nevertheless, it was the rendition that was most often used (3 out of 5) by Carroux for *Garn!* None of the other translators used the same word more than twice.

Sometimes translations are constrained to a "secondary standard" that is not based on the dictionary, but on the translation of the same word used in another well-known text. This is most often applied to the translation of the subtitles of a film based on a book, or the translation of computer games based on a book or a movie, where the target audience of the film or the game being translated will be expected to have read or seen the original from which the film or the game is derived. This is in essence the partial recreation of the literary baggage of the word in the original language in the target language.

In a letter to the editor, in response to Dale Nelson's commentary on *garn* in *Beyond Bree*, David Bratman very accurately classifies *garn* as "a word most strongly associated with Shaw's Eliza Doolittle" (*Beyond Bree*, February 2005, p. 7). For most Americans, this author included, it is probably the only active association with the word *garn*. Given the widespread popular recognition of *garn* from Shaw's *Pygmalion*, or, more likely, the musical based on it, *My Fair Lady*, it could be considered appropriate for Tolkien's translators to use the same word for *Garn!* that is used in the translation of Shaw's (Lerner's and Loewe's) work.

This is obviously an artificial construct for use in the analysis

---

[98] *Groot woordenboek Engels-Nederlands*. Utrecht: Van Dale Lexicografie, 1989, p. 582.

of the first Dutch and the first German translations, because *My Fair Lady* debuted in 1956, but did not attain true popularity until the Academy-Award winning movie came out in 1964, long after these translations had been published. The second Dutch and German translations, however, were done after *My Fair Lady*.

In the Janssen-Pleiter-Gaaikema Dutch translation of *My Fair Lady*,[99] the cue for Professor Higgins' line "It's 'Aoooow' and 'Garn' that keep her in her place" is when Eliza says: "Ach me neus!" This translation produces a viable utterance in all of Tolkien's contexts above, but modern-day native informants consider its use dowdy, old-fashioned, or even cutesy.

This approach also ignores the fact that *me neus!* is a poor translation of *Garn!* in the context of *My Fair Lady*. It entirely misses the point that *Garn!* is a phonetic distortion that is marked for the social stratum to which the speaker belongs. In other words, it needs to be mispronounced and 'vulgar.' The context of the dialogue in *My Fair Lady* at the point that Eliza says *Garn!* is phonetics. Professor Higgins and Colonel Pickering are both phoneticians, and they are discussing pronunciation. The ideal translation of *Garn!*, therefore, should also be a phonetic distortion. In other words, it is the phonetic distortion that is the most important piece of information to convey in the translation of *Garn!* in this context, not the exact semantic value.

The German translation of *Pygmalion* by Siegfried Trebitsch,[100] who knew Shaw, sticks to the definition in *Wildhagen*: *Quatsch!* The German translation of *My Fair Lady* by Robert Gilbert[101] offers an interesting alternative. In Gilbert's version, Eliza says "Dof!"

---

[99] Alan Jay Lerner and Fredrick Loewe, *My Fair Lady* (A musical based on G.B. Shaw's play *Pygmalion*), Amsterdam: H.J.W. Becht, (no date), text translated by Hubert Janssen and Alfred Pleiter, lyrics by Seth Gaaikema, p. 19.

[100] Alan Jay Lerner and Fredrick Loewe, *My Fair Lady* (A musical based on G.B. Shaw's play *Pygmalion*), Berlin: Fischer Verlag, 1913, text translated by Siegfried Trebitsch, p. 17.

[101] Alan Jay Lerner and Fredrick Loewe, *My Fair Lady* (A musical based on G.B. Shaw's play *Pygmalion*), München/Zürich: Droemer Knaur, 1963, text translated by Robert Gilbert, p. 20.

This is an interesting solution, because *Dof!* is not to be found in any of the first-line desktop defining or translating dictionaries,[102] or even in some specialized ones.[103] A German-native speaking informant equated *Dof!* with *Doof!*, and commented that it was heavily marked as slang. Her additional comments largely coincided with those of the Dutch informants about the Dutch translation (*me neus!*). *Dof!* approximates the meaning of *stupid, dumb,* or *silly,* and can be used as a loose synonym for *Quatsch!*. *Dof* it turns out is the pre-war spelling of the modern *Doof,* which is somewhat unusual, because this German translation of *My Fair Lady* dates from 1963. Although any non-standard spelling has a certain stigma attached to it, this is a spoken text and it is the pronunciation and not the spelling that is important to the theater audience. *Dof!,* while a viable utterance in all the Tolkien contexts for *Garn!*, is still not the ideal solution to the problem.

The nine Russian translators[104] of *LotR* also all had a variety of renditions for *Garn!*. The *Galperin* two-volume English-Russian dictionary[105] offers the following translations of *Garn!*: ну да!, иди ты! скажешь тоже!, ух ты! (vol. 1, p. 570) Matorina followed the *Galperin* for Shagrat, but just left *Garn!* out afterwards. "Грр!" [Grr!] and "Гарр!" [Garr!] seemed to be popular with G&G, Bobyr' and Volkovskij. Gruzberg, not unexpectedly, had a "Гарн!" [*Garn!*]. Murav'ev had a number of excellent alternatives, my favorite of which was "Иди врать!" (Go lie!) because it literally captures the underlying sense of *Garn!* < *Go on!* so well.

In the two Russian translations of *Pygmalion*[106] that I have,

---

[102] Duden (1989), Grimm (1860), Muret-Sanders (1910), Wildhagen (1965), Collins (1991).

[103] Heinz Küpper. *Illustriertes Lexikon der Deutschen Umgangssprache* (in 8 Bänden). Stuttgart: Klett, 1983.

[104] See Appendix 'B' for more on the Russian translations.

[105] *New Russian-English Dictionary* (in two volumes), I.R. Galperin (ed.). Moscow: Soviet Encyclopedia Publishing House, 1972.

[106] Бернард Шоу. Избранные произведения в двух томах. Перевод: Е. Калашникова. М.: Государственное издательство художественной литературы, 1956, стр. 206.

Бернард Шоу. Избранные произведения. Перевод: П. Мелкова, Н.

Eliza says what *Galperin* says: "Ух ты!". It is hard to go wrong with *Galperin*, but the translation of *Garn!* that really catches my fancy comes from the Parygin version of *My Fair Lady*.[107] There the cue for Professor Higgins' line "It's 'Aoooow' and 'Garn' that keep her in her place" is when Eliza says: "Чё он!" [chyo on]. This rendition, like *Garn!* is a mispronunciation of "Чего он!" [chego on] that characterizes the person who says it. This translation would be a workable fit in all of Tolkien's contexts above.

Using the translation of *Garn!* in *My Fair Lady* as the secondary standard for the translation of *Garn!* in *LotR* would seem to be indicated because—due to the wide popularity of *My Fair Lady*—that is the most commonly encountered use of *Garn!* to be found in the literary baggage for this word. It may, however, be contraindicated because none of the renditions of *Garn!* in the various translations of *My Fair Lady* are strongly marked as words not to be used in polite company. The angelic face of Audrey Hepburn, and the enchanting melodies of the musical have done much to soften the original impact that the word *garn* once held.

If the 'native habitat' in which Tolkien encountered *Garn!* was indeed the barracks rooms and trenches of World War I, then a stronger anti-social register would seem to be required for *Garn!* This hypothesis would seem to be supported by Tolkien's comments in the Appendices, where he said that while the Orcs used Westron to communicate with one another, the way that they used it did not make it any more pleasant than were the various dialects of Orkish, which Tolkien describes as "brutal jargons," scarcely useful as a means of communication "unless it were for curses and abuse." (Af.511)

Since most present-day readers will have no direct experience with the gritty barracks-room argot of the Tommies of World War I, perhaps a translation to a more modern barracks-room jargon is in order. Unfortunately—for the purposes of this article—I have no personal knowledge of the barracks-room vernacular of

---

Рахманова (предисловие и послесловие). М.: Панорама, 1993.

[107] <www.sinor.ru:8104/~pmv/lady.htm>. Since pulled from the Internet.

the Dutch and German armies. The same, however, cannot be said of the American and Russian armies. Were I to translate *Garn!* to the dialect of the barracks room that was in use when I lived in one, I would render it as *Mofo!* in English and Твою! [Tvoyu!] in Russian, both of which have essentially the same underlying meaning.

Both were, I must point out, sufficiently frequently used in that milieu that they no longer had any actual relationship to their original meanings, which are sufficiently vulgar to shock any polite company. For the socio-linguistic group in which they were used, they had been reduced to mild obscenities of no real significance to the people who used them. For people on the outside of this group, however, they are rather shocking, and that is, quite probably, the effect that Tolkien was looking for with his five uses of *Garn!*.

The modern English translation has the additional advantage of being a condensation and phonetic distortion. The Russian, unfortunately, is only a condensation. These non-standard markings increase the linguistic fit of these two modern translations for *Garn!*, which is commonly perceived to be a linguistic derivative of *Go on!*

While I would find it incongruous to hear Eliza Doolittle use my modern translation of *Garn!*, I would not be at all surprised to hear an Orc or Ted Sandyman or one of Sharky's ruffians use it, which lends credence to my perception that Tolkien, like Shakespeare, occasionally needs to have his vocabulary 'translated' for the modern reader.

Since Tolkien limited the use of *Garn!* to only four speakers in *LotR*, having them all use the same unique word, like Tolkien did, gives them all something in common, and to use the British vernacular, makes them all seem "common." The translator of a tale as long as *LotR*, can certainly be forgiven for missing such a subtle nicety as this, which only a few readers will notice, but it would be nice—given the interest in retranslating Tolkien (there are 2 German, 2 Hebrew, 2 Dutch and 9 Russian translations to name but a few)—if it made it into a future edition, now that his trick has been pointed out.

Spit, Spat, Spittle:
Those Whom Tolkien Wouldst Belittle

In the article above, I commented on the significance of the fact that only four characters in *LotR* use the word *Garn!*, noting that it seemed that Tolkien was using the word *Garn!* to 'keep them in their place.' In discussing my comments on *Garn!*, James Dunning noted Tolkien's garn-ers are very frequently, though not always, his spitters, as well. Ted Sandyman (one of the garn-ers), for example, was described by the narrator as having spat over the wall, just before saying *Garn!* (R.366; VI.8). Dunning suggested that the trait of spitting was also limited to a small group of characters, and could be used to typify them in the same way that the use of the word *Garn!* does.

Tolkien uses the word *spit*, and its derivatives *spat* and *spittle*, a devil's dozen of times in *LotR*. The word *spat* shows up 11 times, and Gollum is the clear winner of the *expectoral* college vote, with 5 of those uses (T.280; IV.1, T.290; IV.2, T.377; IV.6 [2X], T.426; IV.9). The other expectorators are: Bill Ferny (F.244; I.11 [2X]), Ted Sandyman (R.366; VI.8), Wormtongue (T.159; III.6), the Orcs Gorbag (T.443; IV.10) and Shagrat (R.223; VI.1).

This is a less exclusive group than the one made up of garn-ers, but it is every bit as motley, and the two groups do have some overlap. The word *spit* is only used once (T.279; IV.1), and Gollum gets to add that to his score as well. The word *spittle* also shows up only once, where it is used to describe Shelob as she eyes Sam, "her beak drabbling a **spittle** of venom, and a green ooze trickling from below her wounded eye" (T.429; IV.10, **emphasis** added).

Spitting at someone, or on someone is, of course, a gross insult, and Tolkien uses it as such for Wormtongue and Gollum. "Slowly Wormtongue rose. ... with a hissing breath he **spat** before the king's feet, and ... fled down the stair." (T.159; III.6) "Gollum turned and **spat** at him [Frodo]" (T.377; IV.6, **emphasis** added).

In addition to being an intentional insult, spitting is an unsavory habit that is not appreciated by people of refinement. Tolkien's sensibilities with regard to spitting would have most likely had a certain Victorian tint to them, a taste of which can be had in a Victorian-era etiquette book,[108] where it says:

> No lady is ever seen to spit. A gentleman should avoid it, as far as possible. The saliva was intended to be swallowed. ... It is an excrement of the body, and should be disposed of as privately as any other. ...
>
> The use of tobacco has made us a nation of spitters, and no delicate minded person can pass along the streets, enter into a public conveyance, stop at a hotel, or even go to church without being brought into contact with this nuisance of expectoration.

Though Tolkien himself enjoyed a pipe (the cover of the first Russian translation of *LotR* shows Tolkien in profile with a pipe in hand), Tolkien's description of Bill Ferny contains an echo of the complaint about tobacco's relationship to spitting, exhibited in the quote above.

---

[108] *The Illustrated Manners Book: A Manual of Good Behavior and Polite Accomplishments.* New York: Leland Clay, & Co., 1855, <http://chnm.gmu.edu/ lostmuseum/lm/318/>. LVO 12/19/2005.

"Over the hedge another man ... was smoking a short black pipe. As they approached he [Bill Ferny] took it out of his mouth and **spat**. ... He **spat** again." (F.244; I.11, **Emphasis** added)

All his other bad habits aside, Gollum, without even the faint excuse of tobacco to justify his spitting, is clearly an obnoxious personage, as he has almost half (6 of 13) of the total uses of *spit* and its derivatives. Shelob, too, would certainly look ridiculous smoking a pipe, but that does not make her any the less an evildoer, or less worthy of being a member of Tolkien's evil band of spitters.

It would appear that Dunning's hypothesis was correct. The word *spit* can indeed be considered a typifying marker for unpleasant characters in *LotR*.

THE PAPERS OF MASTER FRODO PICKWICK

The Leaf Mold of Tolkien's Mind

Tolkien once said that *The Lord of the Rings* grew out of the "leaf mold" of his mind, "out of all that has been seen or thought or read, that has long ago been forgotten, descending into the deeps."[109] As things climbed out of the leaf mold of Tolkien's mind onto the written page in front of him, he sometimes failed to recognize them for what they were. In a letter to W.H. Auden, Tolkien said that in the telling of his tale, he came upon a number of things that surprised him. He "had never been to Bree," and when he encountered Strider sitting in the corner of the *Prancing Pony*, he "had no more idea who he [Strider] was than had Frodo" (L.216). When Tolkien first encountered Strider, however, his name was not *Strider*, but *Trotter*.

When it came to my attention that Strider had originally been known as Trotter, it stirred up the leaf mold of my mind, and I recalled three points of tangence with Tolkien's tale: a character named Trotter, talking to a servant named Sam at an inn. Since three points of tangence is the threshold at which coincidence begins to give way to a demonstrable relationship, I began to wonder if the leaf that had risen to the surface of my

---

[109] Quoted in: Humphrey Carpenter, *Tolkien*, New York: Ballantine Books, 1977, pp. 140-141.

consciousness from the leaf mold of my mind might not have also been the leaf that fell onto the compost heap of Tolkien's mind to spring phoenix-like into a chair in the corner of the *Prancing Pony* to surprise Tolkien when he walked through the door with Frodo. The author of this particular leaf is a well-known writer, whose work should have been familiar to Tolkien. He is Charles Dickens (1812-1870), and the tale on the leaf is known as *The Pickwick Papers*.

Refreshing my memory with a quick re-read of *The Pickwick Papers* (PP), I discovered that there are indeed a number of parallels between *The Pickwick Papers* and Tolkien's epic. The travelers' arrival at the inn, where the conversation between Sam and Trotter took place is a good example. In PP, when Mr. Pickwick and his manservant Sam Weller step out of the coach that brought them to *The Angel*, Mr. Pickwick warns Sam that: "some caution is necessary. Order a private room, and do not mention my name" (PP 16). Bearing this caution in mind, when Trotter asks Sam Weller for his name, Sam replies that his name is *Walker* and his master's name is *Wilkins* (PP 16).

In the printed version of *LotR*, when Butterbur asks Frodo Baggins what his name is, Frodo replies that his name is *Underhill* (F.210; I.9), bearing in mind the caution that Gandalf gave him somewhat earlier that the name *Baggins* would not be safe to have outside The Shire. (F.97; I.2). The use of an alias at the inn is, therefore, a fourth tangence.

In an earlier draft of Tolkien's chapter, however, there was a fifth tangence. Bingo Baggins (who later became Frodo) introduces himself as Mr. Frodo Walker, Bingo having made this name "up on the spur of the moment, suddenly realizing that it would not be wise to publish their real names in a hobbit-inn on the high road" (HoMe VI.141). This is the same alias that Dickens had used in *PP*. A sixth tangence is that neither Dickens' Trotter, nor Tolkien's Trotter/Strider is taken in by this ruse. They both know to whom it is that they are speaking.

Dickens' Trotter is the sort of scallywag that Strider at first seems to be, but isn't. It is possible that the Trotter whom Tolkien was surprised to see in the *Prancing Pony* in Bree, was initially going to be the same type of character as Dickens' Trotter, who—together with his master Mr. Jingle—proved to be the nemesis of Mr. Pickwick and Sam for a goodly part of Dickens' tale.

The Trotter, who would later become Strider, had not yet fully revealed himself to Tolkien, as can be seen from a number of notes in earlier manuscript versions of the tale that were printed in *The History of Middle-earth*, in which Tolkien asked himself: "Who is Trotter?" It would seem that when Tolkien resolved this question, the name of the character who confronts Frodo at the *Prancing Pony* changed, and the nefarious role of his literary predecessor, Job Trotter, was abandoned, leaving behind only a lingering sense of distrust.

There is also the matter of the opening of the session of the Pickwick Club, during which, as a prelude to his departure on his quest, Mr. Pickwick "slowly mounted into the Windsor chair, on which he had been previously seated, and addressed the club ..., with one hand gracefully concealed behind his coat tails and the other waving in air to assist his glowing declamation" (PP 1). In *LotR*, Mr. Bilbo Baggins likewise rises to address the assembled birthday-party guests as a prelude to his departure. Like Mr. Pickwick, Mr. Baggins stood on a chair (of unspecified type) for this occasion, "waving one hand in the air" and keeping the other in his trouser-pocket, where he had The Ring (F.53; I.1).

The illustration[110] of the momentous occasion of Mr. Pickwick's address by Robert Seymour (d. 1836) supplies the reader with a visual image of what Mr. Pickwick looked like, supplanting the lack of such detail in the narrative. Upon studying the illustration, this reader was prompted to recall Gandalf's description of Frodo to Barliman Butterbur: "a stout little fellow with red checks," to which Sam replies indignantly that this description is of little use, as it could be applied to most Hobbits (F.227; I.10). It is, in fact, more or less what the narrator had said in "The Prologue" and in *The Hobbit*. There, Hobbits are described as being about half the reader's height, varying between 2 and 4 feet, but approximately 3 feet tall on average. They have a tendency "to be fat in the stomach," with good-natured, "broad,

---

[110] Reproduced on the following page from the "Imperial Edition" of Charles Dickens' Collected Works, vol. 24: *The Posthumous Papers of the Pickwick Club*, Boston: Estes & Lauriat, 1895, p. 5.

bright-eyed, red-cheeked" faces (H.16; I, P.19-20). While Mr. Pickwick is taller than an average Hobbit, and somewhat more dour-looking, his other features seem to match the description well enough.

The circumstances of the marriages of the two Sams, are also a point of correspondence for these tales. As he prepared to move to Dulwich in retirement, Mr. Pickwick offers to set Sam Weller and Mary up in a business which would allow them "to earn an independent livelihood," but Sam refuses the offer out of devotion to Mr. Pickwick (PP 56). In the end, though, Sam and Mary do get married. When Mr. Pickwick's old housekeeper died, he gave Mary the job of being his housekeeper, on the condition that she marry Sam at once, a condition that she accepted "without a murmur" (PP 57).

Sam Gamgee's marriage to Rosie has a similar air to it. When Bag End had been restored, and Frodo was ready to move back in, he asked Sam to move in to Bag End with him. Sam Gamgee is more torn between his loyalty to Frodo and his love of Rosie than was Sam Weller. Sam Weller was ready to give Mary up. "'I have considered the young 'ooman. I've spoke to her. I've told her how I'm sitivated; she's ready to vait till I'm ready, and I believe she vill. If she don't, she's not the young 'ooman I take her for, and I give her up vith readiness" (PP 56). Rosie, however, is not quite that patient. She did not like Sam's going away on the quest with Frodo in the first place and now that he has come back, she does not want to "waste" any more time. Frodo's solution to Sam's dilemma is, however, quite Pickwickian. He tells Sam that Sam does not have to choose between the two of them. Sam should get married to Rosie and move into Bag End with her. Although she was never called Frodo's housekeeper, that is what Rosie became for a time (R.376; VI.9).

Another salient similarity between the two tales is that they are both variants of the feigned-manuscript topos, which is a piece of literary sleight of hand to affect the reader's perception of a work. It consists of the author asserting that he is not indeed the author, but merely the editor or translator of the work at hand. In the "Prologue" (P.19), in the "Note on the Shire Records" (P.37), in Appendix F.II (A.513-520) and elsewhere in *LotR*, Tolkien claims that *The Hobbit* and *LotR* are translations from the *Red Book of Westmarch*, "composed by Bilbo [Baggins] himself, the first Hobbit to become famous in the world at large, and called by him *There and Back Again*." Throughout *The Pickwick Papers*, the narrator maintains the pretense that he is merely the 'editor' of a set of papers that had been "carefully preserved, and duly registered by the secretary, from time to time, in the voluminous Transactions of the Pickwick Club."

The similarities of Tolkien's work to *The Pickwick Papers* that are described here are certainly subconscious in origin, because in a letter to *The Observer*, Tolkien stated that his tale was "not consciously based on any other book" (L.31). The coincidences are, nevertheless, interesting for they help to define Tolkien's place in the framework of Literature. If Tolkien has seen farther into the human soul than other writers, it is because, as it says—quoting Isaac Newton—on the edge of the British two-pound coin, he was "standing on the shoulders of giants."

FRODO QUATERMAIN

Frodo Quatermain

Steve Boyum's made-for-television 2004 remake of the movie of Rider Haggard's *King Solomon's Mines*, starring Patrick Swayze[111] is a must see for anyone who thinks that Peter Jackson's cinematic creation does an injustice to Tolkien's epic. By comparison, Jackson hardly changed a word in his effort to bring *The Lord of the Rings* to the screen. The screenplay for *King Solomon's Mines* by Adam Armus, Steven H. Berman and Kay Foster is a politically-correct pastiche of Allan Quatermain meets Indiana Jones and Frodo Baggins. It has very little to do with the book that lent its name to the project.

The screenwriters rewrote the story, supplying it with a number of scenes that project a clearly modern, politically-correct sense of sensibility, such as an anti-hunting episode (0:05:00) and an episode that places Allan Quatermain in a legal battle with his in-laws for the custody of his young son, Harry (0:13:40).

---

[111] *King Solomon's Mines* (mini-series), Directed by Steve Boyum, Hallmark Entertainment, Running time: 173 minutes, 2004. Cites to the movie will be to the elapsed running time at the point of interest: (1:10:10), eg. 1 hour, 10 minutes, 10 seconds.

In the book, Harry is a student in Medical School, and Allan Quatermain admits to having shot 65 lions, and talks of selling ivory from his elephant hunting (KSM I2) and dining on the hearts of two elephants that they had shot (KSM IV). Sir Henry Curtis, a key character in the book, also (un)fortunately has a part in the movie. In the movie, he gets killed. The book ends with a letter from him, telling of his safe return to England and his meeting with Harry (KSM XX).

Amid all the other deviations from the book, one that immediately caught my attention was the scene in which, having been restored to his rightful place, Ignosi the true King asks a final favor of Allan Quatermain. He must destroy the Stone of the Ancestors, because "the one who holds the Stone rules all of Africa" (1:00:15), and "as long as men are interested in the power of the Stone of the Ancestors, my People will not be safe" (2:33:15). The glaring similarity to Frodo's anti-quest was instantly apparent. Allan Quatermain even hesitates like Frodo at Elrond's Council, before agreeing to take up the task.

There is, of course, no such request or stone in the book. In the movie, the Stone of the Ancestors looks like a huge, glowing rock in a sort of ring mount that fits over the head of a statue locked away in the depths of an ancient tomb (2:42:42). Allan Quatermain and his obligatory, beautiful silver-screen companion escape the sealing of the tomb, that they had entered in true Indiana-Jones fashion, just in the nick of time, leaving the Stone behind, supposedly sealed forever underground. Apparently the screen writers forgot that Rings [Stones] like these cannot just be thrown away, they have to be destroyed. "These Rings [Stones] have a way of being found." (F.93; I.2).

Rider Haggard (1856-1925), one of the founding authors of the genre of the adventure novel, wrote *King Solomon's Mines* in 1885, before J.R.R. Tolkien was born (1892). It remained immensely popular in the period of Tolkien's youth, as may be seen from the "Author's Note" to the 1898 edition and the "Post Scriptum" to the 1907 edition, in which Haggard thanked his readers "for the kind reception they have accorded to the successive editions of this tale during the last twelve years" (KSM A.N.), and remarked on "how glad" he was "that my romance should continue to please so many readers" (KSM P.S.). Tolkien would have been 15 in 1907, and squarely in the right demographic to enjoy this novel during the period of its kind reception by the reading public.

In his essay entitled "The Lost Childhood,"[112] Graham Greene (1904-1991) comments on the "deep influence" of books read in childhood, providing his own list of favorite childhood authors, led by Rider Haggard.

> Perhaps it is only in childhood that books have any deep influence on our lives. ... in childhood all books are books of divination, telling us about the future, and like the fortune teller who sees a long journey in the cards or death by water they influence the future. I suppose that is why books excited us so much. What do we ever get nowadays from reading to equal the excitement and the revelation in those first fourteen years? Of course I should be interested to hear that a new novel by Mr. E. M. Foster was going to appear this spring, but I could never compare that mild expectation of civilized pleasure with the missed heartbeat, the appalled glee I felt when I found on a library shelf a novel by Rider Haggard, Percy Westerman, Captain Brereton or Stanley Weyman which I had not read before.

Things that you read in your youth do have an impact on you like no other reading you will ever do, and Haggard's influences can be seen in Tolkien's work in a number of places. Tolkien's story line of the Return of Aragorn to his place as King bears a marked resemblance to the story line of Ignosi in *King Solomon's Mines*. In Haggard's book, the throne that should have been Ignosi's was taken by an usurper who killed Ignosi's father, and Ignosi "wandered for many years" (KSM III), before, having "journeyed into a land of wonders" and "learned the wisdom of the white people" (KSM X), he leads the companions of Haggard's quest through the wilderness before finally returning to claim his birthright.

In "Appendix A(v)", Tolkien tells the tale of Aragorn's

---

[112] Graham Greene. *The Lost Childhood and Other Essays*, London: Eyre & Spottiswoode, 1951, p. 13.

wanderings. Aragorn is left fatherless early in life, and goes to wander "for nearly thirty years" in the fight against Sauron, becoming "a friend of Gandalf the Wise, from whom he gained much wisdom" (Aa.423). Like Strider/Aragorn, Ignosi has another name when he first encounters Haggard's travelers. At that time he gives them the name Umbopa, which means "in vulgar English, he who keeps his eyes open" (KSM III), a not inapt appellation for a Ranger. The name *Ignosi* means "the lightning" (KSM VIII). Aragorn's name in Rivendell was *Estell*, which means "the star" in a number of the Romance languages. (See also the article on *Estell* in this book.)

The battle that Haggard titles "The Last Stand of the Greys" (KSM XIV) is in many ways reminiscent of Tolkien's Battle of Helm's Deep. The approaching armies of Twala, the usurper, find themselves confronted with a "tongue of grass land that ran up into the bend of the mountain, ... [it] was some four hundred yards in depth, even at its root or widest part was not more than six hundred and fifty paces across, while at its tip it scarcely measured ninety." As the attacking force approached, it "hesitated, having discovered that only one regiment could advance into the gorge at a time, and that there, some seventy yards from the mouth of it, unassailable except in front, on account of the high walls of boulder-strewn ground on each side, stood the famous regiment of Greys, the pride and glory of the Kukuana army, ready to hold the way against their power as the three Romans once held the bridge against thousands." (KSM XIV)

Haggard's allusion to "the three Romans" is, of course, to the story of how in 508 B.C. Horatius, the captain of the gate of Rome, together with Lartius and Herminius held the only bridge over the Tiber river against an army of 90,000 Etruscans. (Haggard's attacking army was only 40,000 strong). The approach to the bridge was very constricted and only allowed a few of the attackers to enter it at a time. The three held the bridge for several hours of single combat, while the bridge was destroyed behind them. Just before the bridge fell, Lartius and Herminius crossed to the Roman side, while Horatius continued to hold the bridgehead alone. When the bridge was gone, Horatius—in full armour—jumped into the Tiber, and, in some versions of the story, swam to safety on the Roman side of the river, while in others, he drowned.

This is a story that would have been very familiar to young Victorian and Edwardian schoolboys like Tolkien. It gained 'modern' literary fame in the poem by Thomas Babington Macaulay (1800-1859) known as "Horatius at the Bridge" (1842).[113] Tolkien has his own version of 'three against thousands' in the tale of the Battle of Helm's Deep, As the attacking force of Orcs brings a battering ram to the very gates, Aragorn, Éomer and Gimli go out through a sally port to attack them, and stem the tide for a little while. (T.176-177 III.7)

There is yet another point that ties the three tales together. In Macaulay's poem, Horatius speaks of death as man's fate:

> Then out spake brave Horatius,
> The Captain of the Gate:
> To every man upon this earth
> Death cometh soon or late. (XXVII)

Haggard has a dramatic scene in which the army of Twala the usurper is asked the ritualistic question of "What is the lot of man born of woman?" The 20,000 voices of the assembled companies of his army respond as one: "Death!" (KSM X). The version born of Tolkien's pen was "Nine (rings) for Mortal Men doomed to die." The question of death and immortality is a key one in both Tolkien's works and in Haggard's, especially in his novel *She*. (This topic is considered in a separate article to be found later in this book.)

This, however, does not exhaust the parallels to Haggard's tale of the battle. In a short episode at the end of the chapter, Haggard relates what happened to Captain Good.

> The dead body of the Kukuana soldier, or rather what had appeared to be his dead body, suddenly sprang up, knocked

---

[113] The Project Gutenberg eText of *Lays of Ancient Rome*, by Thomas Babington Macaulay is available at :
<http://www.gutenberg.org/etext/847>. LVO 2/23/2006.

Good head over heels off the ant-heap, and began to spear him. We rushed forward in terror, and as we drew near we saw the brawny warrior making dig after dig at the prostrate Good, who at each prod jerked all his limbs into the air. Seeing us coming, the Kukuana gave one final and most vicious dig, and with a shout of "Take that, wizard!" bolted away. Good did not move, and we concluded that our poor comrade was done for. Sadly we came towards him, and were astonished to find him pale and faint indeed, but with a serene smile upon his face, and his eyeglass still fixed in his eye.

"Capital armour this," he murmured, on catching sight of our faces bending over him. (KSM XIV)

The trick of a soldier playing 'possum,' only to rise up and attack one of the main characters is repeated in Tolkien's rendition of The Battle of Helm's Deep, where "some dozen Orcs that had lain motionless among the slain leaped to their feet, and came silently and swiftly behind. Two flung themselves to the ground at Éomer's heels, tripped him, and in a moment they were on top of him" (T.1177; III.7). Tolkien has Éomer rescued handily by Gimli and his ax.

The joke of Captain Good's armour saving his life from a spear-thrust would seem to be found repeated in The Battle of Moria, in which Frodo is attacked by an Orc Chieftain, who "charged into the Company and thrust with his spear straight at Frodo. The blow caught him on the right side, and Frodo was hurled against the wall and pinned. Sam, with a cry, hacked at the spear-shaft, and it broke" (F.422; II.5). The other members of the Fellowship were all sure that Frodo was dead, and were equally as surprised as Haggard's heroes to find Good/Frodo alive.

The story of the armour that saved Captain Good's life told by Haggard is also suggestive of some elements of Tolkien's story. Each of Haggard's three companions was given "a shining shirt of chain armour, and a magnificent battle-axe" as a gift from King Twala "to the white men from the Stars." The "magic coats through which no spear can pass" that they had received were valuable gifts indeed. Haggard's narrator says that the chain mail shirts were "the most wonderful chain work that either of us had ever seen. A whole coat fell together so closely that it formed a mass of links scarcely too big to be covered with both hands." They "were neither very heavy nor uncomfortable," and the adventurers put them on under their normal clothes. The natives did not possess the skill of making them, and there were but few of them left in the land, so few that only "those of royal blood" could wear them (KSM X).

In *LotR*, Glóin tells Frodo that the Dwarves cannot rival the metalwork of their ancestors, "many of whose secrets are lost. We make good armour and keen swords, but we cannot again make mail or blade to match those that were made before the dragon came" (F. 302 II.1). When Bilbo gave Frodo the corslet of Mithril mail, it is described as being almost as supple as linen and almost weightless when it was worn (F.363; II.3). Bilbo wanted it to be a secret, so Frodo put it on under his normal clothes, like Haggard's adventurers. The same motif is repeated in *The Hobbit*: when Bilbo and the Dwarves left the dragon's horde, they had covered their newly found "glittering mail ... with their old cloaks" (H.229; XIII). The corslet was, like Twala's gift, one beyond price. Gimli calls it "a kingly gift," and though Gandalf tries to quantify its worth, his description is only a meaningless generalization. "[I]ts worth was greater than the value of the whole Shire and everything in it" (F.414; II.4).

Allan Quatermain, strangely enough, has some Hobbit-like characteristics that recall Bilbo Baggins. In the opening paragraph of Chapter I, he says that "I am a timid man, and dislike violence; moreover, I am almost sick of adventure" (KSM I). In the opening chapter of *The Hobbit*, Bilbo says "We are plain quiet folk and have no use for adventures. Nasty disturbing uncomfortable things! Make you late for dinner! I can't think what anybody sees in them" (H.18; I). Quatermain admits, though, that "for a timid man" he has "been mixed up in a great deal of fighting" (KSM I), an admission that makes him sound somewhat like the reluctant participant in the many violent confrontations and various adventures that Bilbo was in *The Hobbit*.

The age of the three characters (Bilbo, Frodo and Allan) at the time that the adventure "befalls" (F.71; I.2) them is unusually similar. Adventure stories are normally the province of younger heroes, but Bilbo is "about fifty years old or so" (H.17; I), returning to The Shire in June of his fifty-second year (S.R. 1342 [T.A. 2942])" (P.35). Frodo was at the "usually more sober age of fifty" (F.71; I.2, F.73; I.2), when he left on his adventure (T.A. 3018). Allan Quatermain remarks that he had turned fifty-five on his last birthday, when his narrative begins (KSM I).

Another interesting parallel between Allan Quatermain and Bilbo is found in Quatermain's ethical evaluation of his life. He admits that he has "never stolen," though once he "cheated a Kafir out of a herd of cattle. But then he [the Kafir] had done me [Quatermain] a dirty turn, and it has troubled me [Quatermain] ever since into the bargain" (KSM I). This sounds like the story of Bilbo's acquisition of the Ring from Gollum, and Bilbo's sensitivity to accusations that he had acquired the Ring by theft (F.60; I.1). Bilbo had not stolen the Ring, but the way that he had won it in the riddle game was cheating.

The irony of a re-working of Haggard's original story, which had had an obvious influence on Tolkien's work, being adapted to include an unmistakable allusion to Tolkien's work struck me as terribly funny. I suspect that the screenwriters did not intend for it to be seen that way, but they were probably not aware of Haggard's influence on Tolkien. I imagine that both Haggard and Tolkien would be appalled, in the same way that C.S. Lewis was appalled at seeing an earlier film version of *King Solomon's Mines*.[114]

---

[114] Lewis was probably referring to Robert Stevenson's 1937 film version of *King Solomon's Mines* (black and white, running time 80 minutes), starring Cedric Hardwicke as Allan Quatermain, with the screenplay by Michael Hogan, Roland Pertwee, A.R. Rawlinson and Ralph Spence. There have since been 3 other remakes in addition to Boyum's: 1) Compton Bennett's 1950 production (color, running time 103 minutes), starring Deborah Kerr and Stewart Granger, with the screenplay by Helen Deutsch, 2) Alvin Rakoff's 1977 production entitled *King Solomon's Treasure* (color, running time 88 minutes), starring John Colicos as Allan Quatermain, with the screenplay by Allan Pryor and Colin Turner and 3) J. Lee Thompson's 1985 production (color, running time 100 minutes), starring Richard Chamberlain and Sharon Stone, with the screenplay by Gene Quintano and James R. Silke.

Lewis' complaints[115] were much the same as mine. He objects to the "totally irrelevant young woman in shorts who accompanied the three adventures wherever they went" (p. 926), and to the change of the ending. In the book, the heroes are awaiting death, sealed in a tomb, surrounded by the mummies of the kings who had once ruled the land. Lewis felt cheated by the new ending, which added an earthquake and the eruption of a volcano, because "there must be a pleasure in such stories distinct from mere excitement" (p. 92). By substituting a different kind of danger for the one in the book, the producer of the film ruined the story for Lewis, because "different kinds of danger strike different chords from the imagination" (p. 94). Where the difference in the chords struck by the movies and those struck by the book rang false to Lewis and myself, Tolkien's borrowings—if they may be called such—from Haggard rang true to my ear.

---

[115] C.S. Lewis. "On Stories," in *Essays Presented to Charles Williams*, London: Oxford University Press, 1947. This volume also includes "On Fairy-Stories" by J.R.R. Tolkien.

A TALE OF DEATH AND IMMORTALITY

Tolkien and Haggard: Immortality

Henry Rider Haggard (1856-1925) was one of the most popular writers of his era. In 1887, Haggard wrote *She: A History of Adventure*, the heroine of which is Ayesha, the Queen of Kôr. The biographical sketch to the *Modern Library* edition of *She* includes J.R.R. Tolkien, C.S. Lewis and Graham Greene among the countless readers whose imagination was captured by this novel.[116]

Haggard's novel is the story of a quest for the mystery of immortality. Though Tolkien's anti-quest is often classified as a tale about power, Tolkien himself rejected this analysis. In a letter to Rhona Beare, Tolkien wrote:

> I might say that if the tale is 'about' anything (other than itself), it is not as seems widely supposed about 'power.' ... It is mainly concerned with Death and Immortality... (L.211)

The similarities of Haggard's and Tolkien's views of immortality are quite remarkable, and they are not the only likenesses shared by their works.[117]

---

[116] H. Rider Haggard, *She: A History of Adventure*, New York: The Modern Library, 2002, p. viii.

Haggard's discourse on immortality is to be found primarily in the dialogue between Holly, the leader of Haggard's quest, and the seemingly immortal Ayesha. She offers Holly the imperial boon of immortality, but he refuses, because, for Holly:

> [T]he world has not proved so soft a nest that I would lie in it for ever. A stony-hearted mother is our earth, and stones are the bread she gives her children for their daily food. Stones to eat and bitter water for their thirst, and stripes for tender nurture. Who would endure this for many lives? Who would so load up his back with memories of lost hours and loves, and of his neighbour's sorrows that he cannot lessen, and wisdom that brings not consolation? Hard is it to die, because our delicate flesh doth shrink back from the worm it will not feel, and from that unknown which the winding-sheet [shroud] doth curtain from our view. But harder still, to my fancy, would it be to live on, green in the leaf and fair, but dead and rotten at the core, and feel that other secret worm of recollection gnawing ever at the heart (SHE XXII).

Haggard's treatment of this significant philosophical question is essentially the same as Tolkien's. In *The Silmarillion,* Tolkien says that even the Powers shall come to envy the gift of death "as time wears." The Elves are bound to the Earth "until the end of days, and their love of the Earth and all the world is more single and more poignant therefore, and as the years lengthen ever more sorrowful. For the elves die not till the world dies, unless they are slain or waste in grief (and to both these seeming deaths they are subject); neither does age subdue their strength, unless one grow weary of ten thousand centuries" (S.42). Tolkien's Elvish span of time finds an echo and an elaboration in Ayesha's discourse to Holly on the history of time. "What is a span of ten thousand years, or ten times ten thousand years, in the history of time? It is as naught—it is as the mists that roll up in the sunlight; it fleeth away like an hour of sleep or a breath of the Eternal Spirit" (XIV).

---

[117] See also: William H. Green. "King Thorin's Mines: *The Hobbit* as a Victorian Adventure Novel," *Extrapolation,* 42.1, pp. 53-64.

The difference in the points of view of Ayesha and Holly is echoed in *The Silmarillion* in the dichotomy that Tolkien has set up between the lives of Elves and the lives of the race of Men. The Elves do not have real immortality, but only a practical immortality that ties them to Arda until the end of days, "[f]or the elves die not till the world dies" (S.42). Ayesha, like the Elves, is not truly immortal, but will only live to "the end of ends ... when Day and Night, and Life and Death, are ended and swallowed up in that from which they came," at which time she knows not what will be her fate (SHE XVI).

Men, on the other hand, are only upon the world for a short space of time, "and are not bound to it" (S.42). At the end of their days, Men depart to a place beyond the knowledge of the Elves, or, in Haggard's parlance, beyond the winding-sheet [shroud] that curtains the unknown from their view. Ayesha's view of immortality is, therefore, that of the Elves, and Holly's that of Men.

Tolkien has Gandalf explain the effects of the practical immortality bestowed on Frodo by the Ring in these terms:

> A mortal, Frodo, who keeps one of the Great Rings, does not die, but he does not grow or obtain more life, he merely continues, until at last every minute is a weariness (F.76; I.2).

Weary is a key word in both Tolkien's and Haggard's examination of immortality. At the end of the Third Age "Elrond grew **weary** at last and" left Middle-earth whither he never returned (Aa.426, **emphasis** added). In Haggard's tale, Ayesha complains to Holly that she cannot die and erase the memory of her lost love. She laments "the **weary** years that have been and are yet to come, and evermore to come, endless and without end!" (XIV, **emphasis** added).

Bilbo has only experienced the practical immortality that the Ring bestows on its bearer for a short while, but he already feels "old" in his "heart of hearts," as if he were being "stretched ... like butter that has been scraped over too much bread" (F.58; I.1).

Gollum has had much longer to experience the effects of the practical immortality granted by the Ring, and is described by Tolkien in even more dire terms, when Sam has a "vision" of the two combatants, as Gollum confronts Frodo for the Ring. He saw Gollum as "a crouching shape, scarcely more than the shadow of a living thing, a creature now wholly ruined and defeated, yet filled with a hideous lust and rage" (R.272; VI.3). Gollum knows that his life is bound to the Ring, and that when it is destroyed he will die too. Sam is inclined to kill Gollum, but the "forlorn, ruinous, utterly wretched" thing that is Gollum "lying in the dust" in front of him awakens his pity, for he [Sam] had also been a Ring-bearer, though for a short time, and could vaguely sense "the agony of Gollum's shrivelled mind and body, enslaved to that Ring, unable to find peace or relief ever in life again" (R.273; VI.3).

Ayesha calls on Holly to rethink his rejection of her boon, but Holly remains steadfast to his decision.

> "And what, oh Queen," I answered, "are those things that are dear to man? Are they not bubbles? Is not ambition but an endless ladder by which no height is ever climbed till the last unreachable rung is mounted? For height leads on to height, and there is no resting-place upon them, and rung doth grow upon rung, and there is no limit to the number. Doth not wealth satiate, and become nauseous, and no longer serve to satisfy or pleasure, or to buy an hour's peace of mind? And is there any end to wisdom that we may hope to reach it? Rather, the more we learn, shall we not thereby be able only to better compass out our ignorance? Did we live ten thousand years could we hope to solve the secrets of the suns, and of the space beyond the suns, and of the Hand that hung them in the heavens? Would not our wisdom be but as a gnawing hunger calling our consciousness day by day to a knowledge of the empty craving of our souls? Would it not be but as a light in one of these great caverns, that, though bright it burn, and brighter yet, doth but the more serve to show the depths of the gloom around it? And what good thing is there beyond that we may gain by length of days?"
> (SHE XXII)

Holly's delineation of the things that are dear to man—ambition, wealth and wisdom—are each, in turn, treated in Tolkien's tale, and shown to be the bubbles that Holly claims they are.

The Ring seems to offer a quick way to quickly climb ambition's ladder to the top rung, but Tolkien has his heroes reject it in powerful scenes that hint at what would become of them were they to climb the ladder. Gandalf rejects Frodo's offer of the Ring, because the Ring would give him "power too great and terrible" and would make him "like the Dark Lord himself" (F.95; I.2). Galadriel rejects Frodo's offer of the Ring, because it would make her the Dark Queen, "beautiful and terrible," "dreadful" and "stronger than the foundations of the earth" (F.473; II.7). "All shall love me and despair!" she says, which is, in essence, a very concise description of the relationship between Haggard's Ayesha and her subjects. Even Billali—basically Ayesha's Prime Minister—whom Holly "believed to be a very fearless person, positively quiver[s] with terror at her words," when she is angered (SHE XII).

Haggard offers a very interesting insight into why despair should be the lot of the subjects of a dark queen like Ayesha. In the scene in which Holly is confronted by Ayesha about a scarab he has in his possession, she says "at times, oh Holly, the almost infinite mind grows impatient of the slowness of the very finite, and am I tempted to use my power out of vexation—very nearly wast thou dead, but I remembered" (SHE XIII). This comment suggests that the Ring Bearers would be affected in the same way, and would become impatient with other, less gifted beings.

In Tolkien's tale, this has an echo in Frodo's pity for Gollum. As the Ring Bearer, Frodo's power of life and death over Gollum was no less than Ayesha's over Holly, yet Frodo did not use it. As they discuss which path to take at the Black Gate, Frodo warns Gollum, that, if need be, Frodo could put on the Ring and command him "to leap from a precipice or to cast [him]self into the fire" (T.314; IV.3). Sam approves of the threat, but, at the same time, is surprised by it, for it is accompanied by a look on Frodo's face and a tone in his voice that Sam had not known before (T.314; IV.3). Frodo has begun to change.

The greed of the Dwarves is what awoke Durin's Bane in Moria, and greed is what brought Smaug the dragon into *The Hobbit*. It is precisely there, in his description of dragons, that Tolkien comes closest to Holly's comment on wealth. Dragons are practically immortal and steal from all and sundry, amassing untold wealth, but "never enjoy a brass ring of it," says Tolkien (H.35; I). This was exactly Holly's point.

Holly's treatise on the inexhaustible nature of knowledge recalls the much more terse Socratic formulation: *All I know is that I know nothing*. The resurrected Gandalf echoes Holly's point about how much there is to know and how long it would take to learn it all in his answer to Aragorn's question of whether he [Gandalf] knows Fangorn Forest well. "Not well," said Gandalf, "that would be the study of many lives" (T.123; III.5). In Haggard's story, Ayesha describes the amount of knowledge that can be accumulated in a single lifetime disparagingly. "Ah, how little knowledge does a man acquire in his life. He gathereth it up like water, but like water it runneth through his fingers, and yet, if his hands be but wet as though with dew, behold a generation of fools call out, 'See, he is a wise man!'" (SHE XIII).

In Tolkien's tale, however, the thirst for knowledge also has an evil side. It was the craving for knowledge that led to the fall of the Elven-smiths of Eregion (F.318; II.2), and knowledge was one of the three temptations offered to Gandalf by Saruman (F.340; II.2).

Interestingly though, both Haggard and Tolkien consider the thirst for knowledge one of the prime motivators for mankind. In Haggard's tale, this can be seen when Holly explains his attitude towards death as he answers a question posed by the elder of the native tribe serving as his guide to Kôr, who wants to know where Holly and his companions come from and why. Are they perhaps "weary of life?" asks his guide (VI). Holly answers boldly that "We came to find new things. We are tired of the old things; we have come up out of the sea to know that which is unknown. We are of a brave race who fear not death, my very much respected father—that is, if we can get a little information before we die" (VI).

This statement finds echoes in both *LotR* and in *The Silmarillion*. The situation in Haggard's book—a white man talking to a native leader—recalls a conversation in Tolkien's epic between Théoden and Ghân-buri-Ghân, the leader of the Wild Men. In this conversation Ghân-buri-Ghân essentially repeats Holly's explanation of where the white men came from. They "come up out of Water" (R.129; V.5).

Tolkien's parallel to the philosophical part of Holly's answer, however, is found in chapter 1 of *The Silmarillion*. There Tolkien explains that Illuvatar "willed that the hearts of Men should seek beyond the world and should find no rest therein" (S.41). The fit in Haggard's time was better than it may now seem to the modern reader. The quest that Holly and his companions undertook was beyond the boundaries of the then-known world. His quest for information would seem to fit well with the desire that Illuvatar places in the hearts of men. The lack of a fear of death that Holly claims for his race points, however, to a time in Tolkien's cosmology before Melkor cast his shadow on Illuvatar's gift of death to Men, confounding "it with darkness, and brought evil out of good and fear out of hope" (S.42).

Ayesha rejects Holly's assessment of the sum total of life as ambition, wealth and wisdom. For her, love is more important than these, for love makes all things beautiful, and breathes "divinity into the very dust we tread." Love has the power to keep life moving "gloriously on from year to year, like the voice of some great music that hath power to hold the hearer's heart poised on eagles' wings above the sordid shame and folly of the earth" (SHE XXII).

Tolkien too places love in the balance to weigh against immortality in the tale of Aragorn and Arwen (Aa.420-428). Tolkien's tale is, however, the mirrored reflection of Haggard's. Arwen rejects immortality to be with her love. Ayesha would make her love practically immortal. Because Haggard's discussion of love and immortality is much more expansive than Tolkien's, studying it helps Tolkien's readers better comprehend Arwen's choice.

Holly rejects even love as an inducement to accept immortality, for "if the loved one prove a broken reed to pierce us, or if the love be loved in vain—what then? Shall a man grave his sorrows upon a stone when he hath but need to write them on the water?" (SHE XXII). Arwen decides that it is better to have shared loved and to die, than to love and then sorrow alone for the loss of that loved one for an eternity. In a sense, she agrees with Holly that it is better to write one's sorrows at the passing of a loved one on the water that will bear the text of the tale for but a short time, than to write those sorrows on a stone where they will continue to torment the immortal writer with there indelibility.

Holly then takes a religious turn in his arguments with Ayesha. He says that he prefers to meet his "appointed death, and be forgotten," because he prefers the real immortality that his faith offers to the practical immortality that Ayesha holds out to him (SHE XXII). Though Tolkien never explicitly replicated this religious argumentation, it is implicit in his outlook. Holly said:

> The immortality to which I look, and which my faith doth promise me, shall be free from the bonds that here must tie my spirit down. For, while the flesh endures, sorrow and evil and the scorpion whips of sin must endure also; but when the flesh hath fallen from us, then shall the spirit shine forth clad in the brightness of eternal good, and for its common air shall breathe so rare an ether of most noble thoughts that the highest aspiration of our manhood, or the purest incense of a maiden's prayer, would prove too earthly gross to float therein (SHE XXII).

The first implied tie in Tolkien's discussion of immortality is in what Holly terms the bonds of the flesh that tie the spirit down. In Tolkien's terms, these are bonds that tie the Elves to the world, of which men are freed at the end of their days. (See S.42 above.) As Aragorn prepares to go to his death, he tells Arwen "In sorrow we must go, but not in despair. Behold! we are not bound for ever to the circles of the world, and beyond them is more than memory, Farewell!" (Aa.428).

Holly's brightness of eternal good in which the spirit shall be clad can be found in the chapter "The White Rider," in which Tolkien replicates Christ's Transfiguration on Mount Tabor and appearance to three of his disciples (Matthew 17:1-9, Mark 9:2-9 and Luke 9:28-36). There Gandalf returns from his journey "through fire and deep water" and appears to the three companions—Aragorn, Legolas and Gimili—clad all in garments shinning as white as the sun (T.124; III.5).

Ayesha rejects Holly's religious beliefs as a mere bauble and attacks his faith.

> "Thou lookest high," answered Ayesha, with a little laugh, "and speakest clearly as a trumpet and with no uncertain sound. And yet methinks that but now didst thou talk of 'that Unknown' from which the winding-sheet doth curtain us. But perchance, thou seest with the eye of Faith, gazing on that brightness, that is to be, through the painted-glass of thy imagination. Strange are the pictures of the future that mankind can thus draw with this brush of faith and this many-coloured pigment of imagination! Strange, too, that no one of them doth agree with another!"

Her argument is that of modern scientific skepticism. Ayesha, like Melkor, redefines mankind's search for eternal happiness in a life after death in her own terms, and criticizes Holly for rejecting the lamp (practical immortality) that she offers him in favor of the star (eternal life of his faith). Her view of happiness is focused on the here and now, rejecting the dream of hope that Holly's religion holds out to him.

> "But so it hath ever been; man can never be content with that which his hand can pluck. If a lamp be in his reach to light him through the darkness, he must needs cast it down because it is no star. Happiness danceth ever apace before him, like the marsh-fires in the swamps, and he must catch the fire, and he must hold the star! Beauty is naught to him, because there are lips more honey-sweet; and wealth is naught, because others can weigh him down with heavier shekels; and fame is naught, because there have been greater

men than he. Thyself thou saidst it, and I turn thy words against thee. Well, thou dreamest that thou shalt pluck the star. I believe it not, and I think thee a fool, my Holly, to throw away the lamp."

Tolkien held out the hope of victory throughout his epic, and it was made manifest by the faith of his heroes that led them on, even when all hope seemed lost. Aragorn dreamed that he could indeed pluck the Lady Evenstar named Arwen (Aa.427), and he did, despite the dangers and obstacles that blocked his path to his goal. It is the Quixotic 'impossible dream' that inspires mankind on to deeds of valor, to explore the unknown, to reach for the stars, spurred on by what—in his poem "To His Coy Mistress"—Andrew Marvell (1621-1678) termed the sound of "times winged chariot hurrying near."

"Carpe Diem!" was the watch word of the poets of Marvell's era, but for those with practical immortality there is no need to seize the day, because there will always be a mañana. They need to light a lamp, rather than wait for the light of the star to come. For those who would achieve something within their short allotted span of life, however, Marvell's advice is best. They must "tear our pleasures with rough strife / through the iron gates of life : Thus, though we cannot make our sun / Stand still, yet we can make him run."

The closing lines of Marvell's poem are considered enigmatic by some, but they are nothing more than the juxtaposition of the wish to make time stand still and the proverbial perception that time flies when you are having fun. Both Haggard and Tolkien offer the reader an exposition on the sense of time's flight for the immortal. Haggard's is essentially a re-telling of an old saw. Tolkien's offers a new insight that better helps the reader to understand the point of view that immortality presents. In Haggard's tale, the body, containing the reincarnated soul of Ayesha's love, is deathly ill and, if the medicine that Holly gives him is to work, it will work within five minutes or not at all. For Ayesha the five minutes she had to wait to learn if he would live or die were longer than the "sixty generations" that she had already waited for his soul to return to her (SHE XVII). Her description of the flow of time shows that even immortals sense a difference in the speed with which time flows.

In Tolkien's tale, Sam is trying to reconcile the phase of the moon with his recollection of how much time they spent in Lothlorien. Sam speculates "that time did not count in there!" Frodo agrees that perhaps they were outside "the time that flows through mortal lands." Legolas, however, corrects their conjecture with the point of view of an Elf:

> Nay, time does not tarry ever,' he said; 'but change and growth is not in all things and places alike. For the Elves the world moves, and it moves both very swift and very slow. Swift, because they themselves change little, and all else fleets by: it is a grief to them. Slow, because they do not count the running years, not for themselves. The passing seasons are but ripples ever repeated in the long long stream (F.503; II.9).

The perception of time is, therefore, clearly relative to the event that is being timed. As an analogy to Einstein's theory of the relativity of elapsed chronological time, the idiosyncratic perception of the passage of time could be defined as changing in relation to the emotional weight attached to the event being timed.

Ayesha's description of *Hell* is time-dependent and finds an echo in Tolkien's tale in his depiction of the *Houses of Lamentation*. Ayesha portrays Hell as "a place where the vital essence lives and retains an individual memory, and where all the errors and faults of judgement, and unsatisfied passions and the unsubstantial terrors of the mind wherewith it hath at any time had to do, come to mock and haunt and gibe and wring the heart for ever and for ever with the vision of its own hopelessness" (SHE XVII). In Tolkien's tale, the Nazgûl threatens Éowyn that he will not slay her, but bear her away "to the Houses of Lamentation, beyond all darkness, where thy flesh shall be devoured, and thy shrivelled mind be left naked to the Lidless Eye" (R.141; V.6). While Tolkien makes no explicit statement about how long this state will last, the suggestion of eternity seems implicit in the logic of his description.

In the end, Holly, like Frodo—his fine speech and resolution to the contrary—gave in to the temptation of Ayesha for "she was more than a woman. Heaven knows what she was—I do not! But then and there I fell upon my knees before her, and told her in a sad mixture of languages—for such moments confuse the thoughts—that I worshipped her as never woman was worshipped, and that I would give my immortal soul to marry her, which at that time I certainly would have done, and so, indeed, would any other man, or all the race of men rolled into one" (SHE XVII).

Ayesha rejected Holly, and in so doing cast him "into the depths ... of despair" (SHE XVII), a pit every bit as consuming as the Cracks of Doom, where he would "always be haunted and tortured by her memory, and by the last bitterness of unsatisfied love" (SHE XXII). This creates exactly the situation that Holly postulated as a reason to reject love as an inducement to accept practical immortality. For an immortal Holly, "always" would have been a much longer time for the memory of Ayesha to hauntingly torture him, than it would have been for the mortal Holly.

If Tolkien is to be taken for his word that his epic is not a tale of power, but one of Immortality and Death, then Frodo's claiming the Ring as his own is much more similar to Holly's surrender to Ayesha's charms (SHE XVII) and his acceptance of immortality (SHE XXV) than it would at first seem. In choosing not to destroy the Ring, Frodo chose not only power, but also immortality. It is the Ring that plays Ayesha's role in Tolkien's tale, and while it may seem absurd to speak of a ring taking on the role of a character in a story, Tolkien has imbued the Ring with a sort of sentience and independence of action that makes it appear to be one of the actors on the stage of his yarn.

Galadriel speaks of "a noble deed to set to the credit" of the Ring, if she had taken the Ring by force from a guest [Frodo] in her house (F.473; II.7). Gandalf talks of the Ring's ability to change its size, and "suddenly slip off a finger where it had been tight" (F.77; I.2). Slightly later, Gandalf describes the Ring in terms that make it sound even more like an animate participant in Tolkien's history. He says that the Ring may slip off its keeper's finger "treacherously" as it "looks after itself," trying "to get back to its master." It "betrayed" Isildur and "abandoned" Gollum (F.87-88 I.2).

In Haggard's tale, Ayesha's immortality, born of the living flame, is destroyed by the flame; just as the Ring was forged in the fires of Mount Doom and is destroyed by them. The agencies of Ayesha's and the Ring's destruction are similar. Ayesha's rejection of Holly's love was based on her love for Kallikrates, whom she herself killed (SHE XXI), and on whose return she had been waiting for some sixty-six generations (SHE I, XVII). The return of the reincarnated soul of Kallikrates is, therefore, the key to her destruction.

Frodo is saved from his decision to take the Ring by Gollum, who, like Kallikrates, had been abandoned by the Ring, yet returns to seal the Ring's (Ayesha's) doom. Leo Vincey, the reincarnate Kallikrates, fears to bathe in the living flame that would give him eternal life, and Ayesha offers to bathe in the flame a second time to show him that the fire will not burn his flesh. Her second bath in the flame, however, removes the spell of her first bath, and she shrivels and dies (SHE XXV-XXVI). Gollum wants his 'precious' back and bites off Frodo's finger to get it, but falls into the flames of Mount Doom, destroying both himself and the Ring.

The parallels are not exact, for Leo Vincey escapes with his mortal life in Haggard's tale and Gollum dies in Tolkien's, but the shared story elements are clearly visible in a parallel reading, and there are too many of them to be the result of pure chance. The leaf mold of Tolkien's mind, to which he attributed his story elements,[118] most certainly contained some tales by Ridder Haggard. Reading Haggard, therefore, can help Tolkien's reader to better understand Tolkien.

---

[118] Quoted in: Humphrey Carpenter, *Tolkien*, New York: Ballantine Books, 1977, pp. 140-141.

TRICKSY LIGHTS: CANDLES OF CORPSES

Tolkien and Haggard: The Dead Marshes

The caves that give entrance to Kôr—the land ruled by Ayesha in Haggard's novel *She*—are "surrounded by measureless swamps" (SHE III) and marshes that can be crossed only "by secret paths." (SHE VII) As Haggard's party crosses the marshes they are preceded by two men with long poles, constantly probing the ground before them to test the firmness of the path, because "the nature of the soil frequently changed ... so that places which might be safe enough to cross one month would certainly swallow the wayfarer the next" (SHE X).

Tolkien's descriptions of the Midgewater Marshes have some interestingly Haggardesque moments. Tolkien calls the marshes "bewildering and treacherous" with "no permanent trail" that even Rangers could find through the "shifting quagmires" (F.246; I.11). In the Dead Marshes it is Gollum who precedes Frodo and Sam, "testing the ground" (T. 295 IV.2).

Many of the details of the swamps and marshes in both tales could have easily been drawn from the common experience of a real-life swamp or marsh. Haggard's narrator comments on the "stench" (SHE V, XXVIII) and on the "clouds of poisonous vapour" (SHE V); Tolkien's of the reek (T.287, T.293; IV.2), vapours (F.248; I.11, T.295; IV.2), and the "black, heavy" air that was hard to breathe. (T.296; IV.2) Haggard's narrator speaks of the "slimy," "sullen peaty pools" (SHE X), "scummy pools of stagnant water" (SHE V); Tolkien's of the "stagnant pools and mires" (T.287; IV.2), "dark and noisome [evil smelling] pools" (T.293; IV.2) and the green of "the scum of livid weed on the dark greasy surfaces of the sullen waters" (T.295; IV.2).

Haggard's narrator recalls that they were attacked by "tens of thousands of the most blood-thirsty, pertinacious, and huge mosquitoes"—"musqueteers," as the narrator's servant Job called them—that came "[i]n clouds," and flew about biting them until they nearly went mad, driving them under their blankets, despite the heat, to spend "the night as quietly as the mosquitoes would allow" (SHE V, X). Tolkien's version of the attack of the insects in the marsh is less detailed and—though it has certain parallels ("clouds of tiny midges")—could be assumed to be drawn from real life were it not for the fact that Sam also makes up a name for the "evil relatives of the cricket" that would not let them sleep. He called them "Neekerbreekers" in imitation of the sound that they made (F.247; I.11). Haggard's neologism (*musqueteers*) is just the type of linguistic aside that would appeal to Tolkien, and seems to have found replication in Tolkien's story.

Corpse Candles

In Tolkien's tale, Gollum warns Frodo and Sam not to look at the "tricksy lights, candles of corpses" (T.296; IV.2). This formulation appears to be a hidden allusion to the Welsh tradition of "corpse candles," which had wide currency in literature in Tolkien's time. It is described here as 'hidden' because it follows the Welsh word order for the term corpse candles (*canwyllau gorf*), not the word order usual in English literature. Because this type of unusual diction is common enough in Gollum's dialogue (compare: "the silver crown of their king" [T.315; IV.3]), it does not seem out of place, but the reader has to 'normalize' it to see the allusion clearly.

In the folklore of Wales, corpse candles are death omens. Tradition states that corpse candles were granted the Welsh in response to a prayer made by Saint David—the patron Saint of Wales—in which he asked for "a sign to the living of the reality of another world (Owen, 299),[119] as a "warning to prepare them for death" (Trevelyan, 178).[120]

Corpse candles have been reported as both stationary and moving lights. Moving corpse candles are observed outside. Stationary corpse candles can be seen either inside or outside. When moving, they often have the appearance of a light floating above the ground at about the height of a human arm bent at the elbow, as if they were the flame of a candle held in a person's hand. The lights generally follow the route of a funeral that is soon to take place, from the house of the person whose death they predict to the church, or from the church to the house. When they are stationary, they are located near the place where the death they are foretelling is destined to occur.

There were also frequent reports of corpse candles floating on the water at spots where someone was soon to be drowned. The American poet Walt Whitman (1819-1892) thought the concept of water-borne corpse candles familiar enough to use it[121] to help convey the image of "the fishermen's little buoy-lights—so pretty, so dreamy—like corpse candles—undulating delicate and lonesome on the surface of the shadowy waters, floating with the current."

Charles Dickens (1812-1870), whose work clearly had an influence on Tolkien,[122] has a mention of corpse candles in *Barnaby Rudge - A Tale of the Riots of 'Eighty.*[123] There the first-person

---

[119] Elias Own. *Welsh Folk-lore*. Oswestry and Wrexham: Woodall, Minshall and Co., 1896.

[120] Marie Trevelyan. *Folk-lore and Folk-stories of Wales*, London: Elliot Stock, 1909.

[121] *Specimen Days and Collect, November Boughs and Good Bye My Fancy* <www.gutenberg.org/dirs/etext05/8cmpr10.txt>. LVO 2/19/2006.

[122] See "The Leaf Mold of Tolkien's Mind" above and Dale Nelson. "Little Nel and Frodo the Halfling," *Tolkien Studies*, volume 2, pp. 245-248.

narrator is preparing to ring the church bell at midnight, when he hears another ghostly bell ring. "It was only for an instant, and even then the wind carried the sound away, but I heard it. I listened for a long time, but it rang no more. I had heard of corpse candles, and at last I persuaded myself that this must be a corpse bell tolling of itself at midnight for the dead."

Haggard likewise has a reference to corpse candles in *She*. In a discussion of death and immortality that bears more than a circumstantial resemblance to Tolkien's examination of the topic (see above), Haggard has his narrator first look at "the eternal stars" above and then at the "impish marsh-born balls of fire" below, that "rolled this way and that." He then speculates "[w]hat would it be to cast off this earthy robe, to have done for ever with these earthy thoughts and miserable desires; no longer, like those corpse candles [the marsh-born balls of fire], to be tossed this way and that, by forces beyond our control; or which, if we can theoretically control them, we are at times driven by the exigencies of our nature to obey!" (SHE X).

Haggard's reference to "forces beyond our control" strikes to the heart of any discussion of free will, but also resonates with the Welsh belief about corpse candles "that there was some charm in the light of this candle so that [people] could not resist following it until it was extinguished" (Jenkins, 84).[124] This is exactly the power that seems to be at work in Tolkien's description of the crossing of the Dead Marshes, when Frodo is lured from the path by the "tricksy lights, candles of corpses" to join the dead of the Marsh (T.296; IV.2).

Haggard's use of *corpse candle* here seems to reflect more of a Shakespearean influence than of a Welsh one. It calls to mind the oft-quoted lines from Macbeth (Act V, Scene V): "Out, out, brief candle! Life's but a walking shadow, a poor player that struts and frets his hour upon the stage and then is heard no more: it is a tale told by an idiot, full of sound and fury, signifying nothing." Tennyson's use, on the other hand, is not marked with this apparent ambiguity.

---

[123] <http://www.gutenberg.org/dirs/etext97/rudge10.txt>

[124] D.E. Jenkins. *Bedd Gelert: Its Facts, Fairies and Folk-lore*, Portmadoc: Llewelyn Jenkins, 1899.

In act III, scene I of his play *Harold*, Alfred Tennyson (1809 -1892) conjures up a sense of foreboding that would not feel out of place in Tolkien's tale of the crossing of the Dead Marshes, when Archbishop Aldred relates what he has heard from someone who had passed Senlac hill three nights previously and was so shaken by what he saw and heard that he could scarcely speak. A ghostly horn accompanied the sounds of battle, "And dreadful lights crept up from out the marsh / Corpse-candles gliding over nameless graves."

The corpse candles in Tolkien's tale likewise mark the nameless watery graves of those fallen in a great Battle at the Black Gates an age ago. The Dead Marshes have grown since the battle and "swallowed up the graves; always creeping, creeping" (T.297; IV.2). In Haggard's tale, an army once tried to cross the swamps to attack the people of Kôr, but it lost its way in the marshes, "and at night, seeing the great balls of fire that move about there, tried to come to them, thinking that they marked the enemy camp, and half of them were drowned" (SHE VII). Though the exact circumstances differ, the faint echo of Haggard's drowned army can still be heard in the faces of the fallen in Tolkien's Dead Marshes.

Tolkien's description of faces visible in the water when the candles are lit bears an eery resemblance to the real Welsh tradition, where it was thought that the identity of the person whose death a passing corpse candle portended could be established "by gazing into the water when it [the corpse candle] passed" (Jones, 208).[125] The fact that Gollum cannot touch the faces in the water makes them seem much like the ethereal Welsh reflections from the other world that, at the same time, weakly echo the visions of Galadriel's and Ayesha's water mirrors.

---

[125] Gwynn Jones. *Welsh Folklore and Folk-customs*, London: Methuen and Co. 1930.

THE RED BOOK OF WESTMARCH

The Feigned-manuscript Topos: A Question of Authorship

In the "Prologue" (P. 19), in the "Note on the Shire Records" (F.37), in Appendix F.II (Af.513-520) and elsewhere in *The Lord of the Rings*, Tolkien claims that *The Hobbit* and *The Lord of the Rings* are translations from the *Red Book of Westmarch*, "composed by Bilbo [Baggins] himself, the first Hobbit to become famous in the world at large, and called by him *There and Back Again*" (P.19). Tolkien even reproduces the title page of *The Red Book*, noting it to be "the memoirs of Bilbo and Frodo of the Shire, supplemented by the accounts of their friends and the learning of the Wise" (R.379-380; VI.9).

Most readers pay little or no attention to this patently fictitious assertion, failing to recognize it for what it is: a literary topos with an impressively long pedigree. Tolkien was not the first author to use the feigned-manuscript topos, nor was he the last. A list of authors who have applied this topos to their works includes such well-known writers as: Rider Haggard, Daniel DeFoe, Sir Walter Scott, Alessandro Manzoni, Charles Dickens, Horace Walpole, Jan Potocki, Jonathan Swift, James Fenimore

Cooper, Sir Arthur Conan Doyle, Nathaniel Hawthorne, Miguel de Cervantes, John Buchan and Umberto Eco.

The feigned-manuscript topos is a literary trick to affect the reader's perception of a work. In the period of its greatest popularity, History was favored over Story. In the academic edition of *Robinson Crusoe,* one of DeFoe's critics—Thomas Babington Macaulay—offers some insight into why an author might want to create a 'fictive' history instead of just writing a novel. "The *History of the Plague* and the *Memoirs of a Cavalier* are in one sense curious works of art. They are wonderfully like true histories; but, considered as novels, which they are, there is not much in them. He [DeFoe] had undoubtedly the knack at making fiction look like truth. But is such a knack to be admired?"[126]

From the controversy surrounding Dan Brown's *The Da Vinci Code*, it is clear that, even in the twenty-first century, this question still lacks a definitive answer. In his recent decision supporting Brown against charges of plagiarism, British Justice Peter Smith, offered an excellent summation of the situation.[127]

> "Merely because an author describes matters as being factually correct does not mean that they are factually correct. It is a way of blending fact and fiction together to create that well known model 'faction.' The lure of apparent genuineness makes the books and the films more receptive to the readers/audiences. The danger of course is that the faction is all that large parts of the audience read, and they accept it as truth."

The feigned-manuscript topos gives a work a sense of authenticity. Many of the authors who use it go on at length about the 'truth' of their works. A number of them—like Tolkien—assume the guise of a scholarly 'translator,' who is concerned with the technical minutiae of the 'manuscript's' origin,

---

[126] Thomas De Quincy, "The Double Character of DeFoe's Works," in Daniel DeFoe, *Robinson Crusoe* (A Norton Critical Edition), Michael Shingel (ed.), New York: Norton, 1994, p. 273.

[127] "The battle of *The Da Vinci Code*" <cnn.com/2006/SHOWBIZ/Movies/05/01/decoding.davinci.ap/index.html >. LVO 5/1/2006.

style, and history. Comments of this type make the 'translator' seem an objective observer whose opinion should be valued.

The sense of authority that the scholarly 'translator' brings to the tale both reinforces the sense of authenticity and acts as a recommendation of the work. If an objective scholar thought the work worthy of translating, it must also be worth reading. Hawthorne's comment that the intent of his 'translation' of the works of the fictitious M. de l'Aubépine was to do what little was in his power to introduce this author favorably to the American public[128] is an explicit example of the otherwise implicit 'translator's recommendation' found in many a use of the feigned-manuscript topos.

The feigned-manuscript topos also offers an author a shield against the stings and arrows of outraged readers and critics. The 'translator' or 'editor' has but to remind them that the tale is not his own to blunt their criticism. Walpole [Q.V.] admitted as much in the "Preface" to the second edition of *The Castle of Otranto*, in which he apologized for having borrowed the personage of a translator.[129]

Henry Rider Haggard (1856-1925) was one of the most popular writers of his era. In 1887, Haggard wrote *She: A History of Adventure*, the heroine of which is "She-who-must-be-obeyed." The biographical sketch to the *Modern Library* edition of *She* includes J.R.R. Tolkien, C.S. Lewis and Graham Greene among the countless readers whose imagination was captured by this novel.[130] In her introduction, Margret Atwood notes: "in Tolkien's *The Lord of the Rings*, She splits into two: Galadriel, powerful but good, who's got exactly the same water mirror as the one possessed by She; and a very ancient cave-dwelling man-devouring spider-

---

[128] "Preface" to his short story "Rappaccini's Daughter," in Nathaniel Hawthorne, *Mosses from an Old Manse* (The Centenary Edition of the Works of Nathaniel Hawthorne, volume X), Ohio State University Press, 1974.

[129] Horace Walpole, *The Castle of Otranto: A Gothic Story*, Philadelphia: Henry Carey Baird, 1854, p. 47.

[130] H. Rider Haggard, *She: A History of Adventure*, New York: The Modern Library, 2002, p. viii.

creature named, tellingly, Shelob,"[131] a conflation of *She* and the OE word for *spider* (*lob*).

The other coincidence between Haggard's *She* and Tolkien's *LotR* is the oft-overlooked feigned-manuscript topos. In his "Introduction" (pp. 3-8), Haggard explains that he is "not the narrator, but only the editor of this extraordinary history," and then continues to explain how the 'manuscript' came into his possession.

Some years previous the editor had been visiting a friend at a University, which for the purposes of his narrative, he calls Cambridge. He and his friend chanced upon two gentlemen of remarkable appearance. The friend knows them and delivers a short introduction for the reader. Some years later the editor received a letter from "Horace Holly," one of the two men he had met briefly in Cambridge. Mr. Holly had read an earlier book by the editor describing an adventure in Central Africa that was "partly true, and partly an effort of the imagination" (p. 5). The two gentlemen are leaving for Central Asia, in search of wisdom, and they anticipate that their stay may be a long one, or that they may indeed never return. In light of this circumstance, they feel that they may not be "justified in withholding from the world an account of a phenomenon which we [the gentlemen] believe to be of unparalleled interest, merely because our private life is involved, or because we are afraid of ridicule and doubt being cast upon our statements. ... [It is] the most wonderful history, as distinguished from romance, that its records can show" (p. 6). They have, therefore, decided to send the manuscript of their tale to the editor, giving him permission to publish it, if he sees fit, on the condition that he not use their real names. In the published version of the manuscript, the letter is signed pseudonymously "L. Horace Holly," in accordance with the writer's request. The "Introduction" closes by entrusting the reader "to form his own judgement on the facts before him, as they are detailed by Mr. Holly in the following pages" (p. 8).

In Chapter II, Haggard introduces the sherd of Amenartas, a potsherd which is inscribed with a text in Greek. The text is presented in block Greek letters and in cursive, and accompanied

---

[131] Marget Atwood, "Introduction," in *Haggard* (2002), p. xxiii.

by a translation. Holly even invites the reader to compare the original Greek text with the translation, so as "to see for himself by comparison" that the translation "is both accurate and elegant" (p. 37). This is not an idle invitation created at the author's whim, but a very real reflection of literary life, for the question of authenticity was sometimes a hotly debated one, as can easily be seen in any discussion of MacPherson or Chatterton.[132]

There is even a facsimile of the potsherd in the book. In her "Introduction" to the *Modern Library* edition of *She*, Atwood notes that the first edition of the book that she read had a photograph of the pot—made to order by Haggard's sister-in-law—to make the tale more convincing. Haggard had intended it to be like the pirate map at the beginning of *Treasure Island*, in hopes of rivaling the popularity of Stevenson's masterpiece. *She* did.[133] In the *Modern Library* edition, the illustration is drawn (pp. 32-33).

As the chapter of the potsherd continues, a Latin text plus translation and an 'OE' text and modern transcription are added to enhance the credibility of the story. The technical discussion of the texts and their translation (p. 31-48) are equally as detailed as are Tolkien's discussions in Appendix F.II. The conclusion of the examination of the potsherd is that the potsherd is "perfectly genuine, and that, wonderful as it may seem, it has come down in your family from since the fourth century before Christ. The entries absolutely prove it, therefore, however, improbable it may seem, the fact must be accepted" (p. 48).

Haggard keeps up the fiction of a manuscript prepared by 'Mr. Holly' in *Ayesha: The Return of She*.[134] (1905) In the "Introduction," Haggard explains that *Ayesha* is really a

---

[132] Louise J. Kaplan, *The Family Romance of the Imposter-poet Thomas Chatterton*, New York: Atheneum, 1988.

Ian Haywood, *The Making of History : a study of the literary forgeries of James Macpherson and Thomas Chatterton in relation to eighteenth-century ideas of history and fiction*, Rutherford : Fairleigh Dickinson University Press, 1986.

[133] Marget Atwood, "Introduction," in *Haggard* (2002), p. xviii.

[134] H. Rider Haggard, *Ayesha: The Return of She*, London: Macdonald, 1956.

manuscript, "badly burned upon the back," that 'Mr. Holly' had sent him in a "dingy, unregistered, brown-paper parcel" (p. xi). 'Holly' is pleased to have seen "a copy of your [Haggard's] book *She*, or rather of my book," which he read in a Hindustani translation. 'Holly' adds: "I see that you carried out your part of the business well and faithfully. Every instruction has been obeyed, nothing had been added or taken away." 'Holly' has, therefore decided to entrust the editor with the final installment of his story, contained in the enclosed manuscript. (p. xii) Again the "Introduction" concludes with an admonition that the reader "must form his or her own judgement" of the manuscript and "its inner significations" (p. xviii).

The *She* novels were not the only ones that Haggard provided with a faux-history that made them seem to be manuscripts. In *Heart of the Wild*[135] (1896), Haggard provides the reader with a "Prologue" (pp. 9-21), in which he explains that "the circumstances under which the following pages come to be printed are somewhat curious and worthy of record" (p. 9). The owner of this manuscript is "a certain English gentleman, whom we will call Jones, because it was not his name" (p. 9). The tale of the "Prologue" is of Jones' friendship with Don Ignatio, a kindly old Indian gentleman, who says that he has seen "the secret city" of the South-American Indians. When Jones expresses his disbelief, Don Ignatio is taken aback, and makes a statement that sounds somewhat like Mr. Holly's fear of ridicule: "I did not in the least expect you to believe me. Indeed, it is because I cannot bear to be thought a liar that I have never said anything of this story, and for this same reason I shall not repeat it to you, since I do not wish that one whom I hope will become my friend should hold me in contempt" (p. 16). Don Ignatio calls Jones to his deathbed, and gives him a Spanish-language manuscript in which "is set out an account of how I [Don Ignatio] and my English friend [James Strickland] came to visit the Golden City, of what we saw and suffered there" (p. 19). The tale that the reader of the *Heart of the World* is presented in the book is a "translation of the manuscript" (p. 21). The translation begins: "I Ignatio, the

---

[135] H. Rider Haggard, *Heart of the Wild*, London: Macdonald, 1954.

writer of this history, being now a man in my sixty-second year, was born in a village among the mountains ..." (p. 22).

Daniel DeFoe (1660-1731) also availed himself of this literary technique. The title page of *Robinson Crusoe* (1719) declares the book to be "the life and strange surprising adventures of Robinson Crusoe ... written by himself." The preface from the 'editor' [DeFoe] says that "the editor believes the thing to be a just history of fact; neither is there any appearance of fiction in it." The story then begins with the statement: "I was born in the year 1632." (DeFoe was born in 1660.) The "Preface" to the third volume of *Robinson Crusoe* is signed Robinson Crusoe and goes on at length about the "real facts in my history" to sustain the fiction of its authorship and authenticity. He was clearly very successful in doing so. In the academic edition of *Robinson Crusoe*, one of DeFoe's critics is quoted as saying: "DeFoe is the only author known, who has so plausibly cicumstantiated his false historical records, as to make them pass for genuine, even with literary men and critics."[136]

The title page of *A Journal of the Plague Year* (1722) records the book as "being observations or memorials of the most remarkable occurrences, as well publick [sic] as private, which happened in London during the last great visitation in 1665. Written by a citizen who continued all the while in London. Never made public before." The citizen is identified on the last page of the professedly authentic account with the initials H.F.

Memoirs of a Cavalier (1720) is identified as "a military journal of the wars in Germany and the wars in England from the year 1632 to the year 1648, written threescore years ago by an English gentleman, who served in the army of Gustavus Adolphus, the glorious King of Sweden, till his death; and after that, in the royal army of King Charles the first, from the beginning of the Rebellion to the end of that war." The "Preface" begins: "As evidence that 'tis very probable these memorials were written many years ago, the persons now concerned in the publication,

---

[136] Thomas De Quincy, "The Double Character of DeFoe's Works," in Daniel DeFoe, *Robinson Crusoe* (A Norton Critical Edition), Michael Shingel (ed.), New York: Norton, 1994, p. 272.

assure the reader, that they have had them in their possession finished, as they now appear, above twenty years: that they were so long ago found by great accident, among other valuable papers in the closet of an eminent publick [sic] Minister, of no less figure than one of King William's Secretary of State."

DeFoe's *The King of Pirates* (1719) is presented to the reader as "an account of the famous enterprises of Captain Avery, the mock King of Madagascar, with his rambles and piracies, wherein all the sham accounts formerly published of him are detected. In two letters from himself; one during his stay at Madagascar, and one since his escape from thence." DeFoe's *The Fortunes and Misfortunes of the Famous Moll Flanders* (1722) is also depicted as a true history, "written from her own memorandums."

In the "Advertisement" to the first edition of *Rob Roy* —published in 1817, before **Sir Walter Scott** (1771-1832) admitted to the world that he was the person behind the *nominus umbra* of 'The author of *Waverley*,' that is while all his novels were still anonymous—Scott created the fiction that *Rob Roy* was not of his invention, but that he was only the editor of a manuscript which he had received from an "unknown and nameless correspondent." He wrote:

> It is now about six months since the author, through the medium of his respectable publishers, received a parcel of papers, containing the outlines of this narrative, with a permission, or rather with a request, couched in highly flattering terms, that they might be given to the public, with such alterations as should be found suitable. ... [The author] takes this public opportunity to thank the unknown and nameless correspondent, to whom the reader will owe the principal share of any amusement which he may derive from the following pages. 1st December, 1817

In the edition of 1829, after Scott had admitted his authorship of 'the *Waverley* novels,' he added a footnote to the first sentence above: "As it may be necessary, in the present edition (1829), to speak upon the square, the author thinks it proper to own, that the communication alluded to is entirely imaginary."

The novel, however, begins with an "Appendix" to the "Introduction," which includes a number of documents about Rob Roy. One of these is an "Advertisement for Apprehension of Rob Roy," from the June 18-21, 1712 edition of the Edinburgh *Evening Courant*. Another is a collection of some letters from the Duke of Montrose, regarding "Rob Roy's arrest of Mr. Grahame of Killearn." The effect is much the same as from Tolkien's Appendices. The Appendix enhances the perception that the novel is in fact a history.

At the same time, Scott soft-pedals the authenticity of his materials in the "Introduction." There he says: "I am far from warranting their exact authenticity. Clannish partialities were very apt to guide the tongue and pen as well as the pistol and claymore, and the features of an anecdote are wonderfully softened or exaggerated, as the story is told by a MacGregor or a Campbell." This type of 'objectivity,' however, only serves to enhance the 'editor's' authority, glossing over his own partialities.

In the same "Advertisement," Scott offers an interesting insight into why he chose to publish anonymously. He said that "he might shelter himself under the plea that every anonymous writer is, like the celebrated Junius, only a phantom, and that therefore, although an apparition of a more benign, as well as much meaner description, he cannot be bound to plead to a charge of inconsistency."

I Promessi Sposi [The Betrothed] by **Alessandro Manzoni** (1785-1873) is a historical novel that came out at a time (the 1820s), when the popularity of Scott's 'the *Waverley* Novels' had engendered imitators of this form of fiction throughout Europe. Manzoni's novel is considered a classic of modern Italian literature, and has been widely translated and retranslated. This first English translation was in 1828. It was followed, in 1834, by three others, and in 1844 and 1845, by yet another two. In the twentieth century, it was retranslated in 1951 and again in 1972.

The Betrothed begins with an "Author's Introduction," in which Manzoni explains that the source of his work is a "scratched and faded manuscript" from the seventeenth century.[137] Criticizing the "hail of conceits and metaphors,: "sentences that don't hang together," "bombastic declamation, full of vulgar solecisms," and "pretentious pedantry" found in the text, he decides to take the sequence of events from the manuscript and recast the language (p. 27). Having made this decision, he finds himself faced with a sense of obligation to give a detailed account of the reasons why he adopted the writing style that he did. When, however, it came time to pull all the arguments and counter-arguments into some kind of orderly whole, Manzoni realized that "they came to a book in themselves. Seeing which, [he] gave up the idea, for two reasons with which the reader will be sure to agree; the first, that a book written to justify another book—not to mention the style of another book—might seem rather ridiculous; the second, that one book at a time is enough, if indeed it is not too much" (p. 28).

Tolkien, apparently, did not agree with Manzoni. While it does not reach book-length, Tolkien's Appendix F.II (Af.513-520) concerns itself with exactly the area of inquiry that Manzoni chose to avoid. It is an explanation of Tolkien's complex writing style, which, on the whole, would probably not have appealed to Manzoni, who chose for a simple idiom instead of a complex one.

Charles Dickens (1812-1870) started his publishing career, as was common in the period,[138] writing under a pseudonym. In 1836, a collection of the humorous sketches that Dickens had written for the *Monthly Magazine* was published as *Sketches by 'Boz'*. These were followed by a series of comic adventures, originally serialized in a 'shilling' monthly, that later came to be published as *The Posthumous Papers of the Pickwick Club* (1837).

Throughout *The Pickwick Papers*, the narrator maintains the pretense that he is merely the 'editor' of a set of papers that had been "carefully preserved, and duly registered by the secretary, from time to time, in the voluminous Transactions of the Pickwick Club. These transactions have been purchased from the patriotic

---

[137] Alessandro Manzoni, *The Betrothed* [I Promessi Sposi], Archibald Colquhoun (trans.), London: The Portfolio Society, 1959, pp. 25-28.

[138] *Oxford Reader's Companion to Dickens*, (Paul Schlicke ed.), Oxford: The University Press, 1999, p. 53.

secretary, at an immense expense, and placed in the hands of 'BOZ,' the author of 'Sketches Illustrative of Every Day Life, and Every Day People'—a gentleman whom the publishers consider highly qualified for the task of arranging these important documents, and placing them before the pubic in an attractive form."[139] In Chapter I ("The Pickwickians"), Dickens begins his tale with the assertion that it "is derived from the perusal of the following entry in the Transactions of the Pickwick Club, which the editor of these papers feels the highest pleasure in laying before his readers, as a proof of the careful attention, indefatigable assiduity, and nice discrimination, with which his search among the multifarious documents confided to him has been conducted."[140]

The Kinsley edition of *The Pickwick Papers* contains a reproduction of the cover of the fourth installment of the original 'shilling' paper-back edition of *The Posthumous Papers of the Pickwick Club* with a 'by-line' that reads: "Edited by 'BOZ'."[141] The Scolar Press facsimile edition of *The Life and Adventures of Nicholas Nickleby*, likewise, shows the original covers of the 'shilling' serials, all with this same 'by-line: "Edited by 'BOZ'."[142]

Horace Walpole (1717-1797)—the first Gothic novelist—published the lead book of the genre—*The Castle of Otranto* (1764)—anonymously, claiming it to be a translation of an old Italian manuscript. The "Preface" to the first edition includes a number of details that give the 'translation' a scholarly air: where it was found, when it was printed and where, when the action in it took place. Speculation on the date of the action of the story, for example, reads: "If the story was written near the time when it is supposed to have happened, it must have been between 1095, the era of the first Crusade, and 1243, the date of the last,

---

[139] Charles Dickens, *The Pickwick Papers* (James Kinsley ed.), Oxford: The Clarendon Press, 1986, p. xxi.

[140] Dickens, p. 1.

[141] Charles Dickens, p. facing the inside cover.

[142] Charles Dickens, *The Life and Adventures of Nicholas Nickleby*, reproduced in facsimile from the original monthly parts of 1838-9 in two volumes, London: Scolar Press, 1982.

or not long afterwards. There is no other circumstance in the work that can lead us to guess at the period in which the scene is laid."[143] There follows a seemingly informed literary and linguistic analysis of the text, clearly intended to give credence to the tale that follows. The 'translator' concludes with an assessment of the veracity of the tale: "Though the machinery is invention, and the names of the actors imaginary, I cannot but believe that the groundwork of the story is founded on truth. The scene is undoubtedly laid in some real castle" (p. 46).

In the "Preface" to the second edition, Walpole admitted his authorship, begging his readers' pardon for having published *The Castle of Otranto* "under the borrowed personage of a translator," hoping since "diffidence of his own abilities and the novelty of the attempt, were the sole inducements to assume that disguise," that the readers will find it excusable (p. 47). His intention had been to let the work "perish in obscurity," if it met with disapproval (p. 47). The public loved it. The press attacked him upon learning that his 'translation' was a fake.

The Manuscript Found in Saragossa by **Jan Potocki** (1761-1815) is a collection of stories recorded, according to the "Foreword," in a manuscript consisting of "several handwritten notebooks."[144] It was 'found' by a French officer who entered the city of Saragossa following its fall to the forces with which he was fighting [in 1809]. The officer did not know much Spanish, but the little that he did know told him that it might be an interesting diversion from the hardships of combat, and he decided to keep the novel, "as [he] was convinced that the book could no longer be restored to its rightful owner" (p. 3). Shortly thereafter, the young officer was captured by Spanish troops. By a fortunate (for the young officer) turn of events, the captain of the forces that had taken him prisoner was a member of the family whose story was told in the manuscript. The French officer was well treated throughout the course of his internment, during which the

---

[143] Horace Walpole, *The Castle of Otranto: A Gothic Story*, Philadelphia: Henry Carey Baird, 1854, p. 41.

[144] Jan Potocki, *The Manuscript Found in Saragossa* (Ian Mclean trans.), London: Penguin Books, 1996, p. 3.

Spanish officer translated the manuscript aloud into French. "I wrote what follows as he dictated it," concludes the "Foreword" (p. 4).

The title page of the 1726 first edition of *Gulliver's Travels*, now generally known to be the work of **Jonathan Swift** (1667-1745), informs the reader that *Travels into Several Remote Nations of the World* (in four parts) is "by Lemuel Gulliver, first Surgeon, and then a Captain of several Ships."[145] The text of the story is preceded by a prefatory letter from Captain Gulliver to the publisher, Gulliver's cousin, Richard Sympson. In the letter, the 'author' calls Sympson to task for prevailing upon him "to publish a very loose and uncorrect [SIC] account of my travels; with direction to hire some young gentleman of either university to put them in order, and correct the style, ... but I do not remember that I gave you power to consent, that any thing should be omitted, and much less that any thing should be inserted ... you have either omitted some material circumstances, or minced or changed them in such a manner, that I do hardly know mine own work" (p. 3). This distances Swift from any inconsistencies in the manuscript, since the changes in it were those of the 'editor.' This is essentially the same concern that Scott displayed in his comment about not wanting to "be bound to plead to a charge of inconsistency." If there are any inconsistencies in the work, it is the fault of the fictitious editor.

The reason for this level of caution in presenting Swift's work is suggested by the editor's reported response to Gulliver's complaint in the prefatory letter. The editor had replied that he was "afraid of giving offense; that people in power were very watchful over the press, and apt not only to interpret, but to punish every thing which looked like innuendo" (p. 3). For such a politically loaded novel as *Gulliver's Travels*, this is certainly a justified caution.

Another reason that authors of the period were not loath to publish their work pseudonymously and/or as 'translators' is

---

[145] Reproduced in: Jonathan Swift, *Gulliver's Travels and Other Writings*, Louis A. Landa (ed.), Boston: The Riverside Press Cambridge, 1960, p. 1.

found in the editor's "Introduction" to the 1960 edition of *Gulliver's Travels*. There the editor quotes "Mr. Spectator," writing in 1711: "I have observed that a reader seldom peruses a book with pleasure 'till he knows whether the writer of it be a black or a fair man, of a mild or choleric disposition, married or a bachelor, with other particulars of the like nature, that conduce very much to the right understanding of an author" (p. vii). "A right understanding of an author" is a relative thing, and is not without some potential—rightly or wrongly—for negative consequences. Obscuring one's true identity can alleviate this problem.

Swift also touches upon the issue of authenticity when he rails against the "censure of yahoos" some of whom "are so bold as to think my book of travels a mere fiction out of my own brain. ... Do these miserable animals presume to think that I am so far denigrated as to defend my veracity?" (p. 5). The 'editor' vouchsafes for the veracity of the 'author' in a note "To the Reader" that follows the prefatory letter. "There is an air of truth apparent through the whole; and indeed, the author was so distinguished for his veracity, that it became a sort of proverb amoung his neighbors at Redriff, when any one affirmed a thing, to say, it was as true as if Mr. Gulliver had spoke it" (p. 7). Haggard uses essentially the same approach by having his fictional author—'Mr. Holly'—praise his 'editor' for carrying out his instructions with regard to the manuscript "well and faithfully (Haggard p. xii).

James Fenimore Cooper (1789-1851) seemingly follows Swift's lead with his "Introduction"[146] to his satirical novel, *The Monikins* (1835), in which the reader learns that Cooper is not the author of the manuscript printed in the book, but rather its publisher. His opening line lets his sense of humor show through.

> It is not improbable that some of those who read this book, may feel a wish to know in what manner I became possessed of the manuscript. Such a desire is too just and natural to be thwarted, and the tale shall be told as briefly as possible.

---

[146] James Fenimore Cooper, *The Monikins*, James S. Hedges (ed.), Albany, NY: New College and University Press, 1990, pp. 1-4.

Cooper then proceeds to relate the tale of a trip to Switzerland in the summer of 1828, during which he saved the beautiful wife of a British viscount from an accidental death in the mountains. In due time, he received "a large packet," which contained "a fairly written manuscript." The note from the viscount that came with the manuscript explained that he had "long hesitated about publishing the accompanying narrative, for in England there is a disposition to cavil at extraordinary facts, but the distance of America from my place of residence will completely save me from ridicule. The world must have the truth, and I see no better means than by resorting to your agency." All that the viscount asks is that Cooper have the book "fairly printed," and send one copy to the viscount and one copy to another American of his acquaintance." The reasoning for the viscount's concern over the publication is essentially the same as was Gulliver's. The tale was indeed poorly received in England, as it was—like Gulliver's—a satire of English society.

Sir Arthur Conan Doyle (1859-1930), begins "A Study in Scarlet"—the first (published 1887) story in the world-famous saga of Sherlock Holmes—with the assertion that the tale is "a reprint from the reminiscences of John H. Watson, M.D., late of the Army Medical Department."[147] This assertion recalls the statement on the title page of *The Red Book* that Tolkien reproduces in Chapter 9 of Book VI ("The Grey Havens"), where it says that *The Red Book* is composed of "the memoirs of Bilbo and Frodo of the Shire, supplemented by the accounts of their friends and the learning of the Wise" (R.380; VI.9). "A Study in Scarlet" concludes with Watson saying: "I have all the facts in my journal and the public shall know them" (p. 123). The fiction is maintained throughout the saga. In "The Five Orange Pips" (published 1891), for example, Watson refers to his "notes and records of the Sherlock Holmes cases between the years '82 and '90," of which the year '87 was particularly remarkable for its "long series of cases of greater or less interest, of which I retain the records" (p.

---

[147] Sir Arthur Conan Doyle, *The Adventures of Sherlock Holmes: A Definitive Text*, Edgar W. Smith (ed.), New York: The Heritage Press, 1950, p. 3.

332). In "The Adventure of the Speckled Band" (published 1892), Watson again refers to his "notes of the seventy odd cases" of Sherlock Holmes that he has collected over the last 8 years (p. 396).

In the lead book of the "Philo Vance" series—*The Benson Murder Case* (1926)[148]—**Willard Huntington Wright** (1888-1939), using the pseudonym S.S. Van Dine, also declares himself to be the chronicler of a famed detective, echoing the assertions of Dr. Watson. He relates that he and Vance were friends from their student days at Harvard. Vance was independently wealthy and Van Dine was a lawyer who served as his "personal legal factotum" (p. 3). Van Dine's and Vance's literary association was, however, somewhat shorter than that of Holmes and Dr. Watson. It only lasted for a "period of nearly four years" (p. 3). During that time, Van Dine not only participated in all the cases that Vance investigated, but also

> being of methodical temperament, I kept a fairly complete record of them. In addition, I noted down (as accurately as memory permitted) Vance's unique psychological methods of determining guilt, as he explained them from time to time. It is fortunate that I performed this gratuitous labor of accumulation and transcription, for now that circumstances have unexpectedly rendered possible my making the cases public, I am able to present them in full detail and with all their various sidelights and succeeding steps—a task that would be impossible were it not for my numerous clippings and *adversaria* [a very bookish word—typical of Wright's style—for *notes*] (p. 4).

The twelve novels that made up the series, claims Wright (Van Dine), "constitute one of the most astonishing secret documents in the police history of this country" (p. 3). He adds an extra touch of verisimilitude to his source materials by including a "verbatim copy" of a document that Vance prepared himself (p. 287).

---

[148] S.S. Van Dine. *The Benson Murder Case: A Philo Vance Story*, New York: Charles Scribner's Sons, 1927.

Manzoni uses the same technique in *The Betrothed*. He refers to *the manuscript* in the text in much the same way as Watson (Doyle) refers to his notes and records. In Chapter XVIII, for example, Manzoni says: "The road of inquiry, observes our manuscript here, is a broad one, but that does not mean that it is comfortable. It has its stumbling-blocks, and rough passages, and its course can be irksome and wearing, for all that it leads downhill" (Colquhoun translation p. 304). In Chapter XXII, he comments: "Our manuscript does not say how far it was from the castle to the village where the Cardinal was staying; but judging from the events which we are about to describe, it could not have been more than a good walk away" (p. 354). In Chapter XXVI, he, once more, reminds the reader of the presence of the manuscript, saying: "And, to tell the truth, even we, sitting with our manuscript in front of us and a pen in our hands, and nothing to contend with except phrases, or anything to fear but the criticisms of our readers—even we, I say, feel a certain reluctance to proceed" (pp. 419-420).

Tolkien's text is likewise sprinkled with mentions of 'notes' and 'records' on which his story would seem to be based. Tolkien's "Prologue" to *LotR* is followed by "Note on the Shire Records" (P.37-39). In it he says that *The Red Book* was "in origin Bilbo's private diary, which he took with him to Rivendell. Frodo brought it back to the Shire, together with many loose leaves of notes, and during s.r. 1420-1 he nearly filled its pages with his account of the War" (P.37). Tolkien repeats this detail near the end of Chapter 6 of Book VI ("Many Partings"), in which he reproduces the dialogue between Bilbo and Frodo, during which Bilbo gives Frodo all his "notes and papers, and [his] diary too" (R.329; VI.6). In part 4 of the "Prologue" ("Of the Finding of the Ring"), the narrator observes that the true story of how Bilbo found the One Ring was "derived no doubt from notes by Frodo or Samwise" (P.35). As the travelers transit Bree in Chapter 7 of Book VI ("Homeward Bound"), Frodo is asked if he has written his book, to which he replies: "Not yet,' he answered. 'I am going home now to put my notes in order" (R.338; VI.7). The effect is much the same as it is in *Sherlock Holmes*, *Philo Vance* and *The Betrothed*. The tales told by Doyle, Wright (Van Dine), Manzoni and Tolkien seem more real because the 'reminiscences' and 'memoirs' contained in them are supported by copious notes and records.

Nathaniel Hawthorne (1804-1864) demonstrated that he had a refined sense of humor when he used the feigned-manuscript topos in the "Preface" to his short story "Rappaccini's Daughter." In it, he informs the reader that the story is a translation of "Beatrice; ou la Belle Empoisonneuse" (French: Beatrice; or the Beautiful Poisoner) by M. de l'Aubépine, whom he richly praises. To add depth to the fiction of an original French author, Hawthorne lists some of the titles of de l'Aubépine's works. These include a collection of stories entitled *Contes deux fois racontées,* and a number of more recent individual short stories. Hawthorne concludes that this "somewhat wearisome perusal of this startling catalogue of volumes has left behind it a certain personal affection and sympathy, though by no means admiration, for M. de l'Aubépine; and we would fain do the little in our power towards introducing him favorably to the American public."

The key to Hawthorne's joke is that *aubépine* is the French word for *hawthorn* (genus Crataegus, family Rosaceae). All the titles that he mentions are French translations of the titles of his own works. The collection of stories entitled *Contes deux fois racontées* is really *Twice Told Tales*, which was published as volume IX of the Ohio State University Press Centenary edition of Hawthorne's collected works.[149] All the remaining story titles can be found—together with "Rappaccini's Daughter"—in volume X of the Ohio State University Press edition of Hawthorne's collected works.[150]

- "Le Voyage Céleste Chemin de Fer" is "The Celestial Railroad" (pp. 186-206)
- "Le nouveau Père Adam et la nouvelle Mère Ève" is "The New

---

[149] Nathaniel Hawthorne, *Twice Told Tales* (The Centenary Edition of the Works of Nathaniel Hawthorne, volume IX), Ohio State University Press, 1974.

[150] Nathaniel Hawthorne, *Mosses from an Old Manse* (The Centenary Edition of the Works of Nathaniel Hawthorne, volume X), Ohio State University Press, 1974.

Adam and Eve" (pp. 247-267)
- "Roderic; ou le Serpent à l'estomac" is "Egotism; or the Bosom Serpent" (pp. 268-283)
- "Le Culte du Feu" is "Fire-Worship" (pp. 138-147)
- "La Soirée du Chateau en Espagne" is "A Select Party" (pp. 57-73), in which "a man of fancy made an entertainment at one of his castles in the air" (p. 57)
- "L'Artiste du Beau; ou le Papillon Mécanique" is "The Artist and the Beautiful" (pp. 447-475), in which the artist creates a mechanical butterfly that was "absolutely lifelike" (p. 470).

The joke would certainly have appealed to Tolkien who put his own name on the map of The Shire in Gothic. In a letter, Tolkien says that he sometimes used the Gothic translation of his surname—Dwalakoneis—for 'Gothic' inscriptions in books that he had read (L.357). In British toponymy, the ending -ing is commonly indicative of a place name derived from a personal name. It names a place occupied by the descendants (-ing) of some founding ancestor-hero (personal name). Doddington (Cambridgeshire, Kent, Lincolnshire, Northumberland, Shropshire) for example, are the towns (town > ton) where the descendants of Dodda lived; Woking (Surrey) is the place where Wocca's people lived; Buckingham (Buckinghamshire) is the home (ham) of Bucca's people; Billingham (Stockton-on-Tees) is the home of Billa's people. *Dwaling*, therefore, would be the ancestral estate of the Family Dwala(koneis), i.e. the Tolkien Family Estate. (See "Dwaling" above.)

The name of **Miguel de Cervantes** (1547-1616) is one that inevitably arises in any discussion of the feigned-manuscript topos. His most famous work is *El Ingenioso Hidalgo Don Quijote de la Mancha* (The Ingenious Gentleman Don Quixote of La Mancha), more widely known simply as *Don Quixote* (published in two parts: 1605 and 1615). In the "Prologue," Cervantes calls himself the "stepfather, though I seem the father of Don Quixote,"[151]

---

[151] Miguel de Cervantes Saavedra, *The Ingenious Gentleman Don Quixote of La Mancha* (in four volumes), Henry Edward Watts (trans.), London: Adam and Charles Black, 1895, p. 6.

alluding to the fiction of the feigned-manuscript topos that the real author is the "sage and sagacious" (DQ1/XXVII) Arab historian named Cid Hamet Benengeli, whom Cervantes mentions at least 33 times in the course of the novel, often describing him in terms of lavish praise. He calls Benengeli the "flower of historians,"(DQ2/LXI) "a historian of great research and accuracy in all things, as is very evident since he would not pass over in silence those that have been already mentioned, however trifling and insignificant they might be, an example that might be followed by those grave historians who relate transactions so curtly and briefly that we hardly get a taste of them, all the substance of the work being left in the inkstand from carelessness, perverseness, or ignorance"(DQ1/XVI). In chapter III of Part II, he asks "A blessing on Cid Hamet Benengeli, who has written the history of your great deeds, and a double blessing on that connoisseur who took the trouble of having it translated out of the Arabic into our Castilian vulgar tongue for the universal entertainment of the people!" (DQ2/III).

The punch line for the joke told above is the same as the one told by Hawthorne. The name of Cervantes' 'historian' is the translation of *Cervantes* into Arabic.[152] The name *Benengeli* is interpreted to mean "son of a stag," the Arabic element *ben* being the same as the Irish and Scottish element *mac*: "son of." In Spanish surnames, the meaning of "son of" is carried by the suffix *-ez*. (*Cervantes* is also attested as *Cervantez*.) *Sanchez*, for example, is 'the son of Sancho.' The closest first name in common modern use is *Cervando*. In his biography of Cervantes, Ormsby observes that the family castle near Toledo was named Cervatos.[153] This is the plural of the modern Spanish word *cervato*, meaning *fawn*, the son (or daughter) of a stag. The coat of arms of the Cervantes family is emblazoned with two gold stags[154]

---

[152] Miguel de Cervantes Saavedra, *The Ingenious Gentleman Don Quixote of La Mancha* (in four volumes), Henry Edward Watts (trans.), London: Adam and Charles Black, 1895, p. 115, note. and <www.bibliomania.com/2/3/174/1112/15814/1.html>. LVO 2/23/2006.

[153] John Ormsby (trans.), <www.web-books.com/Classics/Nonfiction/Biography/Cervantes/Home.htm>. LVO 2/23/2006.

[154] Miguel de Cervantes Saavedra, *The Ingenious Gentleman*

trippant in pale on an azure background. In modern Spanish, the word for *stag* is *ciervo*, and the word for *doe* is *cierva*. In Latin, the word for *stag* is *cervus*. In French it is *le cerf*.

Don Quixote is a parody of the chivalric romances of Cervantes' time. Most modern readers are not familiar enough with the target of Cervantes' parody to see the humor of it, but the Watts translation (1895) has a number of appendices that help make it more understandable.[155] In his section on "The Provençal Romances," Watts observes that this class of chivalric romances is characterized by the fact that nearly all of them have "an original author—Arab, Portuguese, English, or other barbarian—and a translator" (p. 335), pointing to the widespread use of the feigned-manuscript topos at that time in this genre in Spanish.

In the "Preface" to his first novel, *Sir Quixote of the Moors: Being some Account of an Episode in the Life of the Sieur de Rohaine* (1895)[156], **John Buchan** (1875-1940) informs the reader that the narrative in the book was written in English by a gentleman of France, Sieur de Rohaine, "for two reasons: first, as an exercise in the language; second, because he desired to keep the passages here recorded from the knowledge of certain of his kinsfolk in France" (p. 7). As its name suggests, the novel is indeed a chivalric romance, and though Watts' characteristic elements of the genre have been slightly modified, they are all there. The "original author" is a foreigner who offers the reader a different point of view of a situation that is familiar to the reader, but he speaks English well enough to do his own translation. Buchan—like

---

Don Quixote of La Mancha (in four volumes), Henry Edward Watts (trans.), London: Adam and Charles Black, 1895, p. 115, note.

[155] Miguel de Cervantes Saavedra, *The Ingenious Gentleman Don Quixote of La Mancha* (in four volumes), Henry Edward Watts (trans.), London: Adam and Charles Black, 1895, pp. 323-370: A - "The Romances of Chivalry," B - "The Story of Amadis," C - "The Family of Amadis," D - "El Paso Honoroso," E - "Dulcines Del Toboso," F - "La Mancha.".

[156] John Buchan, *Sir Quixote of the Moors: Being Some Account of an Episode in the Life of the Sieur de Rohaine*, London: T. Fisher Unwin, 1895.

Haggard, DeFoe, Dickens, Scott, and Swift—pretends to be the editor, distancing himself from any problems that the reader might discern in the text. He says that he has made few changes in the work, only occasionally substituting an English idiom for a French one, emending "certain tortuous expressions," and, in general, re-writing the portions of the book that were done in Scots dialect, "since the author's knowledge of this manner of speech seems scarcely to have been so great as he himself thought" (p. 8).

In the "Advertisement" prefixed to the first edition of *The Poems of Ossian*,[157] **James MacPherson** (1736-1796) identifies himself as "the translator" 4 times. The verdict of history on the controversy concerning "the authenticity of the poems," as MacPherson termed it in the "Advertisement," did not uphold that claim. In her introduction to the 1996 Edinburgh University Press edition, Fiona Stafford pronounces that "MacPherson drew on traditional sources to produce imaginative texts not modeled closely on any single identifiable original."[158] In her view, MacPherson's work is as much a cultural as a linguistic translation, interpreting "not only between Gaelic and English, but also between the oral culture of the depressed rural communities of the Scottish Highlands, and the prosperous urban centres of Lowland Britain, where the printed word was increasingly dominant."[159]

Stafford's comment prompts this reader to recall Tolkien's comment in "Note on the Shire Records," in which he says that The Shire's inclusion "in the Reunited Kingdom awakened among them a more widespread interest in their own history; and many of their traditions, up to that time still mainly oral, were collected

---

[157] James MacPherson, *Poems of Ossian* (Introduction by John MacQueen), Edinburgh: The Mercat Press, 1971, p. lvii-lviii. Copy no. 50 of a limited print run of 500 copies of the facsimile reproduction of the 1805 edition.

[158] Fiona Stafford, "Introduction: The Ossianic Poems of James MacPherson," in James MacPherson, *Poems of Ossian and Related Works* (Howard Gaskill ed.), Edinburgh: Edinburgh University Press, 1996, p. vii.

[159] Fiona Stafford, p. viii. (See also page xv.)

and written down" (F.37).

In his book on MacPherson, J.S. Smart says that the work is not a translation, but "is really MacPherson's. The older poetry vanished as he wrote, and a poetry which was his, the offspring of his own mind, took its place."[160] That means that MacPherson's role as the 'translator' of *The Poems of Ossian* is much the same as Tolkien's role as the 'translator' of *The Hobbit* and *LotR*, and as Elias Lönnrot's role in the creation of the *Kalevala*. MacPherson is, however, still considered a forger by many. In the library catalogue for my university, MacPherson is cross-indexed under the subject heading "Literary Forgeries and Mystifications," as is Chatterton.

Assertions by these authors that their works were based on old manuscripts that they had 'discovered' were not as improbable when they were first made as they seem to modern readers today. Old manuscripts were indeed being discovered and used by literary authors. The renowned 'Roman Murder Story'—*The Ring and the Book* (1868-69)—retold in narrative verse by **Robert Browning** (1812-1889) is based on an "Old Yellow Book" that Browning bought in Florence in 1860. It tells the story of the trail of Count Guido Franceschini and his coconspirators for the murder of the count's wife in December 1697. The authenticity of Browning's source has been proven by a facsimile reproduction and translation of the "Old Yellow Book" by Professor Charles W. Hodell,[161] a new annotated translation by John Marshall Gest,[162] and by an independent source—the *Cortona Codex*—that was translated by Beatrice Corrigan.[163] The fact that G.K.

---

[160] John Semple Smart, *James MacPherson: An Episode in Literature*, London: David Nutt, 1905, p. vii.

[161] Charles W. Hodell (ed. and tr.), *The Old Yellow Book: Source of Browning's The Ring and the Book*, in Complete Photo-Reproduction with Translation, Essay and Notes, [Washington, D.C.]: The Carnegie Institute of Washington, 1908.

[162] John Marshall Gest (ed. and tr.), *The Old Yellow Book: Source of Browning's The Ring and the Book*, New York, Haskell House, 1925.

[163] Beatrice Corrigan (ed. and tr.), *Curious Annals: New Documents Relating to Browning's Roman Murder Story*, [Toronto]:

Chesterton was well aware of *The Ring and the Book*, devoting a whole chapter to it in his book on Browning,[164] suggests that Tolkien would scarcely have been unaware of Browning's poem and its source.

The 1849 translation of *The Red Book of Hergest* by **Lady Charlotte Guest** (1812-1895), which is more widely known as *The Mabinogion*, is likewise of undoubted authenticity. *The Red Book of Hergest* is a Welsh manuscript known in Welsh as *Llyfr Coch Hergest*, which was written between 1375 and 1425. It is named for the color of its binding and for the location where it was formerly housed: Hergest Manor in Herefordshire. It is now housed in the library at Jesus College, Oxford. Tolkien's well-known love of Welsh suggests that he would have likewise been well-acquainted with the source of Lady Guest's translation.

For the Tolkiennymist, the coincidence of the names of the sources of Lady Charlotte Guest's and Tolkien's translations is striking: *The Red Book of Hergest* and *The Red Book of Westmarch*. Tolkien wanted to write (translate) a mythology for England, and Lady Charlotte Guest's work can easily be said to be a 'mythology for Wales.' The implication of this coincidence is intriguing.

To make matters more interesting, the 'source' of MacPherson's 'translation' of *The Poems of Ossian*, which one could construe as a 'mythology for Scotland,' was also an old red book, here called *The Red Book of Clanranald* to distinguish it from the other two. Quoting from the Highland Society's Report (1805) on MacPherson's work, Smart[165] relates the story of MacPherson's claim that there was an ancient manuscript, known as *The Red Book*, that was given to him by the bard (MacVuirich) of Clanranald, chief of a branch of the MacDonalds in South Uist. Smart notes that this was one of the things mentioned in almost every defense of Ossian. MacPherson's *Red Book* was eventually found, subsequently translated and returned to the

---

University of Toronto Press, 1956.

[164] G.K. Chesterton, *Robert Browning*, London: Macmillan and Co, 1951, pp. 160-176.

[165] Smart, pp. 167-169.

present Clanranald. To the chagrin of MacPherson supporters, it contains an account of the Montrose wars, in which the MacDonalds took part, some poems in Gaelic, but not so much as one line of *The Poems of Ossian*, relates Smart.

The resulting symmetry of three mythologies (for England, for Wales, for Scotland) all being connected to old red books (*The Red Book: of Westmarch, of Hergest, of Clanranald*) seems to defy the laws of chance and to suggest that it is the result of human artifice. It would have undoubtedly tickled Tolkien's sense of linguistic humor. It certainly tickled mine.

Tolkien's attention to this kind of detail is what gives his use of the feigned-manuscript topos its internally consistent feeling of depth and credibility. Unfortunately, factors external to the text do not support Tolkien's fiction, and it has come to be considered just a curious piece of decoration for his books instead of being recognized as the masterful application of an old literary topos that it is.

portal dolmen,
Poulnabrone, Burren,
Co. Clare, Éire

In a Hole in the Ground There Lived a ...

While most modern readers will immediately complete the title sentence for this article with "Hobbit," readers from the time before *The Hobbit* (B.H.) would have been more inclined to say that in a hole in the ground there lived a Neolithic man. The archeological studies of the Victorian Age were full of accounts of "pit dwellings," which can best be described as "a hole in the ground" with a beehive shaped thatched roof supported by a frame of intertwined branches.

The series of Histories of the Counties of England known as the Victoria Histories points to pit dwellings in Shropshire[166] and in Kent.[167] Pit dwellings were reported on Cardunnock, and in Bempton by Bulmer in his *History, Topography and Directory of*

---

[166] T. Auden, "Early Man," in *The Victoria History of Shropshire*, William Page (ed.), London: Archibald Constable and Co., 1908, vol. 1, p. 197.

[167] George Clinch, "Early Man," in *The Victoria History of Kent*, William Page (ed.), London: Archibald Constable and Co., 1908, vol. 1, pp. 315-317.

East Cumberland (1884)[168] and in his *History and Directory of East Yorkshire* (1892).[169] Joseph Stevens devotes an entire chapter to them in his book (1888) on the history of St. Mary Bourne.[170] Volume XI of the *Transactions of the British Archeological Association*[171] reports on pit dwellings on the Isle of Wight. The circular huts on the farm of Ty Mawr are discussed in W.O. Stanley's *Ancient Circular Dwellings in Holyhead Island*.[172] (1862) In his *The Annals of Dunfermline*,[173] Ebenezer Henderson (1809 -

---

[168] T.F. Bulmer, *History, Topography and Directory of East Cumberland*, Manchester: T. Bulmer & Co., 1884.

[169] T.F. Bulmer, *History and Directory of East Yorkshire*, Manchester: T. Bulmer & Co., 1892.

[170] Joseph Stevens. *A Parochial History of St. Mary Bourne with an Account of the Manor of Hurstbourne Priors*, London: Whiting and Co., 1888. (Latest issue containing the addenda of 1895.)

[171] Cited in Stevens, p. 26.

[172] W.O. Stanley, "Ancient Circular Dwellings in Holyhead Island," Archeologia, vol. xxvi; Journal of the British Archeological Association, vol. vii. Cited in Stevens, p. 27.

Stevens lists a number of other articles on pit dwellings in one of his foot notes:

A.C. Smith, *Guide to British and Roman Antiquities of North Wiltshire Downs*, 1884.

Stevens, "Pit Dwellings," Brighton and Sussex Natural History Society, 1872; also Nature, vol.v, 1872.

W.H. Cunnington, "British Dwelling-Pit at Beckhampton, Wilts," Archeological and Natural History Society, vol. xxiii, 1886.

Warne, Charles, 1802-1887. *Ancient Dorset*: The Durotriges. Their stone remains, earthworks, ..., with some account of the Roman, Saxon, and Danish antiquities: including--The ancient mints of the County of Dorset, Poole, 1870, p. 12.

---, Dorsetshire: Its Vestiges, Celtic, Roman, Saxon and Danish, London, 1865.

Spence Bate, "Prehistoric Antiquities of Dartmoor," *Journal of the Anthropological Institute*, July 1871.

Bateman, *Vestiges of Derbyshire*.

A. Hume, "Remarks on Querns," *Archeological Camb.*, Second Series, vol. iv, p. 89.

[173] Ebenezer Henderson (1809-1879), *The Annals of Dunfermline and Vicinity from the Earliest Authentic Period to the Present Time A.D. 1089-1878 Intersperced [sic]With Explanatory Notes, Memorabilia, and Numerous Illustrative Engravings*, Glasgow:

1879) talks of "clay and turf huts, hovels and pit-dwellings", the inhabitants of which "were little better than barbarians." Those were the days, says Henderson, quoting John Dryden (1631-1701) "When wild in woods the noble savage ran."[174]

A clear indication of Tolkien's interest in the prehistory of man during the time that he was working on *The Hobbit* can be seen in his 1932 *Father Christmas Letter*, in which he relates the story of how the North Pole Bear got lost in a cave and found again. In this letter, Tolkien reproduces the drawings on the wall of the chief central cave, and describes what they looked like. His description—less the goblins—is factually accurate, and would make a good summary for children. It contains a number of parallels to the specialist literature on the magnificent cave paintings in northern Spain and south-western France.

These decorated caves were only relatively recently discovered. The Spanish cave at Altamira was only discovered in 1879, but the authenticity of the paintings was hotly debated until 1902, when the last of the major critics of the find finally admitted that he was wrong. In 1903 a young French priest named Henri Breuil (1877-1961) went to Altamira, and began making copies of the paintings. With his arrival, prehistoric art had found its patron. His books[175] and copies of the drawings and paintings made the world aware of the treasures in the cave. He was considered the foremost expert on cave painting, not just on those in Spain, but on those in France as well.

South West France is home to 147 prehistoric sites dating to the Paleolithic era and 25 decorated caves. There seems to be a predominance of one or two animal species among the animals depicted in each of the decorated caves, which gives them a distinctive motif. The cave at Rouffignac (first mentioned in 1575) is especially famous for its paintings and carvings of woolly mammoths and rhinos. Pech-Merle (discovered in 1922) is noted

---

J. Tweed, 1879. Published on the Web at www.tulbol.demon.co.uk/dunfermline/annals1.htm. LVO 2/23/2006.

[174] John Dryden (1631-1701) *The Conquest of Granada*. Part i. Act i. Sc. 1.

[175] H. Breuil. *Four Hundred Centuries of Cave Art*, (Translated from the French by M.E. Boyle), Montignac, 1952.

for its bisons and mammoths; Lascaux for its horse, aurochs and deer. Tolkien's copy of the wall of the chief central cave has a predominance of woolly mammoths: there are four. One of these has a remarkable resemblance to a copy of one of the cave drawings made by Breuil.[176] The trunks are almost identical. Tolkien's lifelike—as opposed to schematic—horse also bears a striking likeness to a drawing[177] of a horse found in Rouffignac. Unsurprisingly, since Rouffignac is known for its rhinos, there is an especially woolly rhino in Tolkien's picture too.

Another parallel between Tolkien's story in his 1932 *Father Christmas Letter* and the cave at Rouffignac is the cave bear, who is so common in the specialist literature that he even has a Latin name (ursus spelaeus). It was the bears who first used the caves and entirely covered the walls with long scratches, says not only Tolkien, but also the specialist literature on the cave.

Because of his detailed interest in the cave art of prehistoric man, Tolkien would almost certainly also have known that the prehistoric inhabitants of England lived in "pit dwellings, exchanging them as time went by for stone huts above ground," as T. Auden put it in his contribution to *The Victoria History of Shropshire* (Auden 197).

The quote from Auden's chapter above seems almost mirrored in Tolkien's history of the Hobbits. "All Hobbits had originally lived in holes in the ground, or so they believed, and in such dwellings they still felt most at home; but in the course of time they had been obliged to adopt other forms of abode" (F.25-26). The burrows of the poorest Hobbits, Tolkien continues, were "mere holes indeed," lacking windows altogether or only having one. Tolkien's description of the architecture of Hobbit houses closely parallels the descriptions of pit dwellings to be found in accounts of the "early men" of England. "The oldest kind were no more than built imitations of smials, thatched with dry grass or straw, or roofed with turves, and having walls that

---

[176] P.M. Grand. *Prehistoric Art: Paleolithic Painting and Sculpture*, vol. III of the Pallas Library of Art, Greenwich, Conneticut: New York Graphic Soviety, 1967, p. 22, illustration 25.b.

[177] Ann Sieveking. *The Cave Artists*, London: Thames and Hudson Ltd., 1979, p. 8, illustration 2.

somewhat bulged," says Tolkien (F.27). Stevens, for example, describes the pit dwellings at St. Mary Bourne as having "their substructures of flint, on which perhaps were placed conical roofs composed of rafters lashed together at the centre, and protected by an outside coat of peat, sods of turf, or rushes. Some of these dwellings might have been constructed of wattles plastered with mud or clay" (Stevens 36).

In his history of Hampshire (1909), Telford Varley proudly describes a settlement of the prehistoric inhabitants of the county, who lived in "curious underground dwellings ... of circular form ... with passages leading to them underground, something like the underground entrances of a modern Eskimo 'mansion'".[178] The tantalizing description could lead one (Tolkien, perhaps) to believe that these remains were from a Hobbit smial of the Third Age. The use of the word "circular" is at first suggestive of Tolkien's "perfectly round" door to Bag End (H.15; I). The description in the original source, cited by Varley, is somewhat less grand, though much more detailed.

The original source is Joseph Stevens' chapter on the pit dwellings discovered at Hurstbourne rail siding near St. Mary Bourne. It too, nevertheless, has some tantalizing Tolkienesque descriptions of the pit dwellings. They were situated "along the brow of the hill," which evokes images of The Hill in Hobbiton. "Circularity of outline and central fireplaces" are also features that Stevens calls attention to that have a certain "Hobbit ring" to them.

Stevens' narrative is accompanied by a sketch of the site dated September 23, 1871. Dwelling number 1 on the sketch (middle, upper right) is pear-shaped, with its entrance opening to the south. The walls of the pit and the entrance way were pitched with flint stones without the use of mortar. The distance from the entrance to the back wall was 22 feet. At its widest point, the pit was 12 feet across. At the center, it was 4 feet deep.

Pits 2 and 3 could not be completely examined because they extended into station property. The entrances to pits 4 and

---

[178] Telford Varley, *Hampshire*, London: Adam & Charles Black, 1909, p. 207.

5 also pointed south. They, like pits 2 and 3, could not be explored because they were under the station road. Stevens identifies the number 6 on the sketch as an entrance way that was apparently never completed.

Pit 7 was completely examined. Its entrance opened to the east, and was 3 feet wide. The distance from the mouth of the entrance way to the back of the dwelling was 42 feet, and the pit itself was 13.5 feet at its widest point. Like pit 1, it was 4 feet deep at the center.

Pit 8, an almost circular hole, is thought to have been a kitchen.

One of the key features of the site is the sloped passageways that serve as entrances. Stevens notes that they had not previously been observed in England, although they had been found at sites in France.

Tolkien hints at Auden and Henderson again later in his tale at the council between Theoden and the Wild Man. In pointing out the antiquity of his people and their knowledge of the territory, the Wild Man says that they know the lay of the land well, having lived on this land since "before Stonehouses; before Tall Men come up out of Water" (R.129; V.5). With this comment, Tolkien touches deftly and subtly on the course of English history.

In this short piece of dialog, Tolkien is hinting at a time when stone houses did not exist, at a time "When wild in woods the noble savage ran." He is also hinting at the great migrations of peoples that swept across the English isles. The race of man that inhabited Neolithic England was short and had long skulls (dolichocephalic). Human remains with this skull type are to be found in many parts of England, Wales and Scotland. They were Iberians, whose most likely modern-day relations are the Basques. They were displaced by a race of tall men with round skulls (brachycephalic), whose arrival ushered in the Bronze Age. It was the descendants of this taller race who met Caesar's legions when they came ashore in England. These are the Celts, who came in two waves. The first was the Goidels, who were, in turn, driven west by the incursion of the Brythons.

Diagram of Pit-Dwellings at Hurstbourne Siding

Tolkien's description of the Wild Man sounds intriguingly like the ones in the Victoria histories of Shropshire and Northhampton by Auden and T.J. George. Tolkien describes the Wild Man as "short-legged" with "short, gnarled," "fat" arms, a "thick and stumpy" stature and a "flat face and dark eyes" (R.129, 130; V.5). George describes Neolithic man as averaging 5 feet 5 inches in height, with a long skull. "Their faces were oval and rather short; their features good, with flat cheekbones, fine jaws and prominent chins. They were evidently dark of skin, hair and eyes."[179] Auden gives a complementary picture, citing Dawkins' book *Early Man in Britain*.[180] The Iberians "were short of stature—the men not exceeding 5 feet 6 inches—and thick-set in figure, their special characteristic being the length of their skull ... The outline of the face was oval and the jaws did not project, but the forehead was comparatively low and the nose was aquiline." Their descendants are still to be found in several parts of England, especially in South Wales, continues Auden. Using the appearance of the modern representatives of the Iberians in Wales and Shropshire as a guide, Auden completes the picture. "They had black hair and black eyes, and except for the shortness of their stature were a handsome race, possessed of considerable mental capacity."

Auden's comment on their mental capacity is echoed by Tolkien in the same dialog between the Wild Man and Theoden. When Éomer asks how the Wild Man knows that the Orcs outnumber them, the Wild Man's sullen voice expresses his displeasure at being thought of as unintelligent, and Theoden reinforces the implication of the Wild Man's response by calling him shrewd (R.130; V.5). Tolkien's close to the dialog is a sad comment on the fate of the Iberians at the hands of the Celts. When offered a reward for his help, the Wild Man says that his

---

[179] T.J. George, "Early Man," in *The Victoria History of Northhampton*, W. Ryland D. Adkins and R.M. Serjeantson (eds.), London: Archibald Constable and Co., 1902, vol. 1, p. 137.

[180] Dawkins, William Boyd (1838-1929). *Early Man in Britain and His Place in the Tertiary Period*, London: Macmillan and Co., 1880, pp. 311-316. Cited in Auden, p. 196.

only wish is that the Rohirrim "leave Wild Men alone in the woods and do not hunt them like beasts any more" (R.131; V.5).

The fact that the indigenous name of the original inhabitants of Scotland was *Caeoill daoin* ("the people of the woods"),[181] which the Romans changed to *Caledonia*, offers an intriguing suggestion as to the origins of both the Wild Men and the element *-dan* in Dunedan.

The Tall Men who came up out of the water represent not only the Celts who displaced the Iberians, but also the Anglo-Saxons, who displaced the Celts. Rohirric was, after all, based on Anglo-Saxon. Auden also has a description for them. "[T]heir faces were angular, their jaws were prominent, and their cheekbones stood out under a high broad forehead. Their height averaged 5 feet 8 inches, and we know from their modern representatives, who are to be seen everywhere in Wales and the borderland, that they had fair complexions with red hair and blue eyes" (Auden 196, see also George 140). Tolkien describes the Riders of Rohan as having yellow, flaxen-pale hair (T.39, 40; III.2) and their leader as "very tall," "a tall man, taller than the rest" (T.39, 41; III.2), as befits their Anglo-Saxon heritage.

This is not the only borrowing from the real history of England in Tolkien's Legendarium. The founders of The Shire were the brothers Marcho and Blanco, who offer an interesting close parallel to the brothers Hengist and Horsa, called "Woden's great-grandsons" by the poet John Lesslie Hall (1856-1928). Hengist and Horsa came to England in the mid fifth century to become the founders of Anglo-Saxon England. The names of both the Anglo-Saxon and the Hobbit brothers mean *horse* in one form or another. *Hengist* means *stallion* in OE and a close linguistic relative of this word can still be seen in Dutch today where *hengst* still means *stallion*. *Horsa*—a form that is transparent for the modern English speaker—is OE for *horse*. Marcho is derived from the OE *mearh*, which survives in modern English as *mare*, in Welsh as *march* (*stallion*) and *marchoglu* (*cavalry*). It can also be seen in Gaelic as *marc* and in Cornish as *marh*. Blanco can be traced to the OE *blanca* (white [horse]), the most famous of

---

[181] Thomas Morgan. *Handbook of the Origin of Place Names in Wales and Monmouthshire*, Merthyr Tydfil, 1997, p. 19.

which is the Uffington White Horse.

The Uffington White Horse is one of England's oldest and most famous hill figures. Carved out of the turf on the chalky upper slopes of the hill, it is 374 feet long, and is recognizable only from the air. Some sources contend that the Uffington horse commemorates Alfred's victory over the Danes in 861 A.D. Yet others maintain that it represents the horse on Hengist's standard. Modern dating techniques, however, place the date of the figure at over 3,000 years, handily discounting both Alfred and Hengist. This date points more in the direction of it being a representation of the Celtic horse goddess Epona. Similar horses can be seen depicted on Celtic jewelry and Iron-age coins. A coin discovered by Stevens in the St. Mary Bourne pit dwellings has a horse on its reverse side. A smooth portion of a rib bone with the head and forepart of a horse inscribed on it with a sharp tool was found in the Robin Hood Cave in Derbyshire (George 136). There is also evidence of horse worship by the Celts in the Iron Age.

Since Middle-earth is a place not of body, but of mind, its artifacts are equally ethereal. Even when they can be found, their purport remains open to interpretation. The cite and the site may have influenced Tolkien, but only he knows that. One of the key things that makes Tolkien's work so enduring is its resonances with the real world, both coincidental and intentional. They offer the reader a background so detailed as to make Niggle's leaves seem like they were done by an impressionist.

In a Fogou in the Ground There Lived a Cornish Hobbit

Fogou is one of the few Cornish words that has made its way into English. It is primarily found in the field of archeology, where it is used to designate a type of man-made, stone-lined, corbelled underground chamber that is found in Cornwall, particularly on the south west tip of Cornwall, the Lizard peninsula. The original Cornish word *ifócw* meant *cave*. Its counterpart in Welsh is *ogof*, which was derived from *o'r cof*. This root can be seen in a number of potentially related words like *cof* = memory, remembrance, *cofeb* = memorial, **cofaint* = memorial, *cofio* = to remember and **cofnod* = monument.

Due to its antiquity, the original purpose of the fogou is unknown. Fogou-s generally have a single, narrow, low-ceilinged entrance that opens into a larger room that could accommodate a fair number of people. The apparent nest of meanings around the word *cof* (memory) in Welsh suggests a ritual usage. Other uses seem counterindicated by the construction of the fogou. It was unsuitable for a defensive structure or as a hiding place. There was no other way out than via the narrow front crawl-way, and that would have made them death-traps for those inside in the event of an attack. The constriction of the crawl-way also makes it unlikely that fogou-s were used to house cattle. It is likewise unlikely that fogou-s were used for storage, as the dampness of the chambers would have ruined anything stored in them.

There is only a limited number of fogou-s left in Cornwall that the inquisitive reader might yet visit. There used to be a great number more, but they were destroyed, apparently as a convenient source of stone for building. There is the Boleigh Fogou, near Land's End, one of the best preserved; the Halligye Fogou, near Mullion (get a big town); the Carn Euny Iron-age village Fogou, near Sancreed; the Higher Boden Fogou, near St. Anthony-in-Meneage; the Pendeen Fogou, near Pendeen Manor House; Pixie's Hall Fogou, near Constantine; the Chysauster Iron-age-village Fogou, near Penzance.

The generic term for underground structures like the fogou is "Souterrain". Unlike the souterrains found in Ireland, Scotland and Brittany, fogou-s are always found together with a settlement or defensive earthwork. In Scotland similar structures are known as "Earth Houses" and "Pict Houses".

Whatever their names, it is clear that structures like fogou-s were used for habitation extensively across Europe, which increases the probability that Tolkien was aware of their existence. Therefore, with a little linguistic imagination and tongue placed firmly in cheek, it is easy to posit that the Cornish word for *smial* is *fogou*. Of course, before a Hobbit moved into one of the currently existing ones, he would have to have the builders over to pretty it up a bit.

A Tale of Tolkien's Woods

Tolkien uses the word *staff* 73 times in *The Hobbit* and *The Lord of the Rings*. Despite there being a large number of uses of the word *staff*, only three of these uses specify what type of wood the staff is made of.

To the modern reader this may be just a superfluous detail of little significance, but in an earlier time when people felt more connected to nature, it was a detail of considerable significance. Tolkien's studied attention to trees throughout the story—for example, the Two Trees, Old Man Willow, Treebeard and the Ents—shows that he had a vast knowledge of tree lore. His attention to the details of the logical flow of his tale suggests that the three types of wood used to make these staffs were not chosen at random, but were intended to convey some additional information of interest to those whose knowledge of tree lore was sufficient to interpret them.

The first staff to be associated with a type of wood is the staff of the Elvenking. He sits on a throne of carven wood and holds a "carven staff of oak" (H.168; IX). The second staff is Gandalf's. In Frodo's commemorative poem about Gandalf, written after Gandalf's Fall in Moria, Gandalf's staff is identified as being of thorn-wood. (F.466; II.7) The third staff is also

Gandalf's, but it is apparently a new staff given to him when he returned to Middle-earth as the White Rider, having "passed through the fire and the abyss" (T.133; III.5) This third staff is made of ash-wood (T.147; III.6).

In Celtic myth, a place where an Oak, an Ash and a Thorn grow in close proximity is a magical one. D.A. MacManus mentions this traditional triad of trees in his book on "the Faerie World of Ireland" (1959). The title of the book even has a Tolkienesque ring to it: *The Middle Kingdom*.[182] "In Ireland," explains MacManus, "the world of *Shee* (*Sidhe*), that is of the faeris [sic] and all those spirits which are elemental and have never been human, was called The Middle Kingdom" (p. 15).

MacManus compliments Rudyard Kipling (1865-1936) on his knowledge of the tree lore about the triad of *Oak, Ash and Thorn*,[183] which Kipling used in his children's historical fantasy set in Sussex, that was published in 1906: *Puck of Pook's Hill*.[184] There, Puck uses "by Oak, Ash, and Thorn!" as an asseveration, in the way that some people might say "by Jove," or "by George," or "by Gosh," when he comes across the children on midsummer's eve doing their abbreviated version of Shakespeare's *Midsummer Night's Dream*. By doing it three times in a row, they have invoked Puck. The number three is significant in Celtic tradition and we will return to it shortly.

Puck is the last of the people of the hills and "oldest Old Thing in England," a description that makes him sound somewhat like Tom Bombadil, whom Elrond describes as "oldest and fatherless" (F.347; II.2). All the rest of the 'Old Things' have left England and Puck is the only one remaining. Puck "came into England with Oak, Ash and Thorn, and when Oak, Ash and Thorn are gone [he] shall go too." Bombadil, on the other hand, was in Middle-earth "before the river and the trees," and

---

[182] Diarmuid A. MacManus. *The Middle Kingdom*, London: Parrish, 1959.

[183] MacManus, p. 53.

[184] Rudyard Kipling. *Puck of Pook's Hill*. Those who would like to see the quotes in context are referred to Project Gutenberg's eText at: <www.gutenberg.org/etext/557>. It is fully searchable. LVO 2/23/2006.

remembers the first acorn (F.182; I.7). Because Puck likes the children of Kipling's story—they were nice to him and shared their food with him—he gives the children a boon of magical sight, by invoking the "right of Oak, Ash, and Thorn."

When Puck sends the children back to the adults, he wisely gives each of them three leaves to chew, one each of Oak, Ash and Thorn. The leaves make them forget their adventures with Puck, because otherwise they might tell the adults about Puck, and if he knows "human beings - they'd send for the doctor."

In the collection of songs from all his works,[185] Kipling repeats the entire text of the "Tree Song" from *Puck of Pook's Hill* and dates it to A.D. 1200.

Charles Kingsley (1819-1875) also invokes the power of Oak and Ash and Thorn in his novel *Westward Ho!, or, the voyages and adventures of Sir Amyas Leigh, Knight, of Burrough, in the county of Devon, in the reign of her most glorious majesty Queen Elizabeth* (1855).[186] When Sir Richard Grenville's godson comes to his house to announce that his father is dead and that Sir Richard must be his father now, Sir Richard "swore a great and holy oath, like Glasgerion's, 'by oak, and ash, and thorn,' that he would" (Chapter II).

The Glasgerion to whom he refers is the subject of a ballad found in Thomas Percy's *Reliques of Ancient English Poetry* (1765), which is one of the cornerstones of English Literature. It is a collection of historical and lyrical ballads that give definition to what is regarded as the canon of popular English poetry. Glasgerion is also mentioned in Chaucer's *The Canterbury Tales* and in the ballad:

> Glasgerion swore a full great oath
>   By oak and ash and thorn,
> 'Lady, I was never in your chamber
>   Sith the time that I was born.'— (XVII)[187]

---

[185] Rudyard Kipling. *Songs from Books*, London: Macmillan and Co., 1914. </www.gutenberg.org/etext/15529>. LVO 2/23/2006.

[186] <www.gutenberg.org/dirs/etext99/wstho10.zip>. LVO 2/23/2006.

[187] Sir Arthur Quiller-Couch, ed. (1863–1944). *The Oxford Book*

Triplism is a prominent feature of Celtic and Nordic tradition. It can be seen in the archeological evidence as images with three heads or cojoined faces. In textual sources, it is seen as three names for a single deity, each name reflecting a different aspect of the deity's power or domain, such as the one that was, the one that is and the one that will be. The Norns, for example, who tend Yggdrasil, are three sisters who each look into a different time, either the Past, the Present, or the Future. Their names were Urd (the Past), Verdandi (the Present) and Skuld (the Future). In the Celtic tradition, Cernunnos, Genius Cucullatus and Iunones are deities whose statuary displays triplistic symbolism.[188]

Try as it may, the Christian Church failed to completely eradicate the old triplistic gods. Some of them became the three-headed giants and others became the three-headed dragons that still are found from time to time in folktales and folklore. Others were co-opted into the Christian tradition, where triplism is represented by the Holy Trinity: The Father, Son and Holy Ghost.

It is not surprising, therefore, to see a triad of trees considered to be of special significance. If Celtic/Nordic triplism, in which the traits of the members of the triad are often seen to overlap, is applied to the triad of Oak, Ash and Thorn in the same way that it was applied to the Celtic and Nordic gods in human form, then each of the types of tree would represent a different aspect of a single sacred tree. The reverence accorded to this triad of trees through swearing oaths by them would seem to make the Tree of Life a likely candidate to be represented by the triad.

The Folk-lore of Plants (1889)[189] by T.F. Thiselton-Dyer (1848-1929) details some interesting overlaps in the mythical characteristics of the trees of the triad that suggest that they could be aspects of a single sacred tree. Thiselton-Dyer notes

---

of Ballads, Oxford: The Clarendon Press, 1910.
<http://bartleby.school.aol.com/243/40.html>. LVO 2/23/2006.

[188] Miranda Green. *Dictionary of Celtic Myth and Legend*, New York: Thames and Hudson, 1992, pp. 60, 72, 104-105, 126.

[189] Thomas Firminger Thiselton-Dyer. *The Folk-lore of Plants*, London: Chatto & Windus, Piccadilly, 1889.
<http://www.gutenberg.org/etext/10118>. LVO 2/23/2006.

that while Yggdrasil, the Tree of Life of Nordic tradition, is an Ash, Thorpe[190] believes that the Tree of Life is "identical with the 'Robur Jovis,' or sacred oak of Geismar," which was cut down by Saint Boniface (c. 672-754[5] A.D.) near the present-day town of Fritzlar in northern Hessen, in 723 A.D.. The same assertion is made by Ellis-Davidson.[191]

A number of traditions hold that man was descended from trees. Thiselton-Dyer points to the Roman and Greek traditions in which men were thought to be the descendants of both the Oak and the Ash. To demonstrate this he quotes Virgil (70-19 B.C.) from *The AEneid*:

> These woods were first the seat of sylvan powers,
>
> Of nymphs and fauns, and savage men who took
>
> Their birth from trunks of trees and stubborn oak.

He continues by quoting Juvenal (c. 60 - c. 40 A.D.), from his sixth satire:

> For when the world was new, the race that broke
>
> Unfathered, from the soil or opening oak,
>
> Lived most unlike the men of later times.

The Greek tradition is represented by a quote from Homer (c. 900 - c. 850 B.C.). In *The Odyssey*, the disguised hero is interrogated about his origins, because he does not appear to "come of the oak told of in old times, nor of the rock."[192]

For the Ash, Thiselton-Dyer points to the Greek poet Hesiod

---

[190] Thiselton-Dyer cites Thorpe's *Northern Mythology, Comprising the Principal Popular Traditions and Superstitions of Scandinavia, North Germany, and the Netherlands*, London: E. Lumley, 1851, i. 154-5.

[191] Hilda Roderick Ellis Davidson, *Gods and Myths of Northern Europe*, Baltimore: Penguin Books, 1964, p. 191.

[192] Thiselton-Dyer cites Walter Keating Kelly's *Curiosities of Indo-European Tradition and Folk-lore*, London: Chapman & Hall, 1863, p. 143.

(8th century B.C.), who said that "Jove made the third or brazen race out of ash trees." He continues with a quote from Hesychius (of Alexandria, 5th century A.D.), who calls "the fruit of the ash the race of men." Phoroneus, the first man of Grecian legend, notes Thiselton-Dyer, was "born of the ash."

In the Nordic tradition, represented by the Eddas, man and woman were created from two tree trunks. The trunk of the Ash-tree became the man Askr, while the other trunk became the woman Embla. In the same tradition, the World Ash-tree Yggdrasil connects Asgard, Earth and Hel.

While the Oak is the tree normally associated with Thor and various other lightning gods, Thiselton-Dyer has a whole chapter on "Lightning Plants" and all three trees of the triad are included in it. In Aryan Indo-European tradition, he notes, the White-thorn was "originally sprung from the lightning."[193] Citing an old couplet—"Avoid an ash / It courts the flash"—as his authority, he also includes the Ash. Palmer has another version of Thiselton-Dyer's couplet that treats all three trees at once, offering advice for those caught by a thunderstorm while out in the open.[194]

> Beware of the oak it draws the stroke;
> Avoid the ash it courts the flash;
> Creep under the thorn it can save you from harm.

The association of the Oak with fairies is supported by the well-known, old rhyming proverb: "Turn your cloaks / Fairy Folks are in old oaks." The first phrase is a reminder that wearing one's clothes inside-out was considered a protection against fairies. The sense of this proverb is supported by Thiselton-Dyer's report of a German belief that the holes in an Oak are "the pathways for elves."[195] In Brittany, reports Thiselton-Dyer, old

---

[193] See also W.G. Wood-Martin. *Traces of the Elder Faiths of Ireland* (in two volumes), London: Longmans, Green and Co., 1902, vol. 2, p. 156. He seems to be quoting Thiselton-Dyer.

[194] Roy Palmer. *Britain's Living Folklore*, London: David & Charles, 1991, p. 158.

and solitary Thorn trees growing in sheltered hollows of the moorland "are the fairies' trysting-places."[196] He continues that, in Brittany and in some parts of Ireland, the Hawthorn is popularly known as "the fairy-thorn." MacManus confirms the association with fairies for all three, the Oak, Ash and Thorn. He, in fact, has a whole chapter on "Fairy Trees" in his book (pp. 51-63).

In his book *Lucks and Talismans* (1934), Charles R. Beard devotes a whole chapter[197] to "Stocks," the OE word for *tree*, in which he examines the role of trees as royal, tribal talismans. Beard tells of the "inauguration trees" of the Irish kings, who, in an earlier time—before the Tudors (1485-1603) introduced hereditary lords—were elected to their office under the ancient trees, that represented "the tutelary deity of the tribe" (p. 136). Branches from these trees were used for the king's scepter,[198] a synonym for staff, according to the Hastings *Dictionary of the Bible*, which remarks that "the long scepter is simply an ornamented staff" (p. 417).[199]

These trees were known in Irish as a "bile," and their presence can still be felt in place names like *Lisnabilla* in Antrim and *Rathvilly* in Carlow, both of which mean "the fortress of the Ancient Tree."[200] In his *Traces of the Elder Faiths of Ireland* (1902), Wood-Martin uses the place name *Billatinny* as an example, which he glosses as "the old" or "sacred tree of the fire" (vol. 2, p. 158).

---

[195] Thiselton-Dyer cites Conway's "Mystic Trees and Flowers," *Blackwood's Magazine*, 1870, p. 594.

[196] Thiselton-Dyer cites "Sacred Trees and Flowers," *Quarterly Review*, July 1863, pp. 231, 232.

[197] Charles R. Beard, *Lucks and Talismans*, London: Sampson Low, Marston, 1934, pp. 130-149.

[198] Patricia Monaghan. *The Encyclopedia of Celtic Mythology and Folklore*, New York: Facts on File, 2004. p. 45.

[199] *A Dictionary of the Bible* (in 5 volumes), James Hastings (ed.), Edinburgh: T. & T. Clark, 1902, vol. 4, p. 613 (*Staff*: see *Rod* and *Scepter*), p. 291 (*Rod*), pp. 416-417 (*Scepter*).

[200] Beard, p. 136. See also P.W. Joyce. *The Origin and History of Irish Place Names*, Dublin: McGlashan and Gill, 1871, whom Beard seems to be quoting, pp. 481-483.

"Beneath these sacred trees the petty kings of ancient Ireland were installed and it would seem to have been accepted that the life of the king and possibly, by an easily understood extension, the survival of his line was bound up in that of the tree" (p. 136). When a tribe was conquered, the 'victors' would chop down the tribe's tree and cut it into pieces. Since these trees were considered the *Crann Bethadh* (Tree of Life), says Ellis in his *Dictionary of Irish Mythology*,[201] destroying the tree would have been a grave blow to the vanquished enemy tribe.

Though the use of Coats of Arms is probably no older than the time of Henry II (1154-1189),[202] Oaks are the most common tree in British Armory.[203] When the blazon of a Coat of Arms states "a tree" without specification of the type of tree, the Oak is to be understood.[204]

Following the Battle of Worcester (1651), the story of Charles II (1630-1685) hiding in an Oak to escape capture became a part of the national consciousness, and the Oak Leaf became a symbol to be worn on Charles II's birthday (29 May). This day came to be known as Oak Apple Day.[205] The custom of wearing oak leaves in one's button hole continued in the U.K. until into the late 1940s.[206] The tradition of Royal Oak Day was still alive enough in the 1990s to be included in *Goodnight, Sweetheart*, a successful, prime-time British TV series.

After the defeat of James II (1633-1701) by William III (1650-1702) in the "Glorious Revolution" (1688-1689), a commemorative medal was minted that showed two trees.[207]

---

[201] Peter Beresford Ellis. *A Dictionary of Irish Mythology*, Santa Barabara, CA: ABC-CLIO, 1987, p. 186.

[202] Thomas Woodcock and John Martin Robinson. *The Oxford Guide to Heraldry*, Oxford: The University Press, 1988, p. 187.

[203] John Woodward. *Woodward's A Treatise on Heraldry: British and Foreign*, Rutland, VT: Charles E. Tuttle and Co., 1969, p. 315.

[204] Julian Franklyn and John Tanner. *An Encyclopedic Dictionary of Heraldry*, Oxford: Pergamon Press, 1970, p. 331.

[205] Jacqueline Simpson and Steve Round. *A Dictionary of English Folklore*, Oxford: The University Press, 2000, p. 302.

[206] Palmer, p. 113.

One of them was an oak tree with a broken trunk. It symbolized the defeat of James II, the brother and successor of Charles II. The other tree was an orange tree fully laden with fruit. It symbolized the victory of William III of the house of Orange, of William-and-Mary fame.

In his *The Origin and History of Irish Place Names*, Joyce[208] comments that the root for *Oak* (*doire*) was one of the most productive place-name elements in Ireland, as it appears in the beginning of over 1300 names, and a great many others end with it (vol. 1, p. 487). This gives a good idea, Joyce says, of how abundant the tree was in the past.

In her book on Welsh folklore, Marie Trevelyan remarks on the pre-eminence of the Oak and the reverence with which it was held by the Druids.[209] The Ash, she continues, was the next most important tree.[210] Wood-Martin has an illustration of a huge Ash-tree, known as the "Big Bell Tree,"[211] very probably, as Wood-Martin points out elsewhere,[212] an Anglicization of the Irish word *Bile*. Trevelyan observes that because Ash was a "charmed wood," it was invariably used by Welsh Bards to carve their *coelbren* (literally: omen wood) on.[213]

The association between wood, writing and knowledge can still be found in the vocabulary of Welsh, where the word for

---

[207] Geoge L. Craik. *The Pictorial History of England, Being a History of the People as Well as a History of the Kingdom* (in X volumes), London: W&R Chambers, 1841, p. 29.

[208] P.W. Joyce. *The Origin and History of Irish Place Names* (in 3 volumes), Dublin: McGlashan and GIll, 1871.

[209] Marie Trevelyan. *Folk-lore and Folk-stories of Wales*, London: Elliotstock, 1909, p. 101.

[210] Trevelyan, p. 102.

[211] Wood-Martin, vol. 2, p. 159.

[212] Wood-Martin, vol. 2, p. 154.

[213] Trevelyan, p. 102.

alphabet is Yr Wyddor, which is related to the word *gwydd* (*woods, trees*) > *gwyddin* (*wooden*). The initial '**G**' is lost when preceded by an article (*yr*) through the process of lenition in Welsh. The root of this word produced a number of other words related to wisdom and learning, like *gwyddon* (*wizard, scientist*), *gwyddionol* (*scientific*) and *gwyddoniadur* (*encyclopedia*). The most probable explanation of this linguistic relationship is the story of how Odin gained the knowledge of the Runes (writing). According to legend, Odin hung "on the windy tree" for nine full nights in exchange for the Runes. It is commonly held that "the windy tree" was the Ash Yggdrasil.

MacManus reports an interesting folk belief that 'ties' the three trees together to create an amulet that would protect the bearer "against any hostile spirits of the night." The amulet consisted of a twig of each of the trees of the triad tied together with a red string (p. 56).

If the three trees represent a trinity of the aspects of a single sacred tree, then it should be possible to identify the prime aspect of the whole that each tree represents, despite the overlap in their characteristics. The three aspects of the Tree of Life would, logically, seem to be Birth, Life and Death.

The Ash would appear to represent birth. It is the tree from which the first man came. It also represents knowledge and wisdom. In *LotR*, these two aspects of Ash-wood can be seen in the fact that it is the type of wood from which the staff of the 'resurrected,' and much enlightened Gandalf was made. "I have forgotten much that I thought I knew, and learned again much that I had forgotten," says the resurrected Gandalf (T.125; III.5).

The Thorn-tree would appear to represent death. Thiselton-Dyer observes that Christian tradition identifies the White-thorn with the crown of thorns worn by Christ on the cross. He also relates that in his time there was a belief in some parts of Essex that bringing the flowers of a White-thorn into the house would inevitably result in sickness or death. The probable source of this belief can be found in a paper by Paul Kendall[214] who reports

---

[214] Paul Kendall. "Mythology and Folklore of the Hawthorn," *Trees for Life: Restoring the Caledonian Forest*, <www.treesforlife.org.uk/tfl.mythhawthorn.html>. LVO 2/23/2006.

that in mediaeval times people said that the smell of hawthorn blossom reminded them of the smell of the Great Plague in London. Kendall provides a scientific basis for this association. Botanists have discovered that one of the chemicals that makes up the scent of the hawthorn flower is trimethylamine, which is also one of the first chemical products of the decay of animal tissue.[215]

In the earlier time at which the association between the smell of hawthorn flowers and death was made, people were more familiar with the smell of death. Unembalmed bodies were kept in the house prior to burial and the rich were entombed in crypts under the church floor from whence the odor of death found its way into the church and into the language. The phrase "stinking rich" comes from being rich enough to be buried in a crypt in the church so that your corpse could stink it up. The use of the Thorn-tree to represent the aspect of death of the Tree of Life matches the context of Tolkien's use of Thorn as the wood of the staff carried by Gandalf at the bridge just before he falls to his 'death.'

The Oak-tree would appear to represent temporal power and life in the present on earth. This is suggested by the inauguration of the Irish kings under sacred "bile" trees, which, given the great number of Oaks in Ireland at the time, were probably mainly Oaks. The association of Oaks with the British Royal family through Oak Apple Day, though, is, perhaps, more to the point for those less well-read in Irish tradition. This aspect of the Oak-tree corresponds well to Tolkien's use of oak as the wood used for the staff of the Elvenking in *The Hobbit*. The fact that he is the King of the Elves and not of men might have been influenced by the old proverb about fairy folks who live in old oaks, but King he was nonetheless, and his staff (scepter) was made of oak.

The context of Tolkien's use of each kind of wood, therefore, seems to fit with the mythological context of the three trees that represent the triplism of the Tree of Life. It is Tolkien's attention to this level of detail that sets his work apart. It would seem

---

[215] See also:
<www.chemguide.co.uk/organicprops/amines/background.html>.
lvo 2/23/2006.

strange, if someone so well-versed in tree lore as Tolkien had not chosen the type of wood for each of the staffs intentionally and with care.

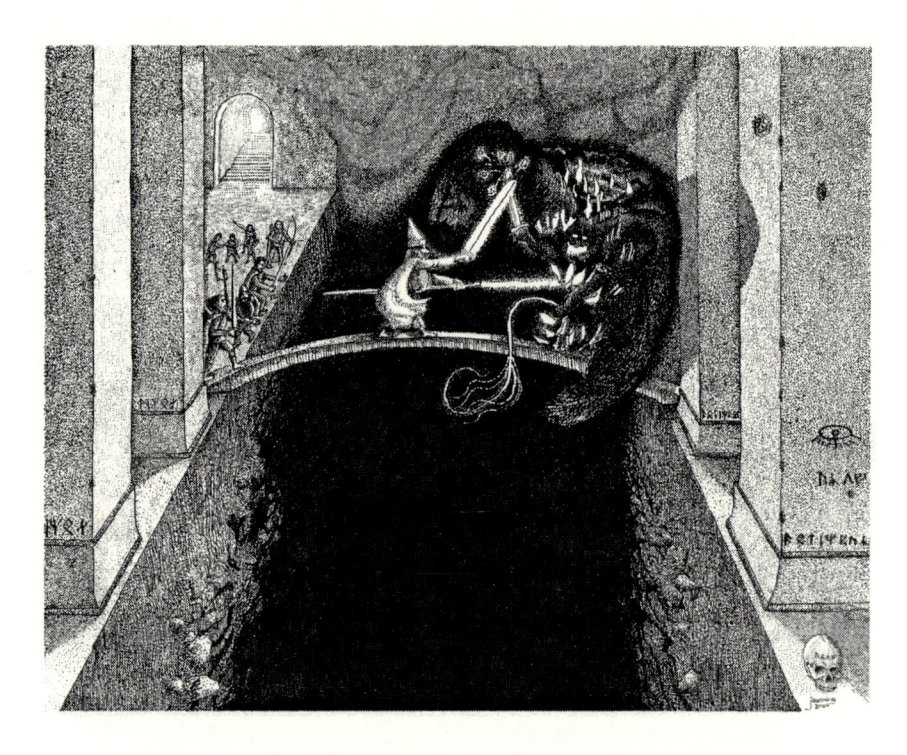

Gandalf fights the Balrog with sword and staff
Drawing: JWD

The Bounders

The **bounders** were the border guards of The Shire. In *Nomenclature*, Tolkien notes that his use of the word *bounder* is a "slender jest" that is "not worth imitating, even if possible." He elaborates that this jest is a play on the meaning of *bounder* that was current in the nineteenth century that would be recognized by, but not actively used by modern English speakers. A quick survey of the Internet, however, shows that it is indeed alive and well in the twenty-first century. The word *bounder* is used in the sense of someone who has overstepped the bounds of propriety, and is often used in a pair with the word *cad*. Tolkien is, in essence, attempting to create a faux-etymology for *bounder*, something he did for other words, for example, the name of the game of *golf* (H.30; I).

Tolkien said that he wanted the English reader to recall the meaning of *bounder/cad*, while clearly comprehending the function of a Hobbit bounder. To this end, the context in which bounder appears in *LotR* is sufficiently elaborated to get his point across. Their job was "to 'beat the bounds', and see that outsiders of any kind, great or small, did not make themselves a nuisance" (P.31).

In his book on Old English Customs[216], Ditchfield notes that the ancient observance of the custom of beating the bounds of the parish was previously practised everywhere, but that it was beginning to fall out of common use at the time that he wrote the book (1896). A procession led by the officials of the parish would actually walk the bounds of the parish, stopping at certain places to beat or duck the boys in the procession "in order to impress their memories with the details of the parish bounds" (p. 116).

Beating the Bounds Round the Boundary Elm, Stratford

Ditchfield quotes an invocation that has a very Hobbitish feel to it from "The Book of Homilies" that was to be read before the beating of the bounds. "We have occasion given to us in our walks today to consider the old ancient bounds and limits belonging to our township, and to other our neighbors bordering about us, to the intent that we should be content with our own, and not contentiously strive for others', to the breach of charity,

---

[216] P. H. Ditchfield. *Old English Customs Extant at the Present Time: An Account of Local Observances, Festival Customs, and Ancient Ceremonies Yet Surviving in Great Britain*, London: George Redway, 1896.

by any encroaching one upon another, or claiming one of the other, further than that in ancient right and custom our forefathers have peacefully laid out unto us for our commodity and comfort." (p. 115)

In *Nomenclature*, Tolkien rejects the initial solution offered by the Dutch translator (*poenen*), implying that Schuchart had gotten the linguistic equivalent of the bends from dictionary diving, having ignored the warning markers in the context. In Dutch, *poen* (singular) is a good match for *bounder* in the sense of *cad*, and the modern Dutch-English dictionary still points in this direction.

Schuchart was apparently made aware of Tolkien's objection, because the first printed edition of the Dutch translation of *LotR* does not use *poenen*, but rather the word *grenswakers* (border guards: grens = border), which is not attested in the 1976 *Van Dale* (the Dutch equivalent of *Webster's*). In the second edition of the translation, *grenswakers* was normalized to *grenswachten*, which is the form found in *Van Dale*. Schuchart's original printed solution (*grenswakers*) was, in my opinion, much better, because, like *bounder*, it made the reader stop to think about what it was that was not just quite right about this word.

Carroux, the first German translator, created the word *Grenzer*, which is a combination of *Grenz* (boundary, border) and the suffix *-er*, essentially the same trick that Tolkien was playing with *bounds* (limits) + *-er*. The normal German word for *border guards* is *Grenzwache* (compare the normalized Dutch translation). Krege, the second German translator, kept this made-up word in his translation. There is no need to argue with success.

The first Polish translator (Skibniewska) used the common word for border guards (*pograniczniki*), while the second Polish translator (Łoziński) replicated Carroux's trick with the unattested *graniczniki* (granica + -nik).

Most of the Russian translators ignored *bounders*, and just omitted it from the text. Gruzberg had the common word for *border guards* (пограничники [pogranichniki]). Nemirova had a very serviceable calque: порубежные стражники [porubezhnye strazhniki] = boundary watchmen). Matorina had a solution with good visual impact: обходчики [obkhodchiki], which literally means those who walk around something. *Obkhodchik* is a name for a type of inspector. K&K followed her lead.

The Czech translator had a simple solution. She used the adjective for *bounds, border*: pomezní.

The second Dutch translator (Mensink-van Warmelo) had another idea. Her solution for the word *bounders* was *Rakkers*, which is an excellent solution with an interesting valence of multiple meanings that can play against the meaning of the verb *rakken* (to clean up). A *rakker* can be:

1) (historical) an assistant bailiff, sheriff or reeve,
2) a bounder or a cad,
3) scallywag, rogue.

Though not attested, *rakker* is also logically someone who carries out the action of the verb *rakken*.

She creates an appropriate context in her translation of Tolkien's description of their job as "to 'beat the bounds', and see that outsiders of any kind, great or small, did not make themselves a nuisance" (P.31). She said that their job was "to keep the border clean (de grens te rakken) and to see that outsiders of any kind, great or small, did not make themselves a nuisance" (p. 30). She successfully did what no one else did. She recreated Tolkien's "slender jest," and rather skillfully at that.

The Cinematographer of Waverley
Reproduction of the Original Handbill from MythCon XXXV

On Sunday at 9.30 p.m.
for the
Entertainment of several Mythconians

Sir Walter Scott's
Much admir'd Comedy
from the Year 1822

The Cinematographer of Waverley
or
Sentience and Sentiments

with additional Dialogue by Mark T. Hooker[217]

will be perform'd without appropriate Scenery or Dress
by
a Cast of Two

Dr. Jonas Dryasdust
Professor of Tolkien Studies at Wolvercote College,
Oxford
Mr. Mike Foster
and
Selhew LLoyd, Cinematographer, Kennaquhair Studios
Mr. Mark T. Hooker

music by Mr. Howard Shore will not be perform'd
designer of graphics, Mr. Geoffrey Crayon
buyer of properties, Mr. Steptoe & Son
designer of costumes, Miss. Annie Menswher
designer of make-up, Count Ehnance Grimm
director of lighting, Mr. Threwyon D'Wend-O'Braekes
catering, The Green Dragon
the producer, Mr. Lloyd

NO MONEY RETURN'D

---

[217] With apologies to Sir Walter Scott, who wrote the original in 1822 as a Prefatory letter to *Peveril of the Peak*.

Dryasdust: Craving, then, your forgiveness for my presumption, would you consider the possibility of venturing yourself amongst a body of critics to whom, in the capacity of skilful literati, the investigation of truth is an especial duty, and who may therefore visit with the more severe censure those aberrations which it is so often your pleasure to make from the path of true Literature.

LLoyd: I understand you. You mean to say these learned persons will have little toleration for a film founded on Literature?

Dryasdust: Why, sir, I do rather apprehend that their respect for the foundation will be such that they may be apt to quarrel with the inconsistent nature of the superstructure, just as every classical reader pours forth expressions of sorrow and indignation when, in viewing a film, he chances to see a snowboard where there is no snow.

LLoyd: But since the situation is most dire at that point, a little comic relief was felt to be in order. Not quite correct according to the narrative, strictly and classically criticized; but presenting something uncommon to the eye, and something fantastic to the imagination, on which the spectator gazes with pleasure of the same description which arises from the perusal of a Star Wars film.

Dryasdust: I am unable to dispute with you in metaphor, sir; but I must say, in discharge of my conscience, that you stand much censured for adulterating the pure sources of Literary knowledge. You approach them, men say, like the drunken yeoman who, once upon a time, polluted the crystal spring which supplied the thirst of his family, with a score of sugar loaves and a hogshead of rum; and thereby converted a simple and wholesome beverage into a stupefying, brutefying, and intoxicating fluid, sweeter, indeed, to the taste than the natural lymph, but, for that very reason, more seductively dangerous.

LLoyd: I allow your metaphor, doctor; but yet, though good punch cannot supply the want of spring water, it is, when modestly used, no malum in se; and I should have thought it a shabby thing of the parson of the parish had he helped to drink out of the well on Saturday night and preached against the honest, hospitable yeoman on Sunday morning. I should have answered him that the very flavour of the liquor should have put him at once upon his guard; and that, if he had taken drop over much, he ought to blame his own imprudence more than the hospitality of his entertainer.

Dryasdust: I profess I do not exactly see how this applies.

LLoyd: No; you are one of those numerous disputants who will never follow their metaphor a step further than it goes their own way. I will explain. A poor fellow, like myself, weary with ransacking his own barren and bounded imagination, looks out for some work in the huge and boundless field of Literature, which holds forth examples of every kind; lights on some personage, or some combination of circumstances, or some striking trait of manners, which he thinks may be advantageously used as the basis of a feature-length film; bedizens it with such colouring as his skill suggests, ornaments it with such romantic circumstances as may heighten the general effect, invests it with such shades of characters as will best contrast with each other, and thinks, perhaps, that he has done some service to the public, if he can present them a lively fictitious moving picture, for which the original narrative that he paid to press into his service only furnished a slight sketch. The stories of Literature are accessible to every cinematographer, and are no more exhausted or impoverished by the films which are made from them than the fountain is drained by the water which we subtract for domestic purposes. And in reply to the sober charge of falsehood against a narrative announced positively to be fictitious, one can only answer by Prior's exclamation:

> Odzooks, must one foreswear cinematic license?

Dryasdust: Nay; but I fear me that you are here eluding the charge. Men do not seriously accuse you of misrepresenting the book, although I assure you I have seen some grave treatises in which it was thought necessary to contradict your interpretations.

LLoyd: That certainly was to point a discharge of artillery against a wreath of morning mist.

Dryasdust: But besides, and especially, it is said that you are in danger of causing the book to be neglected, modern souls being contented with such frothy and superficial knowledge as they acquire from your films, to the effect of inducing them to neglect the severe and more accurate source of your film.

LLoyd: I deny the consequence. On the contrary, I rather hope that I have turned the attention of the public on a work of Literature that has not received elucidation from writers of more learning and research, in consequence of my films having attached some interest to them.

Dryasdust: We severer literati, sir, may grant that this is true; to wit, that your films may have put men of solid judgement upon researches which they would not perhaps have otherwise thought of undertaking. But this will leave you still accountable for misleading the young, the indolent, and the giddy, by thrusting before them a film, while it has so much the appearance of conveying information as may prove perhaps a salve to their consciences for employing their leisure in the viewing, yet leave their giddy brains contented with the crude, uncertain, and often false statements which your films abound with.

LLoyd: It would be very unbecoming in me, reverend sir, to accuse a gentleman of your repute of cant; but, pray, is there not something like it in the pathos with which you enforce these dangers? I aver, on the contrary, that by introducing the busy and youthful to 'truths severe in silver-screened fiction dressed,' I am doing a real service to the more ingenious and the more apt among them; for the love of knowledge wants but a beginning—the least spark will give fire when the train is properly prepared; and having been interested in cinematic adventures, ascribed to an author, the reader begins next to be anxious to learn what the facts of the novel really are, and how far the cinematographer has justly represented them.

But even where the mind of the more careless spectator remains satisfied with the light screen treatment a cinematographer has afforded to a book, he will still leave the theatre with a degree of knowledge, not perhaps of the most accurate kind, but such as he might not otherwise have acquired. Nor is this limited to minds of a low and incurious description; but, on the contrary, comprehends many persons otherwise of high talents, who, nevertheless, either from lack of time or of perseverance, are willing to sit down contented with the slight information which is acquired in such a manner. The great Duke of Marlborough, for example, having quoted in conversation some fact of English Literature rather inaccurately, was requested to name his authority. 'The BBC's *Masterpiece Theatre*,' answered the conqueror of Blenheim; 'the only English literature I ever watched in my life.' And a hasty recollection will convince any of us how much better we are acquainted with those parts of English Literature which the immortal BBC has dramatized than with any other portion of British story.

Dryasdust: And you, worthy sir, are ambitious to render a similar service to posterity?

LLoyd: May the saints forefend I should be guilty of such unfounded vanity! I only show what has been done by the giants of Literature. We pygmies of the present day may at least, however, do something; and it is well to keep a pattern before our eyes, though the pattern be inimitable.

Dryasdust: Well, sir, with me you must have your own course; and for reasons well known to you, it is impossible for me to reply to you in an argument. But I doubt if all you have said will reconcile the public to the anachronisms of your present films. Here you have a warrior of Gondor offend against his nature, an elf maiden take the place of an Eldarin lord, and make light of a Dwarf of high stature.

LLoyd: They may sue me for damages as was the case Dido versus Virgil.

Dryasdust: A worse fault is, that your manners are even more incorrect than usual. Your Gondorian is faintly traced in comparison to your Hobbitonian.

LLoyd: I agree to that charge; but although I still consider hypocrisy and enthusiasm as fit food for ridicule and satire, yet I am sensible of the difficulty of holding fanaticism up to laughter or abhorrence without using colouring which may give offense to the sincerely worthy and learned. Many things are lawful which, we are taught, are not convenient; and there are many tones of feeling which are too respectable to be insulted, though we do not altogether sympathize with them.

Dryasdust: Not to mention, my worthy sir, that perhaps you may think the subject exhausted.

LLoyd: The devil take the men of this generation for putting the worst construction on their neighbor's conduct!

EXIT: Stage left, in a huff.

Post-script

The satire contained in the theatrical reading of *The Cinematographer of Waverley or Sentience and Sentiments* at the Sunday Entertainments during MythCon XXXV seems to have been too subtle by half, because its import was lost on a number of MythConians in the audience, due to the fact that they were unaware of the actual history upon which it was based. A short historical excursion, therefore, seems in order for this edition.

"Sir Walter Scott's Much admir'd Comedy from the Year 1822" was in fact the Prefatory Letter to his novel *Peveril of the Peak*. It was written (1822) before Scott (1771-1832) had acknowledged (1825) that he was the author of a series of novels known only to the reading public as "The Author of *Waverley*," referring to Scott's first successful novel: *Waverley* (1814). His anonymity, to some extent, protected him from the stings and arrows of outraged historians, who took umbrage at his literary treatments of history.

Scott's feigned argument between himself and Dr. Dryasdust (a 'speaking' name meant to convey Scott's perception of the character of the historians who objected to his work) outlines

Scott's view of the controversy. The good doctor's statement "with me you must have your own course; and for reasons well known to you, it is impossible for me to reply to you in an argument" is nothing more than an admission that Dr. Dryasdust is Scott's pawn and that his arguments are hollow. It could not be otherwise with Scott putting words into the good doctor's mouth.

The humor in the play, if it may be called such, arises from the fact that the changes necessary to give it a modern resonance were few. Where the Letter said 'history,' the Play said 'literature.' Where the Letter said 'literature,' the Play said 'cinema.' Some allusions specific to criticisms of Peter Jackson's films were sprinkled about the text, replacing allusions specific to criticisms of the works of 'the author of *Waverley*,' and the BBC's *Masterpiece Theatre* (a cinematic medium) took the role of Shakespeare (a dramatist) in the line in the Play that read: "The great Duke of Marlborough, for example, having quoted in conversation some fact of English Literature [originally: history] rather inaccurately, was requested to name his authority. 'The BBC's *Masterpiece Theatre*,' answered the conqueror of Blenheim; 'the only English literature [originally: history] I ever watched [originally: read] in my life.'" At the Movie Panel, David Bratman had a ready list of (mis)quotes allegedly of Tolkien that were really from Jackson. The gist of the joke is, therefore, that things have not changed all that much in the 180 years since Scott first penned the Letter.

It was thought that a little historical perspective might help in understanding the potential effects of Jackson's films on Tolkien's literature. The inquiring reader is invited to look beyond the parody for something of greater significance. Notwithstanding Scott's glib assurances of the benign nature of his literary enterprise, in this feigned battle of words between himself and the notional Dr. Dryasdust, the march of history has prepared another lesson for the careful reader of these lines. Looking at the process under discussion in this dialogue from the perspective of today offers the modern reader a view of the whole that was not afforded to Scott and his apparitional opponent because they were too close to the proverbial trees to see the forest. In the time since this dialogue was written, Scott's treatments of history have eclipsed the sources that they were based on, as more people began to read literature than read history. I think that I could say, without fear of contradiction, that most people who are aware of Sir Walter Scott as a literary figure will be unaware of the controversy surrounding his works when they were first published, and will be hard-pressed to name even one of his historical sources.

In today's post-literate screen-age, film and television have become the preferred medium for a very large portion of society. The words of Chance the gardener (a.k.a. 'Chauncey Gardiner'), played by Peter Sellers in the movie *Being There*[218]—"I like to watch"—have become the motto of the age. Scott's own monumental work *Ivanhoe* has been retold for the silver screen and television no less than seven times. [See the filmography below.] How many of those reading this article, who know something of *Ivanhoe*, gained their knowledge at first hand, from the book? It seems rather likely that many of the readers of this epistle will be more familiar with the movie or the television productions, and that most of them have never even heard of the novel for which this imaginary dialogue was the prefatory letter. If that is indeed the case, then, since history repeats itself, I am afraid that we can look forward to the same fate befalling Tolkien's works. It is, therefore, not so much Scott's words in this fictional dialogue that are important to the current reader, but the actual fate of Scott's books. They are still readily available (as a quick search on <www.amazon.com> will show), but have you read Scott lately? Do you know anybody who has? Have you read *Being There*, or only seen the movie?

---

[218] *Being There* (runtime: 130 minutes), directed by Hal Ashby, scenario by Jerzy Kosinski (also the novel, New York: Harcourt, Brace and Jovanovich, 1970), 1979.

Filmography

Ivanhoe (runtime: 48 minutes), directed by Herbert Brenon, with King Baggot as Ivanhoe, silent, B&W, 1913.

Ivanhoe (a.k.a. Rebecca the Jewess), directed by Leedham Bantock, scenario by Leedham Bantock, with Lauderdale Maitland as Ivanhoe, silent, B&W, 1913.

Ivanhoe (runtime: 106 minutes), directed by Richard Thorpe, scenario Aeneas MacKenzie, with Robert Taylor as Ivanhoe, 1952.

Ivanhoe (ITV-Series: 39 30-minute episodes), directed by Lance Comfort and Arthur Crabtree, scenario by Bill Strutton, with Roger Moore as *Ivanhoe*, B&W, 1958-59.

Ivanhoe (made for TV: runtime 142 minutes), directed by Douglas Camfield, scenario by John Gay, with Anthony Andrews as Ivanhoe, 1982.

Ivanhoe (six-part BBC miniseries, runtime: 300 minutes), directed by Stuart Orme, scenario by Deborah Cook, with Steven Waddington as Ivanhoe, 1997.

Legend of Ivanhoe, directed by Sergey Tarasov, with John Haverson, 1999.

Estel

Estel (S Hope) was the pseudonym used for Aragorn II while he was being hidden in Rivendell to keep the Enemy from learning that one of Isildur's heirs still lived. (A.420 [Appendix A]) No attempt is generally made to parse this name (eg. Allan[219] p. 78; Noel[220] p. 142). The *Etymologies* do, however, contain elements that suggest that it is possible to parse the name into *est* (first) + *el* (star).

The initial element (EST-) would appear to be a variant of ESE-, ESET- (396). The examples given include *esta* (Q first) and *esse* (beginning). The entry directly above is ES-, which also offers the examples *esta* (Q to name) and *esse* (a name). The note in the *Etymologies* accompanying these two entries considers them "mutually exclusive," but a certain logical explanation for the 'overlap' becomes apparent when considering the quote from Tolkien about the origin of the name Hobbit. "Names always

---

[219] Jim Allan. *An Introduction to Elvish*, Frome, Sommerset, U.K.: Bran's Head Books, 1978.

[220] Ruth S. Noel. *The Languages of Tolkien's Middle-earth*, Boston: Houghton Mifflin, 1974.

generate a story in my mind," said Tolkien, and that was the beginning of *The Hobbit* (Carpenter 193, see also L.163).

This logical underpinning is further strengthened by a somewhat similar Bible quote, which has a certain resonance with Tolkien's statement about names. "In the beginning was the Word," says *John* 1:1. The Personal Study Edition of the *Catholic Bible* (CBPSE)[221] categorizes the term *word* in this passage as a reflection of God's "dynamic creative word," which is able to create something out of nothing, as in *Genesis* 1:3, where "God said, 'let there be light,' and there was light." A name is a type of word that "tells the story of the things they belong to" (T.85-86; III.4), and the giving of names is a part of both the Bible and of Tolkien's tale. The giving of names is one of the first things to be done 'in the Beginning'. In *Genesis* 2:19, God created the animals and brought them to Adam to be named. In Tolkien's tale, the order of the actions was reversed. The names came first and then something or someone was created to match the name. In the fabric of this logic, *names* and *beginnings* are clearly related.

The second element of the name *Estel* (-EL) is glossed as poetic Quenya for *star*, as in *Elrond* (starry dome = vault of heaven), *Elros* (Star Rain,[222] Elrond's brother) and *Elwing* (Star Foam,[223] their mother). The element -EL may be represented in a final position in the word *peredil/peredhil* (half-elven). The first element in *peredil* is *per*, meaning *half*. The *Etymologies* discuss the transposition *edel/edil* under ELED- (star folk), which would coincide with the second element of *per-edil* (half-elven). The transposition suggests that the two elements are semantic morphemes rather than just phonemes. The possible meaning of each of these morphemes can be sought in a combination of the semantics of the original entry ELED- that carried a sense of 'departure from' and of the new entry ELED- (star folk) > *edel*. Joining these two semantic elements into a meaningful whole

---

[221] *The Catholic Bible* (Personal Study Edition), Oxford: University Press, 1995.

[222] See ROS¹ in the "Etymologies."

[223] See LOT(H) [flower] in the "Etymologies," where *Wingelot* is glossed as 'foam flower.' See also: *The Shaping of Middle-earth*, Boston: Houghton Mifflin, 1986, pp. 149 and 152.

suggests that *ed* signifies *from* and *el* signifies *star*, yielding a hypothetical original meaning of 'from star' for the element *edil/edhil* in *peredil/peredhil* (half-elven). Compare "Q Elda 'departed' Elf" from the rejected original entry for ELED-.

If it is, therefore, possible to parse the name *Estel* < est + el, then the combination of its two elements would appear to be read as 'first star'. The word order of the compound (adjective + noun) follows that of Tolkien's other parsable names. The logic behind a compound word with the meaning 'first star' representing the concept of *hope* can be found in a number of traditions that associate the planet Venus—the first 'star' seen in the evening—with hope. Venus is the brightest object in the sky after the sun and the moon.

The modern reader may be most familiar with this association through the wishing rhyme: Star light, Star bright / first star I see tonight / I wish I may, I wish I might / have the wish I wish tonight.

There is sufficient internal evidence in *LotR* to support the logic of the compound on its own, but the tradition is much older. The internal evidence is to be found in Tolkien's tale of Eärendil (Sea Lover) the Mariner, whose ship Vingilot (Foam Flower, named for his spouse Elwing) bears him and the brightest of the Silmarils—the star of hope—through the night. (LT II.266) In *LotR*, Eärendil is referred to as "the Evening star" (F.472; II.7), which is the planet Venus. The original title of Tolkien's poem of Eärendil was "The Voyage of Éarendel the Evening Star" (LT II.267). It is the light of Eärendil's star that is captured in the phial that the Lady Galadriel gave Frodo to be a light for him when all other lights were extinguished (F.488; II.8) that brings Frodo hope as Frodo and Sam are confronted by Shelob in the dark, as if Eärendil "had come down from the high sunset paths" to stand at his side (T.418; IV.9).

Tolkien said that he liked history and considered its finest moments to be those that shed light on words and names (L.205). The study of the history of words and names is called etymology, and the Klein[224] *Comprehensive Etymological Dictionary of the*

---

[224] Ernest Klein. *A Comprehensive Etymological Dictionary of the English Language* (in two volumes), Amsterdam: Elsevier, 1966.

English Language offers an interesting starting point for the further study of the story of the tradition of the Evening Star and its association with hope. The dictionary notes that the English word *star* comes from the hypothetical Proto-Indo-European word *astero, which, it suggests, may have been the name of the Evening Star that was given to it when it was believed to be the goddess Astarte (Klein, II.1505). *Astarte* is the Greek rendition of the name of the Phoenician mother goddess Ashtoreth. The rough equivalent of Astarte in the Greek Pantheon of gods is Aphrodite, with a certain amount of localization to match Greek tastes. (Hastings,[225] I.171a)

Astarte

The consonant envelope STR (*aSTeRo) is seen in the word for *star* in a number of languages such as: Dutch (ster), German (Stern), OE (steorra), French (astre), Greek (astron), Welsh (seren), Breton and Cornish (sterenn). It also shows up in words like *astrology*, *astronomy* and *disaster* (born under an ill-omened star). This consonant envelope is also found in the name of Astarte's counterpart in Babylonian and Assyrian tradition *Ishtar*.

In Babylonian astro-theology, the star of Ishtar was the planet Venus.[226] In a footnote to *Jeremiah* 7:18 (see also *Jeremaiah* 44:17-25), the *CBPSE* says that cakes shaped like stars were baked to be used as burnt offerings to Ishtar, "the Queen of Heaven." The *Encyclopedia Biblica* equates this title with "a cult of Venus" (IV.3993). A similar recurring title for Astarte is "Mistress of Heaven,"[227] but, in *Paradise Lost*, Milton crowns Astarte "The Queen of Heaven." The title of "Queen of Heaven" is the same one given to the Virgin Mary by the Christian Church,[228]

---

[225] *A Dictionary of the Bible* (in 5 volumes), James Hastings (ed.), New York: Charles Scribner's Sons, 1898.

[226] *Encyclopedia Biblica* (in 4 volumes), T.K. Cheyne (ed.), New York: Macmillan, 1899, vol. 1, p. 338. Also Hastings, vol. 1, p. 169a.

[227] *The Anchor Bible Dictionary* (in 6 volumes), David Noel Freedman (ed.), New York: Doubleday, 1992, vol. 1, 493.

and there are indeed a number of authors who consider that certain aspects of the myths of Astarte/Ishtar were co-opted by the Christian Church—as was the case with many other pagan beliefs—for attribution to Mary (eg. Walker,[229] 70, 453; Beard,[230] 28).

Mary—like Astarte/Ishtar—is a mediatrix. The Hastings *Bible Dictionary* quotes a prayer, in which Ishtar is addressed as "Queen of the gods ... Lady of Heaven and earth, who hears petitions, heeds sighs, the merciful goddess who loves justice" (Hastings, I.168b). In a hymn, Ishtar is called "the begettress of all, mother Ishtar .. whose aid and sympathy a supplicant may expect to receive" (Hastings, I.169a).

The mediatrix in the Buddhist tradition is the goddess Tara, whose name is commonly held to be derived from the Sanskrit word for *star* (*tara*). She was born of a tear shed by Bodhisattva Avalokitesvara, who is held to be the savior of mankind. Her iconography often depicts one of her hands in a gesture of boon-granting, indicating a willingness to aid all who call upon her for help. She is believed to work both day and night with unending compassion to relieve the suffering of those who seek her aid. In the Tibetan Buddhist tradition, she is called *The Great Savioress* (Dölma). In this tradition, mariners look to the intercession of Tara in the same way that Catholic sailors call upon the Virgin Mary in her guise as Stella Maris, the Star of the sea.[231] As a devout Catholic, Tolkien could hardly have been unaware of Stella Maris.

The consonant envelope STR (star) developed into STL in Latin, where the word for *star* is *stella*. This envelope is considered the result of a normal development from the hypothetical Latin

---

[228] *The New Catholic Encyclopedia* (second edition), 2003, pp. 282-283.

[229] Barbara G. Walker. *The Woman's Encyclopedia of Myths and Secrets*, New York: Harper and Row, 1983.

[230] Charles R. Beard, *Lucks and Talismans*, London: Sampson Low, Marston, 1934.

[231] *The MacMillan Illustrated Encyclopedia of Myths and Legends*, Arthur Cotterell (ed.), London: Marshall Editions, 1989, p. 165.

word *sterla*. It can be seen in English in words like *stellar* and *constellation*. The hypothetical form can be seen in Spanish and Portuguese, where the word for *star* is *estrella*, and *estellar* is the word *stellar*. Tolkien uses the name *Estella* as the first name of Merry's wife, Estella Bolger (A.476), so it is clear this form of the name had not escaped Tolkien's attention.

There are other elements in the tradition of Astarte that are echoed in Tolkien's story of Eärendil 'the Mariner'. On coins minted in Sidon—the oldest city of the Phoenicians and the principal city of their empire—Astarte is pictured "standing on the prow of a galley, with her right hand holding a crown, stretched forward, as though pointing the vessel on its way" (Hastings, I.168a). In days before geopositioning systems (GPS), sailors relied on the navigational help of the stars, and the light of Venus (Astarte's and Eärendil's star) would have guided many a mariner to port. In Bilbo's song of Eärendil (F.308-311), Elwing crowns Eärendil with the Silmaril that is the light of the star seen on Middle-earth and contained in Frodo's phial. This makes her sound somewhat like Astarte, whose dominion include all the dead "who lived in heaven wearing bodies of light, visible from earth as stars" (Walker, 70).

Another interesting element of Bilbo's song is Eärendil's escape from the Evernight of death. Astarte—and all her other various incarnations, including Elwing—descends into the kingdom of the dead, "the house of darkness" (Hastings, I.168b) to return her husband to life. The ancient symbolism was that of the rescue of the dying winter sun,[232] which rises again to grant hope of new life to those on earth (eg. Walker, 453, Hastings, I.168b). This story line is, perhaps, more familiar to modern Western readers as the story of Aphrodite and Adonis.

One of the key "Astral" passages in Bilbo's song of Eärendil is the one in which Eärendil hears "the weeping sore of women

---

[232] In Semitic sources, the observance of the lamentation of Tammuz is recorded as taking place during the summer. Hastings speculates that in his move from one geographic area to another, Tammuz adapted to the local climate and changed from a sun god killed by winter to a god of growing plants "parched and destroyed by the fierce heat of the summer" (Hastings, IV.677a).

and of elven-maids" (F.311). This ties Eärendil to Ishtar through the reference in *Ezekiel* 8:14 to the women weeping for Tammuz. In a footnote to this passage (p. 1041), the CBPSE remarks that the weeping for Tammuz was a part of the annual cycle of Ishtar and Tammuz, in which Tammuz dies and Ishtar descends into the land of the dead to return him to life. This was commemorated on earth by a seven-day period of lamentation during which the women wept for Tammuz (Hastings, IV.677a). It is significant that it was the women who wept, because the *Encyclopedia Biblica* speculates that making offerings to the Queen of Heaven was part of a "specifically women's cult" (IV.3992). In Gebal, the city where the lamentation for Tammuz was centered, "wailing women tore their hair and lacerated their breasts" (Hastings, IV.677a).

Tolkien has rewritten the story slightly, redistributing the parts and apparently changing the gender of the title character. A change of this type is not entirely without precedent. While Astarte was clearly the name of a female deity, there are records of a male deity with similar attributes who was called Athtar. The *Anchor Bible Dictionary* speculates that perhaps Astarte (feminine) was the Evening-star phase of Venus and that Athtar was the Morning-star phase (I.493). It is more likely that he was a localization that gave preference to male deities. In Assyrian and Babylonian literature, Ishtar describes herself as the goddess of the Morning and of the Evening Star, claiming both phases of Venus to herself (Walker, 451). In *The Shaping of Middle-earth*,[233] Eärendil is hailed as "Star of the Sunset," and "Herald of the morn" (p. 154), claiming both phases of Venus for himself. In Bilbo's song, Eärendil is a flame that runs before the sun, "a wonder ere the waking dawn" (F.310; II.1). Tolkien also classifies Eärendil as the Morning Star in *Lost Tales* II (266).

Tolkien appears, however, to have re-apportioned the parts somewhat. Eärendil is the one who hears the women weeping, which equates him with Tammuz. Elwing has what appears to be Astarte/Ishtar's role in bringing him back from the land of the dead. She flies to Eärendil to save him from the Night of Naught,

---

[233] *The Shaping of Middle-earth*, New York: Ballantine Books, 1987.

carrying the light that will be perceived from Middle-earth as a star upon her carcanet [a type of necklace] (F.308-309; II.1). Her name is glossed as "star foam," which is reminiscent of the gloss of the name *Aphrodite*: "sea foam born." Tolkien had a number of speculations on the origin of the name Elwing, one of which indeed had to do with her birth. She was said to have been "born on a clear night of stars, the light of which glittered in the spray of the waterfall by which his house was built,"[234] which strengthens the correspondence between Elwing and Aphrodite in all her "Astral" incarnations (Astarte, Ishtar, Tara).

The consonant envelope STL is the same one found in Tolkien's name *Estel* (Hope). Tolkien said that he did borrow sound envelopes for his words, but that the purport of the original word was "totally irrelevant, except in the case of Eärendil" (L.297). *Eärendil* was originally an existing Anglo-Saxon name that Tolkien reparsed into 'Sea Lover' (LT II.266). The statement in Tolkien's letter restricting his 'borrowing' only to the name *Eärendil* should not, however, be taken too literally. In volume XII of *The History of Middle-earth*, it is noted that the name of Eärendil's ship (Vingilot) was intentionally "formed to resemble and 'explain' the name of Wade's ship Guingelot."[235]

Tolkien indeed liked to make up 'explanations' (etymologies) for existing words, the most commonly cited example of which is, perhaps, for the word *Golf* (H.30; I). It is not inconceivable, therefore, that the etymology of *Estel* = *first star* = *hope* is another one of his faux etymologies for an existing name. It is not unexpected that the name should be considered unparsable, since it is a Sindarin name composed of Quenya roots. How many people, after all, recognize all the component parts of the word *constellation* or the word *disaster*? Perhaps more importantly, Tolkien classified his creation of names as a private way of entertaining himself, "by giving expression to [his] personal

---

[234] *The Peoples of Middle-earth*, Boston: Houghton Mifflin, 1996. p. 49.

[235] *The Peoples of Middle-earth*, Boston: Houghton Mifflin, 1996. Wade's marvelous boat Guingelot is mentioned in Chaucer's *The Merchant's Tale*. For an explanation of who Wade is, see: <www.northernearth.co.uk/66/wade.htm>. LVO 2/23/2006.

linguistic 'aesthetic' or taste" (L.297). Any evaluation of the success of his endeavor is, by Tolkien's own definition, a very subjective judgement that may not be shared by all, but I am a philologist, and I thought this joke was funny.

A BELTMAKER BY ANY OTHER NAME WOULD NOT BE AS FUNNY

Bracegirdle

Bracegirdle is one of those names in *LotR* that you always assume was made up by Tolkien, until you read his comments in *Nomenclature*, where he says that it is a genuine English surname (p. 172). The origin of the name is an occupation: beltmaker. It is derived from OE *brec* (breeches = trousers) + *gyrdel* (belt). It is variously attested with such spellings as *Brachgyrdyll, Brasgirdell, Breechegirdle* and *Braesgirdle*.

There are a number of real, famous Bracegirdle-s. Anne Bracegirdle (1663?1671-1748) was an extremely popular theater actress of the Georgian Era. Ms. Bracegirdle is described as being "of a 'lovely' height" with "dark brown hair and eyebrows, black sparkling eyes, a fine set of even white teeth, a fresh, blushing complexion ... very handsome feet and legs."[236] She was one of those actresses whom you could "simply die for," and actor/playwright William Mountfort indeed did. In December of 1692, in a failed attempt to kidnap Ms. Bracegirdle, Captain Richard Hill, aided and abetted by the infamous Lord Mohun,

---

[236] John Fyvie. *Tragedy Queens of the Georgian Era*, London: Methuen, 1909, p. 15.

fatally stabbed Mountfort, whom they believed to be her lover. They both eluded justice for their parts in this infamous celebrity crime, but each of them eventually died a violent death.

There is a modern literary allusion to Ms. Bracegirdle in an Inspector Alleyn Mystery by Ngaio Marsh (1899-1982) entitled *Final Curtain* (1947), where the bedrooms in the manor house of the murder victim—the illustrious Shakespearean actor Sir Henry Ancred—are all named after famous actors.

"Miss Bracegirdle Does Her Duty" (1916) is the title of a morbid short story[237] by Stacy Aumonier (1887-1928), that finds the middle-aged miss Millicent Bracegirdle alone in France for the first time in her life. She sounds a bit like Bilbo, when, after a life "particularly devoid" of adventure, she discovers "a sense of enjoyment in her adventure," which is most strange, as "she had a horror of travel, and an ingrained distrust of foreigners" (p. 360). In 1926, the story was made into a black-and-white silent movie directed by Edwin Greenwood. It was later staged for *Alfred Hitchcock Presents*, first airing on 2 February 1958.

In *Trevannion* (1948)[238] by L.A.G. Strong (1896-1958), Mrs. Bracegirdle, a widow of independent means, is "that infallible guide in all affairs of the heart and every form of commerce between the sexes" (pp. 33-34) in the one-horse town of Dycer's Bay. In other words, a stereotypical busybody.

Female characters with the name *Bracegirdle* evoke a certain comic image because of the name's association with an article of lady's underclothing, but there are some male Bracegirdles as well.

Sir Leighton Seymour Bracegirdle, KCVO, CMG, DSO[239] (1881-1970) rose to the rank of Rear Admiral in the Royal Navy. He was an Australian who fought in the Boxer Rebellion (1900-

---

[237] Stacy Aumonier. "Miss Bracegirdle Does Her Duty," *The Second Omnibus of Crime* (Dorothy Sayers ed.), New York: Coward-McCann, Inc., 1932, pp. 359-372.

[238] Leonard Alfred George Strong. *Trevannion*, London: Methuen 1948.

[239] KCVO = Knight Commander in The Royal Victorian Order, CMG = Companion in The Most Distinguished Order of St. Michael and St. George, DSO = Distinguished Service Order.

1901), in the Boer War (1901-1902), World War I (1914-1918) and World War II (1939-1945).

The fictional naval officer Anthony Bracegirdle is a member of the cast of the Horatio Hornblower stories and novels by Cecil Scott Forester (1899-1966), which were successful both in print and on the screen. The first novel of the series (*Mr. Midshipman Hornblower*) appeared in 1950, five years before *LotR*. There should be no implication, however, of cause and effect in this case, as in a letter published in *The Observer* in 1938, Tolkien provided a list of the surnames of the wealthier Hobbit families, which included both *Hornblower* and *Bracegirdle* (L.31).

Tolkien's point that *Bracegirdle* is an existing English surname is well taken, but, having made it, he goes on to explain that the name should be translated by sense with some equivalent of "Tight-Belt," "Belt-strainer," or the like, even if the resulting name is not a valid surname in the target language. This instruction merely serves to confirm the reader's initial impression that Tolkien used the name for the comic effect of the modern interpretation of its component parts.

The translations of *Bracegirdle* do indeed offer some interesting interpretations of the name. The two Dutch translators used the same word for the first element (*brace*) in this compound name, but each selected a different word for the second element (*girdle*). The first element they used was *bras* (*brace* in English), which is a seafaring term that describes the pair of running lines used to control the horizontal movement of a sail. The word *bras* has the added advantage that the Dutch verb *brassen* means *to overeat* or *to make a pig of oneself*. The first Dutch translator's (Schuchart's) second element was *gordel*, a somewhat fancier word for *belt* than the commonplace Dutch word *riem*. His translation of the name was *Brasgordel*. Mensink-van-Warmelo's second element was *plaat*, which suggests that she looked a bit too deep in a comprehensive dictionary like the *OED*, where *girdle* is listed as a variant of *griddle*, which, in Dutch, is *plaat*. Her translation was *Brasplaat*.

The first German translator (Carroux) followed Tolkien's suggestion that the name be translated as "Tight-Belt," producing the calque *Straffgürtel*. The first element (*straff*) means *tight*. It is not to be confused with *Straf* (with one '**F**'), which means *punishment* or *penalty*. The second element (Gürtel) means belt. It is hard to argue with success like that, which is probably why the second German translator (Krege) did not change the name in his version.

The first Polish translator (Skibniewska) did not translate *Bracegirdle*, but just gave the name a Polish adjective ending: *Bracegirdle'owie*. The second Polish translator (Łoziński) combined the word for *belt* (*pas*) with the adjective for *empty* (*pusty*), and added an adjective ending: *Pasopustowie*. Łoziński's name, therefore, would seem to indicate someone thin, rather than someone fat, the opposite sense of what Tolkien had indicated that he was looking for in *Nomenclature*.

The Czech translator (Pošustová) only translated the first half of the name. She stopped looking in her dictionary when she got to the British word *braces*, which are known in American English as *suspenders*. In Czech, this item of apparel is known as kšandy. Her name was Kšandičkov.

The Russian translators who tackled this name (only 6 out of 9) had some imaginative solutions. The Murav'ev and Kistyakovskij translation was Толстобрюхлы (Tolstobryukhly), which would sound something like the "Pot-Bellies" in English (толстой [tolstoj] = fat, брюхо [bryukho] = belly). Matorina's translation was the slightly less successful Тугобрюхи (Tugobryukhi), which would sound something like "Full Bellies" in English (тугой [tyugoj] = tight, full, pumped-up; брюхо [bryukho] = belly). For a name based on the element туго- [tugo-], I should have liked to have seen an attempt at Tolkien's suggestion of "Tight-Belts." *Тугоременники [Tugoremenniki] (ремень [remen'] = belt) could have worked.

Nemirova had a good solution with a certain amount of bilingual humor. Her name was Брюхстоны (Bryukhstony), which at first looks like the English name *Brookstone*, but on closer examination reveals itself to be "Groaning Bellies" (брюхо [bryukho] = belly, стон [ston] = groan). Nemirova's name would have been, perhaps, more successful as *Брюкстоны [Bryukstony], "Groaning Trousers" (брюки [bryuki] = trousers [a loanword from Dutch: *broek*]), but that is just my opinion.

Karrik and Kamenkovich had the equivalent of "Redo (your buttons)," which is a subtle hint that one's clothes are too tight (перестегнись [perestegnis'] an imperative form = re-close a fastener). Volkovskyj did not put as much effort into this name as he put into others, and ended up with Толстинги (Tolstingi), which would sound like the "Fattings" in English (толстой [tolstoj] = fat + -ing[240]).

Grushetskij and Grigoreva came up with an excellent parody of Tolkien's tautological, snobbish hyphenated name *Sackville-Baggins* (sack = bag). Their version was Помочь-Лямкинс (Pomoch'-Lyamkins), which would sound like "Suspender-Brace-ins" (помочи [pomochi] = braces [suspenders], лямки [lyamki] = braces [suspenders]).

---

[240] See also my article on the name *Dwaling*.

Roman Fighting Elephants

Whence an Oliphaunt?

In *Nomenclature*, Tolkien said that the name *Oliphaunt* was intended to be a "rusticism" for the word *elephant*. It was to be slightly deformed on the premise that the names of foreign animals, seldom or never seen, should sound somewhat strange as well. He was disappointed that the Dutch translator (Schuchart) used *Olifant*, which is the modern Dutch word for *elephant*, because this translation did not have the archaic coloration that he wanted this name to have. Despite this criticism, the official Dutch translation retained the word *Olifant* in all three of its revisions.

Tolkien classified the word *elephant* as probably having come from the Old French *olifant*, with the shift from the initial '**O**' to an initial '**E**' having taken place in OE or Old German. Tolkien's suggestion was to reverse this shift, and that was essentially what the German translators (Carroux and Krege) did. The modern German word for *elephant* is *Elefant*, and the German translation for *Oliphaunt* is *Olifant*. That trick does not work in Dutch, where the shift never took place, so the unofficial Dutch translation by Mrs. Mensink-van Warmelo adopted Tolkien's final vowel sound (Olif**au**nt) instead, which does give the name a strange flavor in Dutch.

Recently, while reading an early-twentieth-century novel of South Africa by John Buchan (1875-1940)[241] entitled *Prester John*[242], I was surprised to come across the name *Olifants*. This novel was originally written in English, and, as Buchan notes in his autobiography, became "a school reader in many languages."[243] Needless to say, the book has fallen out of fashion of late in the current politically-correct, post-literate age. In Tolkien's time, however, it was clearly widely appreciated, and it is not unreasonable to conjecture that Tolkien might have read *Prester John*. He would have been 18, when it came out in 1910. He was within the demographic at which the book was aimed (the hero was only 19), and he would have had an interest in South Africa, since he was born there in Bloemfontein. It is clear that he read Haggard's stories about Africa.[244] In a letter to *The Observer*, Tolkien commented that he had "read several books on African exploration" (L.30).

The *literary baggage* of each word and name in a language is built up out of all the usages of a word that a reader has ever been exposed to. Tolkien called this "the leaf mold" of one's mind (*Carpenter* 140-141). If the name *Olifants* from *Prester John* was a part of the leaf mold of Tolkien's mind, then it would have indeed been "archaic" by the time that Tolkien wrote *Nomenclature*, which was only written as an aid to translators after *LotR* had come out, over 45 years after the first publication of *Prester John* in 1910. At the time that *Prester John* came out and was in wide circulation, however, the coloration of the name *Olifants* would have been that of exotic, faraway places full of adventure.

---

[241] Perhaps most famous as the author of *The Thirty-nine Steps*.

[242] John Buchan. *Prester John*, New York: George H. Doran Co., 1910.

[243] John Buchan. *Memory Hold-the-Door* (an autobiography), London: Hodder and Stoughton, Ltd., 1940, p. 194.

[244] For a discussion of Tolkien and Haggard, see "Frodo Quatermain" "Tolkien and Haggard: Immortality" and "Tolkien and Haggard: The Dead Marshes" above.

The name *Olifants* appears in *Prester John* in a description of the landscape in chapter IV, "My Journey to the Winter-veld," in which the hero acquaints the reader with the local geography, because an understanding of the geography is important to comprehending the tale that follows.

> The Berg runs north and south, and from it run the chief streams which water the plain. They are, beginning from the south, the Olifants, the Groot Letaba, the Letsitela, the Klein Letaba, and the Klein Labongo, on which stands Blaauwildebeestefontein (p. 58).

What strikes the linguistic eye in this passage is the number of Afrikaans (originally XVII-century Dutch) elements in the place names. The element *veld* in chapter title is the word for *field* in Dutch. *Berg* is *mountain* in Dutch. *Groot* is *great* or *large*, as in The Greater Letaba. *Klein* is *small* or *the lesser*. *Blaauwildebeestefontein* is the *blue wild animal* (wildebeest = gnu) *spring*. *Olifants* is *elephants*.

Tolkien was right. For the Dutch reader, the name *Olifant* does not sound as exotic or archaic as it does to a reader whose literary baggage for the name *Olifants* includes *Prester John* in English, but then again, there are not that many modern English-speaking readers who have read *Prester John* these days. Reading Buchan's novel offers a new perspective on the question of "Whence an Oliphaunt?". Perhaps it crept up out of the leaf mold of Tolkien's mind from a leaf that was once a tale of adventure in South Africa, the land of Tolkien's birth.

COUNTLESS SLOPPY MISTAKES

Tolkien in Chinese: A Thesis[245] Review

Comparative Translation Studies

Tolkien is increasingly becoming the topic of Comparative Translation Studies.[246] The second volume of Walking Tree Publisher's "Translating Tolkien" series is due out this spring, and I recently came across a thesis written in English on the two Chinese translations of *The Lord of the Rings*. It was done in 2000 by a Dutchman—David van der Peet—at Fu Jen Catholic University in Taiwan. The thesis discusses the two Chinese

---

[245] A Thesis Submitted by David van der Peet to the Graduate Institute of Translation and Interpretation Studies of Fu Jen Catholic University entitled *"The Lord of the Rings*: Critique of the Two Chinese Translations" (April 15, 2000).
<www.lucifer.hoolan.org/paper/paper/paper02.pdf>. LVO 2/23/2006.

[246] *Comparative Translation Studies* examine the translations of a text in order to come to a better understanding of the source text. Tolkien may—to some extent—be regarded as an proponent of Comparative Translation Studies, though he was not talking about his own work, but of the work of another chronicler, dear to his heart. In "The Monsters and the Critics," he said: "The effort to translate, or to improve a translation, is valuable, not so much for the version it produces, as for the understanding of the original which it awakes."

translations of *The Lord of the Rings*, concluding that both versions made "countless sloppy mistakes," failing to convey the meaning of the original, because the translators did not understand it correctly, or because they lacked a knowledge of "the complicated linguistic and cultural backdrop" against which Tolkien's epic plays.

The author of the thesis devotes a considerable amount of space to summarizing Tolkien's major works, pointing to their roots in "Norse mythology and Christianity." This is a necessary first step in the analysis of any translation, because the quality of the translation cannot be judged without an understanding of what it was that needed to be translated.

The Analysis

Within the main body of the thesis, the author looks at the translations of seventeen prose passages and three poems, selected to provide examples of the characteristic mistakes and problems encountered in the two Chinese translations. Drawing on this analysis, the author demonstrates how "the unique character and genesis of Tolkien's fantasy world, ... the invented languages, plot, and humorous style of *The Lord of the Rings* require special attention during the translation process." He finds that without a complete understanding of the "elaborate historic, linguistic, cultural, geographical and mythological setup," the translator will be unable to "preserve the content and spirit of the original."

Punctuation

In his analysis of the prose segments the author looks at a number of areas, pointing out that "Tolkien's sometimes lengthy sentences, often held together by generous use of colons, semicolons, and dashes, are a tough challenge for the Chinese translator." Tolkien's use of brackets for humorous asides also seems to have been a considerable problem for the Chinese translators, for the same reason. "After all, these punctuation marks (like the use of brackets) are a relatively new addition to Chinese literary usage—not to mention that the use of any punctuation marks was unknown in classical Chinese literature up to the Ching dynasty."

Forty leagues

One of the lexical elements that the author examines is the measurement 'Forty leagues.' This is a part of Tolkien's description of how large The Shire was. In Tolkien's first edition (1954), The Shire was 50 leagues east to west by nearly 50 north to south. With the fourth edition (1965), it changed to 40 by 50, omitting the "nearly."

One of the Chinese translators apparently interpreted *league* as an organization, instead of a unit of measure. The other Chinese translator converted Tolkien's dimensions for The Shire (40 by 50 leagues) into 120 by 150 miles, a solution that the author considers satisfactory, because "'miles' are for the Chinese reader probably roughly as 'exotic' as 'leagues' for the English reader, since China directly adopted the metric system after abandoning its own traditional measures of length."

This would indeed appear to be a viable solution, as the Polish, the Czech, the German and the Dutch translations[247] of the title of Jules Verne's famous *20.000 lieues sous les mers* all use the word *miles* for the translation of *lieues*, which is rendered in the English translation as *20,000 Leagues Under the Sea*.

The leagues-to-miles solution (120 by 150 miles) was also the one taken by the Czech translator, the unofficial Dutch translation and the revised edition of the official Dutch translation. The first edition of the official Dutch translation had said: "50 miles ... almost 50 miles," following Tolkien's original description, but substituting miles for leagues on a one-to-one basis, which is the case in the translation of the title of *20,000 Leagues Under the Sea*. The 'mile to a league' conversion was also repeated by the Russian Grigor'eva and Grushetskij translation. It was, however, based on Tolkien's revised dimensions (40 by 50) for The Shire. Their smaller Shire was also kept company by the second Polish translator's version of 30 by 40 'miles.'

The first Polish translation (Skibniewska) used the archaic word *staje* for *league*. This is a unit of linear distance equal to 1.067 kilometers. Her Shire was 40 by 50 staje, which is 42.68

---

[247] 20.000 mil podmorskiej żeglugi (Polish), 20.000 mil pod mořem (Czech), 20.000 Meilen unter den Meeren (German), 20.000 mijlen onder zee (Dutch).

kilometers by 50.34 kilometers, or 26.46 by 31.2 miles. The Karrik and Kamenkovich (K&K) Russian translation used the more widely recognized archaic Russian unit of measure, the *verst*. One verst is equal to 1.06 kilometers, essentially the equivalent of the Polish staje. The K&K Shire was 60 by 70 versts, making it only slightly larger than the Skibniewska Shire.

The Matorina Russian translation introduced the archaic, dialectical word гон [gon], which is variously defined as between 50 and 80 сажень [sazhen']. One sazhen' is 2.13 meters. This makes her Shire either 4.260 kilometers by 5.325 kilometers or 6.816 kilometers by 8.52 kilometers, depending on the number of sazhens per гон [gon].

The most inventive re-arrangement of the dimensions of The Shire was in the first edition of the Murav'ev and Kistyakovskij Russian translation, where The Shire was described as being 100 leagues from east to west and 150 leagues from north to south. The second edition corrected this mistake.

Most of the Russian translations used the word лига [liga]. In the standard, modern, desk-top dictionaries, лига [liga] is an organization, not a unit of measure, though in the classic dictionary of nineteenth-century Russian, лига [liga] is also defined as a unit of measure. Modern Russian dictionaries list льё [l'ë] as the unit of measure, as in the title of Jules Verne's famous novel 20,000 *Leagues Under the Sea*: 20.000 льё под водой [20.000 l'ë pod vodoj].

Both the German translations used an interesting, old-fashioned measurement to define the size of The Shire. In German, The Shire was 40 by 50 *Wegstunden* ('road-hours'). This is not the modern—especially American—concept of an hour's drive by car, but rather the distance covered on foot in an hour, approximately 3 miles, which exactly matches the conversion of leagues to miles found in the majority of the other translations: 120 by 150 miles. This is the most elegant of all the solutions to this problem. It matches the decidedly slow, pre-industrialized pace of life in The Shire.

Daddy Twofoot

The author of the thesis also ponders the translation of the name *Daddy Twofoot*, which Tolkien, in his notes to translators, says to "translate by sense." The author is perplexed about how to do that, because in Chinese, the ambiguity of the name "Twofoot" needs to be resolved. Is the element *foot* in this name a unit of measure, or does it mean that the old Hobbit has two feet? The author believes that it is a unit of measure. In his view, "tallness varies, and may deserve some special comment, whereas there is nothing worth mentioning about the fact that someone has two feet, be he Man or Hobbit—two feet is the normal thing, and only less (or more feet) would deserve any particular attention."

This same conundrum exists in the Slavic languages. In Russian, for example, the words for 'foot' (unit of measure) and 'foot' (appendage) are not the same. The unit of measure is фут (fut), and the appendage is нога [noga] for humans and лапа [lapa] for animals. Most of the nine Russian translations said 'two paws' (Двулап [Dvulap]). The CD-ROM Gruzberg translation said 'pair of paws' (Паралап [Paralap]), and the Grigor'eva and Grushetskij read "bigger feet' (Большеног [Bol'shenog]), while the Nemirova rendered *Twofoot* as 'three feet' (Триног [trinog]). The first Polish translator left it untranslated ("Twofoot"), as did the print version of the Gruzberg translation (Туфут [Tufut]), while the second Polish translator (Łoziński) changed it to Dwustopczyk ('two foot,' stopa = foot). The Czech translator (Pošustová) made it Dvounožka ('two foot,' nožka = little foot).

More important for the resolution of this name than the question of whether it is a unit of measure or an appendage, is the fact that the element *foot* is a component part of a number of Hobbit names, like Whit*foot*, Har*foot*, Proud*foot* and Puddi*foot*. The element *foot* should be the same in all of them for best effect. Most translators fail on this score.

Tolkien's Style: Repeats

The author similarly addresses Tolkien's stylistic predilection for repeating text elements within close proximity to each other, pointing specifically to the segment where *The Shire* is defined:

> The Hobbits named it the Shire, as the region of authority of their Thain, and a district of **well-ordered business**; and there in that pleasant corner of the world they plied their **well-ordered business** of living ... . [P.24, **emphasis** added.]

Avoiding repeats is the universal admonition of language arts teachers everywhere, but the author of the thesis rightly feels that this repeat deserves to be preserved. Tolkien layers the information in his text with studied repeats, that often fall prey to translators who 'normalize' the text for their readers, depriving them of the subtle significance that Tolkien's repeats give to the text.

All of the Russian translators avoided a repeat here, as did the second Polish translator, the second German translator and the first (official) Dutch translator. Even the translators who did include a repeat, apparently found Tolkien's phrase "well-ordered business" clumsy to deal with, and only the Czech translator had a good rendition of it. Tolkien's phrase is clumsy on purpose. The reader is meant to stumble over it, and having stumbled over it the second time, to remember it. Tolkien uses this trick repeatedly. It is a recognizable part of his style that few translators manage to replicate.

The Czech translator gets credit for half a repeat. She had a wonderful rendition of "district of well-ordered business" (oblast spořádaného podnikání), but could only bring herself to repeat the adjective half of the phrase 'well-ordered business.' Her version of the repeat was: "led a (well-)ordered life" (se zabývali spořádaným žitím). The first Polish translator did even less well, because, while she does have a repeat, it is not a full repeat, but only an echo: peace ... peaceful (spokój ... spokojny), which is true enough, but not the point that Tolkien was trying to make. The unofficial Dutch translator got the point across, though even she was not prepared to repeat a linguistic unit as large as "well-ordered business." She said that The Shire was a region where everything that happened was *orderly* and that the Hobbits led an *orderly* life (alles ordelijk toeging ... hielden zij zich bezig met hun ordelijke leventje). Only the first German translator came close to producing a viable repeat that was nearly as clumsy as Tolkien's. Her repeat was "well-ordered work" and "ordered work" (wohlgeordneter Arbeit ... geordneten Arbeit). Even she could not bring herself to replicate the entire thing.

Tolkien's Neologisms: Gentlehobbit

I would, however, take exception to the author's evaluation of the translation of Tolkien's neologism 'Gentlehobbit.' The author feels that "since both the person speaking and his audience are Hobbits, the subject of their talk also being Hobbits, there is really no specific need to come up with the slightly awkward [Chinese characters that hopefully say: *Gentlehobbit*], since it is clear from the context that Bilbo is a Hobbit." Tolkien's neologisms are part and parcel of the "elaborate historic, linguistic, cultural, geographical and mythological setup" of which the author speaks in his evaluation of the translations. As such, the translator should make an effort to recreate them in the target language.

Although the word *gentleman* is well enough accepted in Russian to have its own dictionary article (джентльмен [dzhentl'men]) and some derivatives with Russian word formation elements (джентльменство [dzentl'menstvo], gentlemenliness), only one of the Russian translators (Gruzberg) was daring enough to use it to recreate Tolkien's neologism, producing (джентльхоббит [dzentl'khobbit]). The same is true of Dutch, where the second translator (Mensink-van Warmelo) simply imported *gentlehobbit*, apparently considering it recognizable enough in Dutch, where *gentleman* is also an entry in the standard Dutch defining dictionary. In German, the first translator (Carroux) created a very readable neologism of her own: *Edelhobbit*, which is transparent as an analog of the German words for *nobleman* and *noblewoman* (*Edelmann/Edelfrau*). The second German translator took it out. The first Dutch translator (Schuchart) likewise made a readable neologism, combining *Hobbit* with the Dutch word for *gentleman* (*heer*), to form *Hobbitheer*. The Czech and the two Polish translators all avoided *gentlehobbit*.

Hybrid Text

Tolkien's use of repeats and his neologisms are two of the things that add to the illusion that *The Lord of the Rings* is a translation from the long-lost *Red Book of Westmarch*. They are types of otherness that mark his fictional translation as what is known in academic translation studies as a hybrid text.

> A hybrid text is a text that results from a translation process. It shows features that somehow seem 'out of place'/ 'strange'/'unusual' for the receiving culture, i.e. the target culture. These features, however, are not the result of a lack of translational competence or examples of 'translationese', but they are evidence of conscious and deliberate decisions by the translator. [248]

Tolkien's use of repeats and his neologisms are conscious and deliberate decisions that Tolkien the 'translator' took in order to convey a sense of the 'out of place' to the target culture, i.e. English Literature. Translators translating Tolkien's 'translation' should be conscious of the hybrid nature of Tolkien's text and attempt to replicate it. "Hybrid texts allow the introduction into a target culture of hitherto unknown and/or socially unacceptable/unaccepted concepts through a medium which, by its non-conformity to social/stylistic conventions and norms, proclaims the otherness of its origin and thereby legitimizes its right to be heard. There is freedom of expression which is unhindered by said conventions," say Schäffner and Adab in their "The Concept of the Hybrid Text in Translation."[249] Translators who ignore the hybrid nature of Tolkien's text are rejecting the legitimate claim of the otherness of his text to be heard.

---

[248] Christina Schäffner, Beverly Adab, "The Concept of the Hybrid Text in Translation," <www.les.aston.ac.uk/hybridhypotheses.html>. LVO 2/23/2006.

[249] Schäffner and Adab.

Conclusion

In general, I found the author's comments interesting, but regretted that he had not included a back translation for the Chinese text for those readers interested in the translation process, but unable to read Chinese. On the whole the thesis was readable, but there were a number of English mistakes (there are two examples in the paragraph below, marked by corrections in square brackets []), which, considering that the thesis was written by a non-native speaker, is not surprising, or necessarily disturbing.

In his conclusion, Van der Peet notes that for a novel as long as *The Lord of the Rings*, replete with so many plot lines and different characters (many of whom have more than one name), "careful reading and consistency are of quintessential importance." In the Chinese translations, "neither the translators nor the editors seemed to have made much effort at harmonizing the completed translation and making 'everything fit' the way Tolkien had done so masterfully in the original." The author's conclusion is that the ideal translator for Tolkien's novel, where "everything is interwoven in an intricate pattern," would be "an intimate 'cognoscente,' or a very thorough and professional translator (ideal would be a combination of both) with [a lot of] time on his hand[s]." His appraisal of the Chinese translations is much the same as the one that I expressed in my book on the Russian translations.[250] He has "the hope of one day seeing a better translation of *The Lord of the Rings* into Chinese."

---

[250] Mark T. Hooker, *Tolkien Through Russian Eyes*, Switzerland: Walking Tree Publishers, 2003.

Mathom House from an old engraving circa 2950 s.r. ☺

Appendix 'A'
The 39 Historic Counties of England

Changes to the administrative map of England in the 1970s and 1990s mean that modern administrative maps of England can be more of a hindrance than a help in a linguistic analysis of Tolkien's toponymy. The table below shows the names of the 39 historic counties (sometimes referred to as the traditional counties) that Tolkien (1892-1973) would have been familiar with.

Bedfordshire	Leicestershire
Berkshire	Middlesex
Buckinghamshire	Norfolk
Cambridgeshire	Northamptonshire
Cheshire	Northumberland
Cornwall	Nottinghamshire
Cumberland	Oxfordshire
Derbyshire	Rutland
Devon	Shropshire
Dorset	Somerset
Durham	Staffordshire
Essex	Suffolk
Gloucestershire	Surrey
Hampshire	Sussex
Herefordshire	Warwickshire
Hertfordshire	Westmorland
Huntingdonshire	Worcestershire
Kent	Wiltshire
Lancashire	Yorkshire
Lincolnshire	

THIS IS A BLANK PAGE

Appendix 'B'
A Brief Guide to the Translations Cited

The first **Dutch** translation (published 1956-1957) was by Max Schuchart (1920-2005). It was the first translation of *The Lord of the Rings* (published 1954-1955) into any language. The "second" Dutch translation was prepared in the late 1970s by Mrs. E.J. Mensink-van Warmelo, who did her own unofficial translation of *The Lord of the Rings*, because she did not like the Schuchart translation. Schuchart revised his translation in 1996. While there are two translations, there is only one map, and consequently only one version of place names that only appear on the map. For a more detailed examination of the differences in these three versions, see: Mark T. Hooker, "Dutch Samizdat: The Mensink-van Warmelo Translation of *The Lord of the Rings*," *Translating Tolkien*, volume 2, Switzerland: Walking Tree Publishers, 2004. Published in Dutch as: "Nederlandse Samizdat: De Mensink-van Warmelo vertaling van *The Lord of the Rings*, *Lembas* (the journal of the Dutch Tolkien Society), number 113, 2004; "Schuchart vs. Mensink-van Warmelo: Round Two," *Lembas-extra* 2004, Leiden: De Tolkienwinkel, 2004, pp. 75-99; and "A Newly Revised Dutch Edition of The Lord of the Rings." *Translation Journal*, volume 9, No. 1, January 2005, <http://accurapid.com/journal/31review.htm>.

The first **German** translation by Margaret Carroux was published 1969-1970. Many still consider it to be the best of the two. A new translation by Wolfgang Krege came out in 2000. For a discussion of the two see: Rainer Nagel, "The New One Wants to Assimilate the Alien," in *Translating Tolkien*, volume 2, Switzerland: Walking Tree Publishers, 2004.

The Russian book market offers its readers a much greater "choice" than does the English-language book market. There are seven **Russian** translations and two re-tellings. If a Russian reader does not have much time, and just wants the plot highlights, there are the Bobyr' and the Yakhnin re-tellings. If a Russian reader wants a Russian story instead of an English one, there are the Murav'ev & Kistyakovskij and the Volkovskij. If a Russian reader wants a new-age Tolkien, there is the Grigor'eva & Grushetskij. If the Russian reader wants an annotated *LotR*, there is the Kamenkovich & Karrik. If a Russian reader wants a text with all the big words simplified, there is the Matorina. If the Russian reader wants to read Tolkien, however, they have to read him in the Original, and to help them get their English up to speed, there is the Gruzberg and the Nemirova. Choice is the hallmark of a market economy, and the Russians are obviously doing their best to become one. For a detailed who's who of the Russian translations, see: Mark T. Hooker, "Nine Russian Translations of *The Lord of the Rings*," in *Tolkien in Translation*, Thomas Honegger (ed.), Switzerland: Walking Tree Publishers, 2003; or Mark T. Hooker, *Tolkien Through Russian Eyes*, Switzerland: Walking Tree Publishers, 2003.

The first **Polish** translation by Maria Skibniewska (published 1961-1963), was right on the heels of the Swedish one (published 1959-1961) and ahead of the Danish (1968-1970) and German (1969-1970). A revised Polish translation was done by Jerzy Łoziński in 1996.

Illustration Credits

Astarte (p. 220): *The Iconographic Atlas of the Arts and Sciences*. Philidelphia: Iconographic Publishing Co., 1886, plate 17.7.

Mr. Bilbo Baggins, esq. and the corslet of chain mail he is donating to Mathom House (p. 6): courtesy of *The Hobbiton Daily News* ☺: Drawn by JWD

Bill Sticker (p. 51): Oscar Browning. *The New Illustrated History of England* (in 4 volumes), London: J.S. Virtue and Co., 1888, vol. iv, p. 218.

Boundary Elm, Stratford (p. 204): Browning, vol. ii, p. 80.

Bredon Hill Map (p. 12): computer layout by the author.

Bucklebury (p. 33): Browning, vol. ii, p. 112.

Commemorative Medal with Orange and Oak Trees (p. 199): George L. Craik. *The Pictorial History Of England* (in 10 volumes), London: C. Knight, 1841, vol. IV, p. 29.

Crest of the Taille Bois Family (p. 55): *The Novels and Miscellaneous Works of Daniel DeFoe*, Oxford: D.A. Talboys, 1940, title page.

Illustration Credits

Diagram of Pit-Dwellings at Hurstbourne Siding (p. 185): Joseph Stevens. *A Parochial History of St. Mary Bourne with an Account of the Manor of Hurstbourne Priors*, London: Whiting and Co., 1888.

Deverills Map (p. 45): computer layout by the author.

Faversham Moot Horn (p. 100): P.H. Ditchfield. *Old English Customs Extant at the Present Time: An Account of Local Observances, Festival Customs, and Ancient Ceremonies Yet Surviving in Great Britain*, London: George Redway, 1896.

Gandalf fights the Balrog with sword and staff (p. 202): original drawing by JWD.

Harbottle Castle (p. 57): M.A. Richardson. *The Local Historian's Table Book of Remarkable Occurrences, Historical Facts, Traditions, Legendary and Descriptive Ballads, etc., Connected with the Counties of Newcastle-Upon-Tyne, Northumberland and Durham* (in 4 volumes), Newcastle-Upon-Tyne: M.A. Richardson, 1843, vol. iv, p. 48.

Lake Town (p. 18): *The Iconographic Atlas of the Arts and Sciences*. Philidelphia: Iconographic Publishing Co., 1886, plate 4.7.

Llyfrawr Logo (p. i): George L. Craik. *The Pictorial History of England* (in 10 volumes), London: W. & R. Chambers, 1856, vol. ii, p. 205; Charles Knight. *The Popular History of England* (in 7 volumes), London: Bradbury and Evens, 1857, vol. i, p. 104.

Mathom House ☺ (p. 246): Oscar Browning, 1888, vol. iv, p. 174. The original caption read: "Old shop, corner of Fleet Street and Chancery Lane, early in the nineteenth century." Also in: Craik, 1856, vol. ii, p. 850, and in: W.H.S. Aubrey. *The National and Domestic History of England* (3 volumes in 11 fronts), London: J. Hagger [1870?-80], front 6, p. 550.

Mathum Sword (p. 82): Craik, 1856, vol. ii, p. 859.

Mr. Pickwick addresses the Pickwick Club (p. 120): Reproduced from the "Imperial Edition" of Charles Dickens' Collected Works, volume 24: *The Posthumous Papers of the Pickwick Club*, Boston: Estes & Lauriat, 1895, p. 5.

Newbury Map (p. 30): computer layout by the author.

Owen Gledur's Oak (p. 75): *Cassell's Illustrated History of England* (in 9 volumes), London: Cassell, Petter and Galpin, 1865-1874, vol. i, p. 486.

Pershore Map (p. 13): computer layout by the author.

Poulnabrone Dolmen (p. 178): Original drawing by JWD.

Roman Fighting Elephants (p. 232): Knight, vol. i, p. 18.

Roman Soldiers (p. 96): Browning, vol. i, p. 9.

Standing Stone (p. 70): Richardson, vol. iii, p. 73.

Stonehenge Restored (p. 78): *Cassell's*, vol. i, p. 4.

Town Hall (p. 20): Richardson, vol. iii, p. 61.

Yale map (p. 43): computer layout by the author.

About The Artist

The artist contributing three prints to this volume is James Dunning, who has served as jack of many trades, to include linguist, soldier-clerk, free-lance translator / interpreter, teacher, professional student, chemist and pharmaceutical researcher, archivist, author and editor of scientific reports (*et al.*), and musician in Irish and international music. He has acquired no *formal* art training other than the casual observation and homage of the eye to nature and to works and techniques admired, but is now accumulating a portfolio nevertheless, including these pen-and-ink drawings.

The artist has read and digested Tolkien's various works for forty years and has constructed evolving mental landscapes of scenes in Middle-earth. Having read *The Hobbit* and *The Lord of the Rings* over twenty times, each time he picks up fresh details. He has tried to depict Tolkien themes presented here in a style consistent with J.R.R. Tolkien's own illustrative style.

About The Art (*Artist's descriptions*) - Drawings are executed in drawing ink, black, white and grey with standard drawing pens on paper or on Bristol board, with occasional traces of tortillon stump shading (2 and 3). Most pieces have a story behind them, and these are no exception. In keeping with *A Tolkienian Mathomium's* linguistic landscapes of Middle-earth, 2 and 3 feature linguistic content: Tolkien's scripts.

1. Portal Dolmen, Poulnabrone (1986) - This fine dolmen is situated on *The Burren*, a natural rock table fractured into many fine crevices. In springtime many of these crevices contain a microcosmos of breathtaking flora blossoming on a Lilliputian scale. This extensive table rock also platforms a number of imposing ruins, among them this dolmen, a Neolithic monument of unknown function, perhaps a burial chamber. *The Burren* is in the northwest of the County Clare, in Ireland. I was there in 1978.

2. Bilbo and the Mathom House (2006) – Back again in *The Hobbit*, Bilbo lends his *mithril* coat to a museum, later identified as the Mathom House in Michel Delving. Inspired by his *Tolkienian Mathomium*, I conceived this piece and hereby dedicate it to Mark T. Hooker. The Mathom House is depicted in classic Hobbit-style, reflecting their closer kinship with the earth: underground construction with round door and window, surrounded by lush botanical splendor. Inscriptions above its door read M.D. (for Michel Delving) in the Tengwar and in Daeron's Runes. Bilbo stands beside his *mithril* coat and helm on display, as if posing for a write-up in the *Hobbiton Daily News*. He has blown some fine smoke rings and is drawing pensively for the next ring. Speaking of *Rings*(!): judging from Bilbo's constrained (*confusticated and bebothered*?) expression, he may be becoming uncomfortable with the unwanted attention, or impatient posing for the slow and methodical artist (no Nikon® or Polaroid® cameras in Middle-earth), or perhaps he has spotted Lobelia Sackville-Baggins approaching, for he is wishing he were somewhere else; his left hand is in his pocket absent-mindedly fingering his *Ring*.

3. The Bridge of Khazad-Dûm (2006) – *The Fellowship of the Ring* pits Gandalf (the artist's most-favoritest LOTR character) against the Balrog, a dreadful winged spirit of the underworld, on a narrow ribbon of stone arching over a fathomless abyss. The eye is drawn immediately into the horror of the immense yawning void. Despite the valiant intentions of his cohorts (Aragorn is mounting the bridge despite Gimli's caution, and Boromir chafes to spring into action), Gandalf is seen brave but utterly alone against a menacing paradox of shadow and flame with fiery sword and whip of many thongs. Gandalf's staff, at the wizard's will or even spontaneously, is discharging the Secret Fire of Anor in defense, and his sword has just shattered the sword of the Balrog. His eight companions look on aghast. Men, Elf and Dwarf are in defensive or protective postures, Hobbits are either overcome or offering support.

The massive pillars of Moria are inscribed at the base with runic names and patronymics of various Dwarf rulers. The right foreground pillar is that of Durin: its inscription in entirety would read "Durin of Khazad-Dûm." However it bears sickening scars of the Orcs' desecration. This pillar has been damaged by warfare. Above its Dwarvish inscription may be seen Orc graffiti, namely a ghastly *Eye of Sauron* with nine rays (think: the Nine *Nazgûl*), and the name of *Azog* the Goblin King.

Below in the lower right-hand corner: can you identify the foreground skull from its inscription? The skull has been branded with the name of AZOG. In Appendix A of *The Lord of the Rings* the Goblins brand the head of Thrór with Azog's name: could this be the fabled skull of Thrór, preserved as a trophy by Azog, unheeded by the Fellowship in their haste? These Orkish artifacts are a vile insult to the grandeur of Khazad-Dûm, but also the artist's further reminder how the servants of Morgoth and Sauron have usurped Durin's kingdom and defiled the glory of the ancient mansions of the Khazad.

* * * * * * * * *

ARTIST'S NOTE - The above pieces are property and copyright [©] of James Dunning, and are used by Mark T. Hooker in *A Tolkienian Mathomium* with express permission. Those interested in purchasing high quality prints of these pieces or others from his portfolio may contact the artist at jwdunning@bellsouth.net.

Index

A

A Journal of the Plague Year (DeFoe)   159
"A Study in Scarlet" (Sherlock Holmes)   167
Adansonia digitata (baobab tree, Latin name of)   76
admonition of language arts teachers   242
Adonis   222
adventures, no use for   129
"The Adventure of the Speckled Band" (Sherlock Holmes)   168
Ædward the Unconquered   23
Æthelflæd   23
afon (Welsh word for *river*)   66, 85
African exploration   234
Afrikaans   235
age of the hero at the start of his adventure   129
Alfred (king)   188
alias, Tolkien's and Dickens' use of   118
alliteration   101
alliterative alarm   101-102
alliterative Anglo-Saxon poetry   103
alliterative rhyme   103
Altamira   181
ambiguity   26, 42, 54, 150, 241
amulet from trees of the triad   200
ancient "inauguration trees"   71, 197
Ancient Tree, fortress of the   71, 197
"The Angel" (Dickens' inn)   118
Anglo-Saxon   187
Anglo-Saxon England   2, 187
Anglo-Saxon tradition of Gift Giving   2
Anglo-Saxon language   10
Anglo-Saxons   66, 187
anti-quest   124, 133
Aphrodite   220, 222, 224
Appendix F.II to *LotR*   162
appointed death   140
Aragorn   4, 93, 98, 125-127, 138-142, 217
Archet   7-8, 15, 67

Argoed 8, 67
armour 2, 128-129
Arwen 4, 139-140, 142
ash tree 42, 192-197, 199-200
    man descended from 196
ash-wood 41, 192, 200
Ashton under Hill 12
Astarte 220-224
Aston Bampton 63
Ashtoreth 220
Athtar 223
Auenbronn (German translation of *Shirebourn*) 25
Auenland (German translation of *The Shire*) 24-25
authenticity 154-157, 159, 161, 166, 174-176, 181
Avon (see river Avon)
Avon river valley 13
Ayesha 133-145, 147, 151
Ayesha: The Return of She 157

B
Bag End 34-35, 37, 42, 120-121, 183
Baggins iii, 37
Baggings, Bilbo 34, 101, 119, 121, 129-130, 135, 153, 167, 169, 243
    Bilbo's song of Eärendil 222-223
    Bilbo and adventures 5, 228
Baggins, Frodo < Bingo 118
Bagshot (real place) 31, 34-35
Bagshot Row 34, 37
balewort (plant name) 40
ballads, lyrical 193
baobab tree 76
Baranduin (see river Baranduin)
barracks-room argot 111
Battle at the Black Gates 151
Battle of Greenfields 101
Battle of Helm's Deep 126, 128

Battle of Moria 128
Beal (real place) 67
beans and bacon 32, 32 n.
beat the bounds 203-204, 206
Beeford (real place) 67
The Benson Murder Case (Philo Vance) 168
Beowulf 1-4, 38, 52, 237
The Betrothed (Manzoni) 169
Bhagavad Gita 75
bile (Irish word: "ancient tree") 71-72, 77, 197, 199, 201
Bill Stickers 51
Bindbale Wood 37-39, 40
Bindbole Wood 37, 40-42
bindweed (plant name) 40
Blackpool (real place) 68
blacksmith 85-88
blacksmith's anvil 88
Blanco (brother of Marcho) 187
blue (the color) 89-91
blue blade of true fierceness 89
Boann (Irish water goddess) 85, 90
bole (tree trunk) 41
Bombadil, Tom 192-193
book written to justify another book 162
bootless (the word explained) 20
Bored of the Rings 19
botanical names of Bree 39
bounder and a cad 203, 205-206
bounder (borderguard of The Shire) 203, 205-206
bounds, beat the 203-204, 206
Bracegirdle 55, 227-231
brachycephalic (type of scull) 184
Brandy Hall 10, 33, 47, 63
Bredon (real place) 7, 11-12, 14
Bredon Hill (real place) 8, 11-13

Bree	7-8, 12-14, 17, 93, 117
Bree Hill	7-8, 13, 59
Bree mile	95, 97
Bree-Land	7-8, 12, 15, 17
Breedon (real place)	7, 11
Bree-men, language of the	10
Brereton (real place)	125
Brill (real place)	7
bronze weapons	89
Brown, Dan	154
Browning, Robert	175
Buchan, John	173, 234-235
Buckland	10, 13, 29, 31-33, 67, 101, 103
Bucklebury	31-33
Buddha	90
Buddhist tradition	221
Büttel (German word)	56
Bywater	67
Bywater Pool	68

C

cadence, marching	96-97
Caerlleon ar Wysg (real place)	67
Caerwysg (real place)	16
Caesar	89, 98, 184
Caledonia (origin of the word)	187
"candles of corpses"	49, 148, 150
canon of popular English poetry	193
The Canterbury Tales (Chaucer)	193
carcanet	224
Carpe Diem!	142
carreg (Welsh word)	79
Carrock	79-81
Carroux (German translator)	24, 49, 57, 103, 108, 205, 229, 243, 249
The Castle of Otranto (Walpole)	155, 163-164
Castell Carreg Cennen (real place)	80-81
Castell Dinas Bran (real place)	44
Castellnewydd ar Wysg (real place)	68
cauldron	86, 89-90
cave bear	182
cave paintings	181
Celduin	67
Celtic culture	10
Celtic elements in place names	8-10, 15, 17
Celtic horse goddess	188
Celtic hydronyms	66, 85
Celtic jewelry	188
Celtic lore	86
Celtic myth	192
Celtic river names	66, 85
Celtic tradition	192, 194
Celts	184
Cervantes, Miguel de	154, 171-173
Cervantes (the meaning of the name)	172
Charles I	34, 159
Charles II	198-199
"charmed wood" (ashwood)	199
Chatterton, Thomas	157, 175
Chaucer	40, 193
Chesterton, G.K.	175
Chetwood	8
Chinese translations	237-245
Christ's Transfiguration on Mount Tabor	141
Christian-era writers	70
Christianity	70, 72, 77, 194, 200, 220-221, 238
pre-Christian religious site	74, 78
church (the place-name element)	77
Churchstoke (real place)	58
Cid Hamet Benengeli (faux	

author of *Don Quixote*) 172
"The Cinematographer of Waverley" (pastiche of Scott) 207-215
Civil War (1633-1642) 28, 30, 34
Coats of Arms 198
Cockney 105-108
coelbren (Welsh word for dendroscript) 199
Combe 7-8, 12, 31, 36
Comparative Translation Studies 237
condensation (linguistic process) 36, 112
consonant envelope 11, 19, 20
consonant envelope b*l 72
consonant envelope *p*ll* 72-73
consonant envelope STL 221, 224
consonant envelope STR 220-221
contraction (linguistic process) 33, 52, 58, 103
Cooper, James Fenimore 166-167
Cornish language 189
Cornwall 189-190
corpse candle 148-151
Cotswold Hills (real place) 11
counties of England 22-23, 247
Coventry (real place) 27, 28, 29
Coventry blue 28, 29
"The Cow Jumped over the Moon" (nursery rhyme) 101
crown of thorns worn by Christ 200
cry of alarm 101-103
Culann 85-86
Culhwch and Olwen 88

D

Daddy Twofoot 241
Danelaw 23, 25, 60
The Da Vinci Code 154
Dead Marshes 147, 150-151
Deadmen of Dunharrow 81
death 127, 133, 134, 138, 140, 144, 145, 149-150, 200-201, 222
   appointed death 140
   fear of 138-139
   gift of 134, 139
   life after 141
   man's fate 127
   death omens (corpse candles) 149-151
decorated caves 181
Deephallow 63
DeFoe, Daniel 154, 159-160, 173
Dern Dingle 12
description of Hobbits 119
Deverills (real place) 45
Dickens, Charles 94, 118, 121, 149, 153, 162, 173
dictionary diving 47
Dingle (real place) 12
dolichocephalic (a type of scull) 184
Don Quixote 171-173
Doyle, Sir Arthur Conan 167-169
dragons 39, 138, 194
Drill and Ceremonies 96
druids 199
Dryden, John 181
duin (Ilkorian word for *water*) 67
Dunedan 187
Dutch translation 248
Dutch translator (Mensink-van Warmelo) 47, 61, 206, 229, 233, 242-243, 248
Dutch translator (Schuchart) iv, 10, 25-26, 29, 33-35, 37-38, 42, 46-47, 50-52, 57, 60-61, 93, 205, 229, 233, 239, 242-243, 248
duty to fight 2

A Tolkienian Mathomium 263

Dwalakoneis (Gothic translation of *Tolkien*) 51, 171
Dwaling   iv, 49-52, 171
Dwarf of high stature   211
Dwarvish smiths   88
dwfr   45, 66, 85

E

Eärendil   219, 222-224
Eärendil's ship   224
Eärendil's star   219
Earth Houses   190
Eddas   196
Edward the Elder   23
Einstein's theory of relativity   143
elephant, word for   233
element Church   77
element -dan   187
element -EL   218
element ELED-   218
element ESEK-   15
element EST-   217
element *foot*   241
element *hop*   52
element -hall   47
element KEL-   67
element *shot*   35
Ellen Lluyddog   58
Elven-smiths of Eregion   138
Elvenking   191, 201
Elves   134-135, 140, 143, 197
Elvish smiths   89
Elwing   218-219, 222-224
enchanted weapons   85-86
ending *-ing*   iv, 50, 171, 231
Entmoot   12
Entwade   54
Epona (Celtic horse goddess)   188
Esgaroth   15-17
Estel   126, 217, 219, 224
etymologies, made-up by Tolkien   101, 203, 224

Evening Star   219-220, 223
Evernight of death   222
Evesham (real place) 11, 13-14

F

faces in the water   151
"faction" (fact + fiction)   154
fair (event)   31-32
    etymology   32
fairies   196-197
Fairlop Fair   32
Fairlop Oak   32, 74
fairy folk   196, 201
Fairy Trees   197
fairy-thorn (hawthorn tree)   197
faith (religious)   140-142
false historical records (DeFoe)   159
fame, the worth of   141
Father Christmas Letter (1932)   181-182
faux-etymology (Tolkien) 203, 224
faux-history (Haggard)   158
FEAR! FIRE! FOES!   101, 103
Fee Fi Fo Fum   102-103
feigned-manuscript topos   121, 153-156, 171, 173, 177
"The Five Orange Pips" (Sherlock Holmes)   167
film   207-212, 214-215
film
    based on a book   108
    founded on Literature   208
film version of *King Solomon's Mines*   130-131
filmography for *Ivanhoe*   216
flame, living   145
flame of a candle   149
flame that runs before the sun   223
flames of Mount Doom   145
FM 22-5 (*Drill and Ceremonies*)   96-97

fogou (Cornish word) 189-190
folklore of Wales 149
The Folk-lore of Plants
 (Thiselton-Dyer) 194
Fonthill (real place) 46
foot (appendage or unit of
 measurement?) 241
forge water, curative power of
 86-87
*The Fortunes and Misfortunes
 of the Famous Moll
 Flanders* (DeFoe) 160
Foster, Mike 207
four gifts of the ancestors 89
free will 150
Frodo, change brought on by
 the Ring 137
Frodo's age at the start of his
 adventure 129
Frodo's decision to keep the
 Ring 145
Frodo's anti-quest 124
Frodo's housekeeper 121

G

Gá (ancient Germanic word for
 a 'district') 22-23, 25
Gaelic language 16, 88, 174
Galadriel 137, 144, 151, 155
Gandalf 93, 118, 126, 137-138,
 141, 191-192, 200-201
 resurrected Gandalf 138,
 200
Garn! 105, 107-113
garn-ers 113-114
Gau (German word) 22, 24
Gawd lumme! (Cockney slang)
 106
Geismar, sacred oak of 195
gentlehobbit 243
George IV 34
German translation 249
Ghân-buri-Ghân 55, 139
gift of death 134, 139
Glasgerion 193

Glorious Revolution 198
Goblin's Hollow Tree 74
goddess Ashtoreth 220
goddess Astarte 220-224
goddess of the Evening Star
 223
goddess of the Morning 223
gold 3-4
golf, the etymology of 101,
 203, 224
Gollum 114-115, 136-137, 145
Gorhendad (Welsh word for
 grandfather) 10
Gothic language 51, 171
Gouw (Dutch word) 22, 24
Govannon (mythic
 blacksmith) 87-88
Great Comberton (real place)
 12
Great Hall with a Thousand
 Soldiers 90
great migrations 184
Great Plague 201
Great Savioress 221
greed of the Dwarves 138
Greene, Graham 125, 133, 155
Greywood 55
Gruzberg (Russian translator)
 46, 48, 58, 110, 205, 241, 243,
 249
Guingelot (Wade's ship) 224
Gulliver's Travels 163-166, 167
Guest, Lady Charlotte 176

H

Hadrian's Wall 55
Haggard, Henry Rider 94, 97,
 123-128, 133-135, 137-138,
 142, 145, 147-148, 150, 153,
 155-158, 166, 173, 234
 Haggard's influence on
 Tolkien 130
half translation 57-58
Ham (real place) 31, 36
happiness, search for 141

Harbottle (real place)   54-55
Harbottle Castle   55
Hardbottle   53-57
Harwood Forest (real place)   55
Hawthorn (tree)   170, 197, 201
Hawthorne, Nathaniel   154, 170-171, 172
Hay (real place)   44
hay (hedge)   31
Haysend   31, 63
Heart of the Wild (Haggard)   158
hearts of Men, as shaped by Illuvatar   139
Hell   143
helmet   4
Hengist   187-188
Herald of the morn (Eärendil)   223
Hergest Manor in Herefordshire   176
Het Boze Woud (Dutch translation of *Bindbale Wood*)   37-38
High Hay   31
hill figures   188
Historic Counties of England   23, 247
history, Tolkien on   21, 38
history of time, Ayesha on   134
Hitler   24
Hobbit, description of   119
Hobbitania (Russian translation of *The Shire*)   25
Hobbitshire (Russian translation of *The Shire*)   25
holes in the ground (smials)   182
holm(e) (place-name element)   60-62
Holme (real place)   74
Holmes, Sherlock   167-169
Holy Cow   90
Homer   195

homonym-pun   20
honor (trait)   2-3, 5
Honour (district)   24
Horatius at the Bridge   126-127
horn (mathum)   3
   ancient   2
   Faversham Moot Horn   100
Horn-call of Buckland   101
Hornblower   13, 229
Horsa   187
horse worship   188
housekeeper   120-121
Houses of Lamentation   143
Housman, Alfred Edward   11
humor   2, 5, 7, 11, 19-20, 170, 173, 177, 214, 230, 238
Hybrid Text   244
hydronyms   16, 65-66, 84-85, 87

I

I Promessi Sposi [The Betrothed]   161-162
Iberians   184, 186-187
Ignosi (Haggard character)   125-126
Illuvatar   139
immortal soul   144
immortality   127, 133-135, 139-140, 142, 144-145, 150
   bestowed on Frodo by the Ring   135
   love and immortality   139-140
   real immortality   140
   practical immortality   136, 140-141, 144
Imran Brain   44
inauguration trees   71, 197
inverted tree   75
iron weapons   89
Iron-age coins   188
Isbourne   16
Ishtar   220-221, 223-224
Ivanhoe   215-216
   Filmography   216

J

James I 34
James II 198
jest (see also *humor*) iv, 7, 20-21, 51, 56, 81, 128, 170-173, 203, 206, 214, 225
Jupiter 91

K

Kabala 75
Kalevala 175
Keukenhof (real place) 61
kilometer (unit of measurement) 94-95
King Arthur 81
King Eliseg 43-44
King Ethelred of England 39
King Gustavus Adolphus of Sweden 159
King Henry the Sixth (Shakespeare) 20
King Lear 103
King of the Elves 201
King of the Milesians 91
The King of Pirates (DeFoe) 160
King Olaf 39
King Olave II 85
King Solomon's Mines 94-95, 123-125, 130
King Theoden 3
King Twala 128
King, Eudaf "Hen" (Octavius) 58
kingdom of Powys 44
kingdom of the dead 222
kings of ancient Ireland 198
kings of Powys 44
Kingsley, Charles (novelist) 193
Kipling, Rudyard 192-193
Kirkby Lonsdale (real place) 83-84
Klaarbeek (Dutch translation of *Shirebourn*) 25-26
knowledge 89, 138-139
  literary 208
  love of 210
  of tree lore 191-192, 199-200
  superficial 210
  tree of 76
Krege (German translator) 57, 103, 205, 249

L

Lady of Heaven 221
Lady of Mercia 23
Lake Town 15, 17, 18, 73
lamentation for Tammuz 223
Lancaster (real place) 84
land of the dead 223
language of the Bree-men 10
language of the Hobbits, original 9
language of the Orks, Orkish 111
language of the southern Stoors, older 10
language arts teachers, admonition of 242
language usage, marked 95, 107-111
lár (unit of measurement) 97-98
Lascaux (cave painting site) 182
"The Lay of the Smithy" (Irish *Lays of Fin*) 85
leaf mold of the mind 19, 117, 145, 234-235
leagues (unit of measurement) 93-99, 239-240
The Legends of the Jews (Ginzberg) 76
lenition (term used in Welsh morphology) 8, 16, 53, 67, 81, 200
Lewis, C.S. vi, 130-131, 133, 155
Lhûn/luin 83-85
Liberty (district) 24

A Tolkienian Mathomium 267

life after death 141
lightning gods 72, 91, 126, 196
lightning plants 196
linguistic aside 148
linguistic fossil 65, 84
linguistic taste: Tolkien,
 private 10
Lisse (real place) 60
literary baggage iii-iv, 105, 108, 111, 117, 234-235
Literary Forgeries and Mystifications 175
Lithe 31
Little Comberton (real place) 12
Little Delving 50
Liverpool (real place) 68
llan (Welsh place-name element) 77
Llyn Hir (real place) 17
Lockholes 46
Lon (hydronym) 86
Lon (name of several blacksmiths) 85
 name Lon (blackbird or ousel) 88
Lon mac Liomtha 85, 87-89
London, the place name 84
Long Lake 15, 17, 67
Longbottom 14
Lönnrot, Elias 175
love 120, 134, 135, 137, 139-140, 142, 144-145
 love and immortality 139-140
 love of knowledge 210
Lucan (Roman poet) 91
Lune (hydronym) 83-85
Lune river valley 83-84

M

The Mabinogion 44, 58, 176
Mac an Luin 85-86
Macabuin 85

MacPherson, James 157, 175-176
Macsen Wledig 58
Magnus Clemens Maximus 58
Magnus Maximus 44
mail (armour):
 chain armour 128-129
 corslet of Mithril mail 129
 corslet of ring-mail 4
Major Oak (name of a tree) 74
Major Road Ahead (a pun created by Tolkien) 51
man descended from trees 195
Manannan Mac Lir 86
manuscript 157-169, 175-176
The Manuscript Found in Saragossa (Potocki) 164
Manzoni, Alessandro 161-162, 169
map of The Shire 19, 22, 171
marching day 98
Marcho (brother of Blanco) 187
marked language usage 95, 107-111
marriage of Sam 120-121
marsh-born balls of fire 150
marsh-fires in the swamps 141
marshes 147-148, 150-151
Marvell, Andrew 142
Mary (the mother of God) 220-221
mathom 1-2, 5
Mathom-house 5, 246
mathum 1-5
 mathum-gifu 2-3
 mathum-hus 5
 mathum-sigla 4
 mathum-sword 4
Mayor of Michel Delving 31-32
 Mock Mayor 31
Meavy Oak (name of a tree) 74
mediatrix 221
Melkor 139, 141

memoirs 153-154, 159-160, 167, 170
Memoirs of a Cavalier (DeFoe) 159-160
Mensink-van Warmelo (second Dutch translator) 47, 61, 206, 229, 233, 242-243, 248
Mercian England 23
Michel Delving 5, 50, 57
Micronesia, legends of 75
The Middle Kingdom (MacManus) 192
Midgewater Marshes 147
mile (unit of measure) 93-95, 239-240
    Bree mile 95, 97
    English mile 98
    Irish mile 95, 97
    Roman mile 97
    statute mile 96
Milton 220
misrepresenting the book in a film 209
Mistress of Heaven 220
Mithril chain mail 129
Mock Mayor 31
modern scientific skepticism 141
The Monikins (Cooper) 166
monsters 38-39
Morning Star 90, 223
mortal life 145
mosquitoes 148
"musqueteers" 148
My Fair Lady 106-111
mythologies 176-177
    mythology for England 176
    mythology for Scotland 176
    mythology for Wales 176

N

names generate a story 51, 218
navigational by the stars 222
"Neekerbreekers" 148
Neolithic 179, 184, 188

neologisms 243-244
Newbold (real place) 54
Newbottle 53
Newbury 29, 31-32, 45
Newton, Isaac 17, 121
Newton (real place) 17
Newtown 30, 58
Night of Naught 223
"no use for adventures" 129
Nobottle 53, 55-56
Norbury 24, 29, 33
Nordic tradition 194-196
normalization 46, 63
Norns 194
Northamptonshire 23, 25
"Note on the Shire Records" 121, 153, 169, 174
notes and records 167-169
nursery rhymes 39

O

Oak 192, 195-196, 198-199, 201
    and lightning 91, 196
    and Fairies 196, 197
    Oak Apple Day 198, 201
    men born of the 195
    oak of Geismar 71-72, 195
    oak wood 72, 191, 201
    oak wood posts 74, 76
    place-name element *oak* 199
"Oak and Ash and Thorn" (incantation or oath) 193
Oak, Ash and Thorn, triad of 194
Oak, Ash and Thorn, association with the fairies 197
Oak Leaf 198
oak tree (symbol) 74, 77, 91, 199
Odin 200
The Odyssey 195
old gods 70
oldest Old Thing 192

olifant (Dutch word) 235
Olifants (hydronym) 234-235
Oliphaunt 233-235
oral culture 174
orange tree (symbol) 199
Orcs, language useage 111
"original author" 173
Orkish 111
Ossian (see *The Poems of...*)
ousel 88
Ousel of Cilgwri 88
Owain Llawgoch 81
Owen Glendower's Oak 74

P
pakkeman (Dutch word) 37-38
parody 19-22, 42, 54-55, 173, 214
Pech-Merle (cave painting site) 182
Pembroke Castle 81
Pencoed (real place) 36
Pensham (real place) 13
Penwood (real place) 31, 35-36, 57
Percy, Thomas 193
Pershore (real place) 12-13
personal aesthetic, Tolkien's 22, 39-40, 91
Perun (pagan god) 91
Peter Jackson 123, 214
Peveril of the Peak (Sir Walter Scott) 207 n., 213
Philo Vance (fictional character) 168-169
philological jest (see *jest*)
phonetic distortion 109, 112
Mr. Pickwick 119-120
illustration 120
The Pickwick Papers (Dickens) 118-121, 162-163
Pict Houses 190
*pile (hypothetical Welsh equivalent of the Irish *bile*) 73-74, 77

Pillar of Eliseg 43
Pincup 52-53
pipe, Tolkien with 114
pipeweed 13-14
pit dwellings 179-183, 188
pity for Gollum 136-137
The Poems of Ossian (MacPherson) 174-177
Polish translation 102, 239, 249
Polish translator (first) 102, 205, 230, 239, 241-243
Polish translator (second) 61-62, 102, 205, 230, 239, 241-243, 249
post-literate screen-age 215, 234
Potocki, Jan 164
power 144
  given by The Ring 137
  LotR, a tale of 133, 144
  symbol of 71
  of life and death 137
  of love 139
  of the Stone of the Ancestors 124
Powers (the gods) 134
Powys (in Wales) 17, 43-44
practical immortality 136, 140-141, 144
  bestowed on Frodo by the Ring 135
Prague (real place) 62
Prancing Pony, Tolkien's inn 117
pre-Christian religious site 74, 78
prefix *Ar-* 8
Prester John (Buchan) 234-235
prestige 2-5
pseudonym 21, 156, 162, 165, 168, 217
publish anonymously 160-161, 163
Puck of Pook's Hill 192-193
pun, transference of 61

Index

Pygmalion (Shaw) 105, 108-110

Q

Quatermain (fictional character) 123-124, 129-130
   ethical evaluation of his life 130
Queen of Heaven 220, 223
Queen of the gods 221
quest 119, 121, 124, 125, 133-134, 139
Quixotic 'impossible dream' 142

R

"Rappaccini's Daughter" (Hawthorne) 170
records: "Note on the Shire Records" 121, 153, 169, 174
records, notes and 167-169
records, false historical (DeFoe) 159
Red Books 176
   The Red Book of Clanranald 176
   The Red Book of Hergest 176
   The Red Book of Tref-y-Blodau viii
   The Red Book of Westmarch 10, 35, 121, 153, 167, 169, 176, 244
Redbourn (real place) 60
Redbridge (real place) 60
reed (place-name element) 15, 60-63
Reedlake (see *Esgaroth*) 15
Reedmire (real place) 60
reincarnated soul of Kallikrates 142, 145
religious beliefs 140-141
religious establishment 70
religious site 70
   pre-Christian religious site 74, 78
Reliques of Ancient English Poetry (Percy) 193
reminiscences (see also *memoirs*) 167, 170
repeating text elements (Tolkien's style) 241-242, 244
respect, honor and prestige 5
resurrected Gandalf 138, 200
Ring, the 137, 144
   Ring, abandoned by the 145
   Ring, acquisition of the 130
The Ring and the Book (Browning) 175
Ring Bearer 137
river names (hydronyms) 65
river Avon 9, 11-12, 66, 67, 85
river Baranduin 59
river Boyne 85
river Celduin 67
river Cennen 80
river Dover 66, 85
river Esk 16, 66
river Ex 66
river Exe 16
river Gavenni 87
river Gelion 59
river Is 16
river Kennet 30
river Lhûn 29, 83-84
river Lon (alternate spelling of Lune) 84
river Lune 83-85, 87, 91
river Thames 66
river Usk 16, 66, 68
river Wye 44
river Wylye 45
river Wysg 66-67
river, The Water 16, 65-67
river Stour 23
Rob Roy (Scott) 160-161
Robinson Crusoe (DeFoe) 154, 158
Rohirric 8-10, 187

Rohrau (real place) 60
Rohrbach (real place) 60
Rohrholm 60
Roman league (unit of measurement) 97
Roman Legion in Britain 95
Roman Legionnaire 99
Roman marching pace (see also *cadence*) 98
Roman mile 97
Roman pace 96-97
Roman roads 96
Rosie (Sam's sweetheart) 120-121
Rouffignac (cave painting site) 181-182
Roverandom (Tolkien) 13
Rowan-tree 41 n.
Runes 200
Rushey 59-63
Rushy 59-60
Russian translations 24, 36, 46, 50, 53, 56-58, 63, 102, 110-112, 114, 205, 229. 239-243, 245, 249

S

Sackville-Baggins 231
sacred tree 28, 71-74, 91, 194-195, 197-198, 200-201,
Saint Anne 31
Saint Boniface 71-72, 195
Saint Mary Bourne 31, 180, 183, 188
Sam Gamgee 94, 119-121, 136-137, 143, 148
Sam Weller 119-120
Sam, marriage of 120
Sarn (element in Welsh place names) 58
Sarn Ellen 58
Sarn Ford 57-59
Sarn Lleng 58
Saska Kępa (real place) 62
satire 167, 211, 213

scepter 32, 71, 197, 201
Schuchart (see *Dutch translator*)
Scott, Sir Walter 153, 155, 160-161, 165, 173, 207, 213-215
screenplay for *King Solomon's Mines* 123
Seahenge 74-77
search for eternal happiness 141
secondary standard for a translation 108, 111
Senlac hill 151
Severn river valley 13
Shakespeare vii, 150, 192, 214
Shakespearean English 20, 112
Sharnford (real place) 59
She (Haggard) 127, 133, 155-156
Shelob 114-115, 156, 219
Sherbourn 26, 29
Sherbourne 28
sherd of Amenartas 156
Sheriff 10
shire (scir) 10
  political subdivision 25
  Mericain shire 23
The Shire 19, 22, 24, 93
Shirebourn 25, 27
Shirriff 28, 56
Silmaril, in Eärendil's crown 222
Silmarils, brightest of the 219
silver 3-4
silver screen 124, 210, 215
Sir Quixote of the Moors (Buchan) 173
skepticism, modern scientific 141
Skibniewska (see *Polish translator*)
Smaug iv, 21-22, 38, 40, 51, 138
smial 34, 42, 182-183, 190
snowboard 208

Somerset 23, 25
Souterrain 190
South Africa 234-235
spear 85-86, 88-90, 128
    spear Luin 89
    spear of Destiny 89
    spear of Lugh Lamfhota 90
spit 113-115
Staddle 7-10
    Staddle Hobbits 10
staff 191-192, 197, 200-202
    type of wood used for 191
standard, great, golden 3
star(s) 4, 90, 126, 128, 141-142, 150, 217-224
    the word *star* 220
Stevenson, Robert Lewis 157
"stinking rich" 201
stocc (OE) 69-70, 77-78
stock (place-name element) 31, 36, 42, 58, 63, 69-72, 77, 197
    Stock im Eisen (Vienna) 77
    stocks and stones 70
    "trees" 71
    spelled "stoke" 31, 36, 58, 69-70, 72, 76-77
stone
    one of the four gifts of the ancestors to the Irish 89
    Stone of Destiny 90
    Stone of the Ancestors (object of cinematic fiction) 124
    Welsh word for *stone* 79
Stonehenge 74
    origin legend for 79
stories: Tolkien, love of 1
Strabo (Greek geographer) 89
Stratford (real place) 9, 67, 85, 204
Strider 98, 117-118, 126
swamps (see also *marshes*) 147-148, 151
Swift, Jonathan 163-166, 173
sword 89
    blue and swords 88
    Dwarf-made 129
    enchanted 85
    Mathum sword 4, 82
    one of the four gifts of the ancestors to the Irish 89
    river name containing the element *sword* 85-86
    sword of Nuada 90
    sword Sting 89
    Welsh word for *sword* 86

T

Taillebois (surname of French origin) 55
Tal y bont ar Wysg (real place) 68
tall men who came up out of the water 184, 187
Tammuz 222 n., 223
Tara of Buddhist tradition 221, 224
Tara, the Hindu goddess of war 90-91
Tara, the place 89-91
taran (Welsh and Cornish word for *thunder*) 91
Taranis (Celtic god) 91
tautology 7-8, 16, 59
television displacing books 215
temptation offered to Gandalf by Saruman 138
temptation offered to Holly by Ayesha 144
Tennyson, Alfred Lord 95, 150-151
Theoden-mathum (OE) 4
things that are dear to man 137
thirst for knowledge 138
Thiselton-Dyer, Thomas Firminger 194
Thor 91, 196
Thorn-tree 192, 196-197, 200-201

see also *Oak, Ash and Thorn* (triad)
thorn-wood 192
three Romans (three against thousands) 126-127
three times 192
three trees 201
thunder (German word for) 72
thunder (Welsh and Cornish word for) 91
thunder god 72, 91
timber circles 76
time, perception of 143
time, span of 134
tobacco 114-115
tobacco farming 13
Tolkien (age when) 125, 234
Tolkien the 'translator' 244
Tolkien's place in the framework of Literature 121
Tolkien's Style: Repeats 241
Tolkien, the artist 181
Tolkien, the meaning of the name 49-51
Tolkiennymy 19
Took, Belladonna 49
toponymical history 19
toponyms 19, 65, 91
    Tolkien, invention of 10
The Town Hole (pun) 20
Tradition of Gift Giving 2-3
translation 19, 121, 154-158, 163-165, 170, 172-176, 244
    of computer games 108
    of movie subtitles 108
    translations of *LotR* 112, 248-249
Treasure Island (Stevenson) 157
tree-bole 41
tree lore, Tolkien's store of 191
Tree of Life 71, 76, 194-195, 198, 200-202

tree of religious significance 72
"Tree Song" (Kipling) 193
trees as royal, tribal talismans 71, 197-198
triad of Oak, Ash and Thorn 192, 194
tribal talismans 71, 197-198
"tricksy lights" (Gollum) see also *corpse candles* 49, 148, 150
trinity 200
triplism 194, 202
Trotter 117-119
"true blue" 29
Tuatha De Danann 89, 91
tutelary deity of the tribe 71, 197

U
Uffington White Horse 187
uisge (Irish word) 15, 66
underground chamber 189
underground dwellings 183
underground structures 190
Underhill (psuedonym) 118
Upton Snodsbury (real place) 13

V
valor 142
veneration of water 85
Venus 219-220, 222-223
Verne, Jules 95, 239-240
Victorian-era etiquette 114
Vingilot 219, 224
Virgin Mary 220-221
Vortigern 44

W
Wales 14, 42-44
Walker (alias) 118
Walpole, Horace 155, 163-164
water mirror 151, 155

Waverley Novels (Scott) 160-161
wealth 141
weary 135, 138
weeping 222
Wegstunden (German word) 99
Welsh v, 10, 16, 31, 35, 72, 81, 84-88, 91, 148, 176
   lenition 8, 16, 53, 67, 81, 200
Welsh folklore 149, 199
Welsh manuscript 176
Welsh place-name elements 8, 35, 53, 58, 66-68, 72-74, 79, 85
Welsh river names 85
Welsh tradition 148, 151
West-Saxon England 23
Westerman, Percy 125
Westron 9, 15, 84, 111
Westward Ho! (Kingsley) 193
Weyman, Stanley 125
whiskey 15, 66
White-thorn 200
Whitman, Walt 149
Wild Men 184, 186-187
   "When wild in woods the noble savage ran" 184
William III 198
windy tree 200
wishing rhyme 219
Withypool (real place) 68
Withywindle 68
woad 89
Woden's great-grandsons 187
woman 75, 127, 131, 144, 196
woodbine 40
Woodhall 42, 47-48
   Woodhall Spa (real place) 48-49, 61
Woodhay (real place) 31, 36
Woody End 31, 35-36, 47
word histories 101
World War I 106-107, 111
Woses 36

Wright, Willard Huntington (S.S. Van Dine) 168-169
Wyre Forest 12

Y
Yale 42, 44-46
Yale University 46
Yale [cylinder] lock 47
Yggdrasil 194-196, 200

About the Author

Mark T. Hooker is a specialist in Comparative Translation at Indiana University's Russian and East European Institute (REEI). Retired, he conducts research for publication. His articles on Tolkien have been published in English in *Beyond Bree, Para Nölé* and *Tolkien Studies*, in Dutch in *Lembas* (the journal of the Dutch Tolkien Society) and in Russian in *Palantir* (the journal of the St. Petersburg Tolkien Society). He has presented papers at a number of MythCons and at the fourth Lustrum of the Dutch Tolkien Society. He is the author of *Tolkien Through Russian Eyes* (Walking Tree, 2003), *Implied, but not **Stated*** (distributed by Slavica, 1999) and *The History of Holland* (Greenwood, 1999). He has also written on the Harry Potter vs. Tanya Grotter controversy. He is a graduate of the Russian Advanced Course at DLIWC. He speaks Dutch at home.